The 22nd Maine
Volunteer Infantry
in the Civil War

The 22nd Maine Volunteer Infantry in the Civil War

A History and Roster

NED SMITH

McFarland & Company, Inc., Publishers
Jefferson, North Carolina, and London

LIBRARY OF CONGRESS CATALOGUING-IN-PUBLICATION DATA

Smith, Ned, 1947–
　　The 22nd Maine Volunteer Infantry in the Civil War : a history and roster / by Ned Smith.
　　　　p.　　cm.
　　Includes bibliographical references and index.

　　ISBN 978-0-7864-4893-7
　　softcover : 50# alkaline paper ∞

　　1. United States. Army. Maine Infantry Regiment, 22nd (1862–1863)　2. Maine — History — Civil War, 1861–1865 — Regimental histories.　3. United States — History — Civil War, 1861–1865 — Regimental histories.　4. Port Hudson (La.) — History — Siege, 1863.　5. Banks, Nathaniel Prentiss, 1816–1894. I. Title.
E511.522nd.S65　2010
973.7'441—dc22　　　　　　　　　　　　　　　　　　2010033922

British Library cataloguing data are available

©2010 Ned Smith. All rights reserved

No part of this book may be reproduced or transmitted in any form or by any means, electronic or mechanical, including photocopying or recording, or by any information storage and retrieval system, without permission in writing from the publisher.

Front cover: General Nathaniel Banks (Library of Congress); *The Battle of Irish Bend*, from a sketch by William Hall, 22nd Maine (*Harper's Weekly*, May 16, 1863)

Manufactured in the United States of America

McFarland & Company, Inc., Publishers
　Box 611, Jefferson, North Carolina 28640
　　www.mcfarlandpub.com

For my best friend and wife,
Diane Monroe Smith, with many thanks.

Acknowledgments

This book would not have been written without the help and support of many people.

First, there is Bill Cook, from the Bangor, Maine, Public Library. Bill brought to my attention the Francis Ireland letters that form the backbone of this work. Bill was also very helpful in providing material on Bangor and Central Maine during the years leading up to the Civil War.

Carol Feurtado and Rick Whitney, from the Dexter, Maine, Historical Society, were superb in their assistance with the background material on the Ireland family and the large number of the 22nd's men who came from Dexter.

Sylvia Sherman from the Maine State Archives has been a friend for years and was a great help in this project. Also from the Maine State Archives, Jeff Brown, Art Dostie, Anthony Douin, and Ann Small gave valuable assistance and showed commendable patience with my frequent visits and requests.

Diane Smith from the Isaac W. Case Memorial Library in Kenduskeag, Maine, was a great help with material on Captain Case. Lynn Rogers from the Levant, Maine, Historical Society provided valuable information about Colonel Simon Jerrard and others from that town.

And then, of course, the help of my wife, Diane Monroe Smith, was the most important of all. The hours she spent reading and discussing various chapters and the suggestions and critique she provided were incredibly helpful in getting the work into its final form. The work she did on her excellent books about Maine's Joshua Chamberlain has given her a great perspective on how to write history.

Table of Contents

Acknowledgments vi
Preface 1
Introduction 3

1. Maine and Louisiana: Two States in a House Curiously Divided — 7
2. The Raising of a Maine Regiment — 17
3. Francis Ireland and the Boys from Dexter — 25
4. Leaving Maine — 34
5. New Camps, New Sights — 44
6. The 22nd Settles in to Camp Life — 56
7. Heading South: Banks' Expedition Sails for New Orleans and the Lower Mississippi — 64
8. The Reoccupation of Baton Rouge — 74
9. At Baton Rouge: Balmy Breezes and Deadly Diseases — 84
10. More Sickness, Surviving the Cure, Longing for Home — 95
11. The First Advance Toward Port Hudson — 107
12. The Men of the 22nd "See the Animal" — 119
13. New Iberia and St. Martinville: A Slave Uprising; an Escort for an Ailing Rebel Officer — 131
14. No Spring Mustering Out — 140
15. On to Port Hudson — 149

16. Assault on Port Hudson	166
17. The Fall of Port Hudson, Up the Mississippi and Home	178
Appendix A: Raising the Regiments	185
Appendix B: Causes of Death in the Different Theaters of War	203
Appendix C: Roster of the Twenty-Second Regiment	205
Chapter Notes	233
Bibliography	245
Index	247

Preface

From the beginning of the American Civil War, the opening of the Mississippi River had been a part of the Union strategy — the 3-part "Anaconda Plan." That plan involved a blockade of the Confederate ports, an advance by the Union army toward the Confederate capital, and the taking of the Mississippi River to separate the eastern Confederacy from its western states and supply routes.

But, what was the importance of that latter part of the plan — in particular, the war in Louisiana and the lower Mississippi? When I was in school and during my undergraduate history classes, that aspect of the war received very little attention. OK, there was a brief mention of Farragut and the capture of New Orleans, but that was about it. Even the capture of Vicksburg (eventually) by General Grant's forces was overshadowed by the attention given to Gettysburg.

And what about those 9 month regiments that were raised by the Union in 1862? They just sat around the defenses of Washington, while other regiments did the actual fighting — right? Well, not in all cases.

This book tells the story of one of those 9 month regiments, the 22nd Maine Volunteer Infantry, and its part in the campaigns in Louisiana. These boys from Maine did indeed see real fighting — and dying. They also experienced, with other northern regiments sent to the Deep South, the deadly effects of disease on young men who had no previous exposure to those diseases, and who were living in conditions that promoted the spread of illness.

I hope that this story will appeal not only to students of the Civil War and military history, but also to those who appreciate a dramatic human story told from several different points of view. By including many letters from soldiers, as well as letters from home, we get a very personal view — the story of the average soldier and his family. Along with this personal view, of course, are the letters and reports from officers and commanders, and the material from official records that give the "big picture." By including material from all these sources, we can get a feeling for history that goes beyond the usual official language and puts into context the "spin" that some in command may attempt to use to glorify (or excuse) their own actions.

While teaching U.S. history, I try to make it clear to my students that history is not about memorizing dates, places, and names. History is primarily about people — what they did and why they did it — the flow of circumstances that led to important events, and the thoughts of those who were caught up in those events.

I'm very pleased to present this new addition to the history of the Civil War, and hope it will not only tell the story of less known events, but will also clearly show the reactions, observations, and feelings of the young men involved.

Introduction

On the evening of October 3, 1889, Joshua Chamberlain, former colonel of the 20th Maine and general of Union volunteers, addressed a gathering of veterans and their families and friends at the Gettysburg courthouse. In his speech, as was often the case in the many addresses he was called upon to give, Chamberlain put into perspective the causes of the war and the ideals for which he and his fellow veterans had fought. He commented on the valor shown by men who were inspired by these ideals and the strength they had gained from each other: "The inspiration of a noble cause involving human interests wide and far, enables men to do things they did not dream themselves capable of before, and which they were not capable of alone." In words that are perhaps his best known, he went on to say, "In great deeds something abides. On great fields something stays. Forms change and pass; bodies disappear; but spirits linger, to consecrate ground for the vision-place of souls."[1]

Indeed, the actions of these men, as a group, have been entered firmly in our national consciousness. But what actually abides in our memory? The names of a relatively few well known individuals — the generals and other officers, the broad stories of the troops they led, and the names of major battles. But what abides of the individual soldiers involved? Each of these thousands of men had his unique story, had his own reasons for enlisting, was engaged in desperate battle, and if he was lucky, came home. For many it was the one truly great event of their lives, and all were changed by their experiences. Many would return time and again to the old battlefields to revisit and remember what had come and gone. In 1888, 25,000 veterans returned to Gettysburg for the 25th anniversary of the battle — each with his own memories of moments of fear or bravery, hope, despair, or simple stubbornness that would stay with him always.

And yet, with time, these men would die, stories told to others would fade, and what would remain, in many cases, would be a monument in a town square or a grave marker indicating that here lie the remains of one who fought for his regiment, or his battery, or his ship — a name perhaps no longer remembered even in his own town as new generations lost interest and families moved away or simply died out.

Over the last 10 years or so I have assisted my wife, Diane Monroe Smith, as she researched and wrote her books about Maine's Joshua Chamberlain. I have been very pleased to see an accurate and thoughtful biography of that Civil War figure brought to the public. In her second book, it was exciting to see the story of Chamberlain and the 5th Corps at Petersburg have a thorough telling.

On the other hand, I have for years been frustrated that more was not told of the Civil War's individual soldiers who also ventured far from their homes and took their chances in the great struggles. As special projects with some of my students, we have compiled lists of local Civil War veterans and tried to find as much as we could about their lives before the war, their experiences in the army, and for those who survived, what their lives were like after they came home. In most cases this has led to little more than a list of names, a generic understanding of the battles their regiments fought in, and some records from the census or town tax lists regarding their early and later life.

Therefore, when a friend mentioned seeing some promising Civil War letters written by a young man from nearby Dexter, Maine, I was hoping to find the chance to tell a more detailed personal story. But would this soldier's letters be more than a few scattered notes home about the weather and the food? The collection that I found was quite wonderful. A young man named Francis Ireland, who enlisted in one of Maine's volunteer regiments, wrote to his parents over his entire period of service, sharing with them his observations and thoughts and recording his regiment's story. And, as I had always suspected, it is especially interesting to see the war from the perspective of an individual soldier, recorded as the "great deeds" or just everyday events were happening. These letters, it seemed, could well form the basis for a regimental history, with a substantial part of the story told from the perspective of one soldier.

To add to my excitement, Francis Ireland's regiment, unlike some of those mustered for 9 months, was tested in battle, and this action came in southern Louisiana, a theater of war often overlooked in favor of Virginia, Maryland, and Pennsylvania. More primary source material on the regiment came from an unpublished "brief history" written by their colonel, as well as reports and letters from other soldiers. And the story of the colonel's dismissal from the service provided a look at the questions and choices faced by many officers in many battles — the need to make quick decisions under incredible pressure that would determine the fates of those under their command.

Dexter, Maine, Town Hall and Civil War Monument (author photograph).

The Ireland letters date from September 1862 to the end of June 1863 and provide a remarkable account of the travel, camp life, and action seen by this young man and his regiment. The letters that his parents sent to Francis give us an eye on the home front as exemplified by a small town in Maine. We read about news of the war that was reaching the hometowns of the soldiers at the front, and see the reactions of those at home to specific events and to the war in general. In addition, we have a window on the feelings of parents who often heard about the "big picture" of the war, through newspapers and telegraph, but then had to wait for days or weeks to hear whether their sons had been involved or indeed had survived those same events. In reading their letters, I've come to respect and like these people, and to appreciate the opportunity they have given us to see into their world.

When quoting from the Ireland letters, I have corrected a few spelling mistakes; there were few in the originals, and I felt that putting "[*sic*]" when called for only distracts from the reading of the letters. Misspelled place names and personal names which were unfamiliar to this young man from Maine are given as written and in corrected form. Some spellings that were consistent, such as "altho" and "tho" (which appear to have been common in informal letters of that time period) have been left as they were. I have inserted some punctuation when the intent of the writer was clear. Otherwise, the text is as written. In some other letters, largely those written by another private in the 22nd, Charlie Farrar, I have left spelling as it was in the original. The reason for this difference in treatment is hard to articulate, except to say that the Ireland letters contained very few spelling mistakes, while the spelling in the Farrar letters seemed to add flavor.

1

Maine and Louisiana
Two States in a House Curiously Divided

Maine's history presents a series of seemingly conflicting events that relate to subjects of states' rights and slavery. In order to understand these events, we must forget preconceptions about Maine as a firmly Republican and strongly abolitionist state — although these characteristics gradually became true in the years leading up to the Civil War. For a time, Maine's history involved strong ties to slavery and the slave trade, positive attitudes toward states' rights proponents, and even, at times, saw people from Maine advocating their own secession from the Union.

It is clear that Maine played a role in the slave trade. Ships made in Maine, often captained and crewed by men from Maine, had transported many captives from their African homeland to their forced labor in the New World. And a number of the impressive homes of sea captains in Maine's picturesque coastal towns and cities were built with the money from the slave trade. As late as 1860, Portland, Maine, native Nathaniel Gordon was captured for attempting to illegally bring slaves from Africa — importing slaves having been illegal for over 50 years and punishable by death for over 40 years (the importing of slaves into the U.S. became illegal on January 1, 1808, and in 1820 the U.S. Congress made participation in the international slave trade an "act of piracy"). When Gordon's ship, *Erie*, was stopped off the African coast by the U.S. Navy ship *Mohican*, 897 Africans were found on board. Tried and convicted of illegally attempting to import slaves as an act of piracy, Gordon was sentenced, in 1861, to be hung. The execution was delayed by Abraham Lincoln, but was carried out in New York on February 21, 1862.[1]

The issue of slavery's place in this country, and the issue of states' rights versus a strong central government, and indeed the issue of the right of secession from the Union, had been unresolved since the United States became a nation. As early as 1802 many of the Federalist Party in Maine (then a part of Massachusetts) had talked of secession if the federal government should grow too powerful, and they also opposed the addition of large areas of new land to the United States — the Louisiana Purchase. Federalists believed the purchase of this new land unconstitutional, while those in New England feared that the power and influence of New England would be diminished if new lands to the west were developed and entered the Union as new states. And then there was the question of slavery that concerned many in the Northeast — would these new lands provide areas for the expansion of slavery and add new slave states to the Union?

Then, in 1814, the people of Maine were even more strongly involved in the issue of states' rights and the threat of secession. At that time Maine was still a part of Massachusetts and its coastal areas were heavily dependent on shipping and trade. Many people in Maine and the rest of New England were very displeased with Thomas Jefferson's Embargo Act of 1807 — an attempt to keep the U.S. out of the Napoleonic Wars by stopping trade with Europe. That act was repealed in 1808, but was followed by the Non-intercourse Act of 1809, which attempted to prevent U.S. trade with Britain and France. Then, the War of 1812 ended legal trade with England and made shipping from any U.S. port very difficult due to a British blockade. Massachusetts (including Maine) and Connecticut had refused to place their state militias under U.S. government control, deciding that their militias would be used only for their own defense. As a result, President James Madison's government would not pay for the expenses of defending those states. And so, in 1814 secession from the Union was once again being discussed in New England.

In 1814 the governor of Massachusetts had sent a delegation to Britain to discuss a peace settlement — with Massachusetts hoping to establish its own peace with Great Britain regardless of Britain's relations with the U.S. In that same year, a convention was held in Hartford, Connecticut, to discuss New England's response to the war and the effect on trade. One of the delegates to that convention from what would become Maine, and a member of the Federalist Party, was Stephen Longfellow, the father of poet Henry Wadsworth Longfellow. During the convention the Federalist members argued repeatedly for secession from the U.S. In the final report of the convention, there is no specific mention of secession, but there is a strong statement to the effect that the federal government was making unconstitutional limitations on the sovereign rights of the states. Representatives from New England eventually were sent to Washington to negotiate terms based on the report of the Hartford Convention. However, by the time they arrived, in February of 1815, the Treaty of Ghent had been signed, the war was over, and the major reason for their discussion — non-interference with shipping — no longer appeared relevant.

In the May 15, 1861, *New York Times*, the newspaper looked back at the Hartford Convention and, using a response from the leading Southern newspaper in 1814, made a clear editorial statement regarding secession:

> Virginia on Secession in 1814
>
> In 1814, the New-England people became dissatisfied with the conduct of public affairs and in the celebrated Hartford Convention they took action which looked like asserting the right of secession. Whereupon the Richmond *Enquirer*, Nov. 1, 1814 said:
>
> "No man, no association of men, no State, nor set of States has a right to withdraw itself from this Union, of its own accord. ... The same formality which forged the links of the Union is necessary to dissolve it. ... Any other doctrine, such as that which has been lately held forth by the *Federalist Republican*, that any one State may withdraw itself from the Union, is an abominable heresy....
>
> "We call, therefore, upon the Government of the Union to exert its energies when the season shall demand it, and seize the first traitor who shall spring out of the hot-bed of the Convention at Hartford. ... The Union must be saved when any one shall dare to assail it."[2]

Six years after the Hartford Convention, when Maine became a state in 1820, the unresolved questions regarding slavery played a major part in that process. That process was a part of the balancing act regarding slavery that had gone on since the U.S. declared independence from Britain. In Jefferson's rough draft of the Declaration of Independence, he had included a condemnation of slavery. The context was more specifically a condemnation of King George III's support of slavery, but certainly applied to slavery within the American colonies. A committee of five was created to draft the Declaration, made up of John Adams, Benjamin Franklin, Thomas Jefferson, Robert Livingston, and Roger Sherman, with Jefferson being given the task of writing the document. Upon reading a draft of this document, the committee, largely at the insistence of Franklin and Adams, deleted this antislavery section since, they realized, it would alienate slave owners and pro-slavery sympathizers. Those hoping to separate from England knew they needed the support of all the colonies in order to make their bid for independence have a chance.[3]

It is of further interest that Benjamin Franklin, who for pragmatic reasons had argued to delete the antislavery section of the Declaration, was elected, in 1785, the president of the nation's first anti-slavery society — the Pennsylvania Society for the Abolition of Slavery.[4]

The failure to directly address the slavery issue while including the phrase "all men are created equal" in the Declaration of Independence set the stage for antislavery speeches of the 1800s. Abolitionists could quote from the very document that had brought the country into existence for a statement that slavery ran contrary to the founding fathers' ideals.

Prior to 1820, the Northern states had made slavery illegal within their borders — the earliest state to free slaves being Massachusetts in 1780. Those who owned slaves in the South were very concerned that, if a majority of states became "free states," the U.S. Congress would act to further restrict slavery in the states where it existed, and would prevent new slave states from being admitted to the Union as statehood expanded westward in various territories. This desire to keep the number of slave and free states equal was a fairly recent concern, however, since the numbers had only been made equal at the end of 1819 with the admission of Alabama into the Union as a slave state. In January of 1820, when a bill was introduced to allow Maine to enter the Union as a free state, Congress passed that bill but included an amendment providing statehood for Missouri as a slave state. And so, Maine's admission to the Union was very much a part of the ongoing debate about slavery.

The pro- and anti-slavery positions would, of course, be a factor in the admission of other states to the Union. When American colonists in Texas, for example, had fought for independence from Mexico in the 1830s, one of their complaints against Mexico was the Mexican government's refusal to allow colonists to legally bring their slaves into that Mexican territory. In 1845, when Texas was admitted to the Union (the act that led to the Mexican American War), it was as a slave state, over the objection of many in the North.

The feelings of some in Maine toward states' rights (and the issue of slavery) were an interesting mixture of self-interest and political philosophy which could become rather complicated. Why, for example, would the brother of Maine's Civil War hero, Joshua Lawrence Chamberlain, be named John Calhoun Chamberlain, after the U.S. vice president and senator from South Carolina? Calhoun was, after all, a Southern firebrand who was a militantly outspoken defender of both states' rights and slavery, and a fiery proponent of "nullification," the right of a state to nullify a federal law with which that state disagreed.

1. Maine and Louisiana

The circumstances leading to John Calhoun Chamberlain's name are stated in Diane Monroe Smith's biography of Joshua Chamberlain, *Fanny and Joshua*: "Many Maine people, feeling they had suffered from the national government's high tariffs and policies on trade and currency, saw John C. Calhoun, the mastermind behind nullification and its challenge to federal authority, as a champion." Joshua Chamberlain's grandfather was involved in shipping, primarily as the owner of a shipbuilding yard. He had suffered from losses to the shipping industry created by President Jefferson's embargo on trade from 1807 to 1809, the effect of the War of 1812 and the Tariff of 1816. The book goes on to say that when Joshua Chamberlain's father was an adult,

> there was still considerable opposition in Maine to what was viewed as the national government's interference on issues of trade and currency, which were believed to have impacted negatively on Maine's fortunes. In 1833, five years before John Chamberlain's birth, John C. Calhoun, in order to openly oppose national tariffs and defend South Carolina's nullification law, resigned as vice-president of the United States to again become senator for his state. As a champion of nullification, he was credited by many with forcing the confrontation that would result in compromise and a lowering of tariffs. In the year before John Calhoun Chamberlain's birth, many Americans also believed that the economic panic of 1837 was caused by President Jackson's policies on the nation's banks and currency. Senator Calhoun's previous denunciation of both Jackson and his policies had seemingly proved right, and Calhoun enjoyed such popularity in Maine that a movement in the state's Democratic Party advocated his candidacy for president.[5]

Of course, the feelings of the people of Maine specifically toward slavery is more complicated. While many apparently saw slavery as the "necessary evil" upon which Southern economic health was based, others were merely ambivalent toward slavery. On the other hand, Maine, and other New England states, contained a substantial number of ardent abolitionists. As the Democratic Party became more clearly associated with a pro-slavery stance, the Republican Party emerged from an odd mixture of "Know-nothings" (a "nativist" anti-immigrant and anti–Irish Catholic movement), remnants of the Whig Party, temperance supporters, and abolitionists.[6]

The election of Maine's governor in 1856 can be seen as a clear reflection of the feelings of Maine's people on the issues of slavery and state's rights. The Republican candidate, Hannibal Hamlin, was opposed to slavery, and as a U.S. senator had opposed the Kansas-Nebraska Act, which repealed the Missouri Compromise's limitations on the expansion of slavery. Hamlin had left the Democratic Party in June of 1856, when the Democrats voted to support the Kansas-Nebraska Act, and joined the newly formed Republican Party. When Hamlin won the gubernatorial election by a wide majority over the Democrat and Whig candidates, it was not only a victory for an anti-slavery candidate, but a boost to the national efforts of the Republican Party.[7]

The presidential election of 1856 was also, to a large extent, a referendum on slavery. The Democrat, James Buchanan, ran on a platform that included opposition to federal interference with slavery. Millard Fillmore, former president of the U.S., ran as a Know-nothing candidate, and is therefore a representative of that party's anti-immigrant, anti–Catholic policies. The candidate of the new Republican Party, John Fremont, ran on a platform that included strong anti-slavery statements. The voters of Maine gave Fremont a large majority with 67,279 votes (61 percent) as compared to Buchanan's 39,140 (36 percent), and Fillmore's 3,270 (3 percent). But Buchanan won the national election, with all of the electoral college votes from the South, as well as the states of Pennsylvania, Indiana, Illinois, California, and Missouri.[8]

In the presidential election of 1860, Maine once again came down strongly on the Republican side and voted overwhelmingly for Abraham Lincoln and his running mate from Maine, Hannibal Hamlin. The Republicans received 62,811 votes in Maine (62 percent), while the Democrat, Stephen Douglas, received less than 30,000 (29 percent). It is interesting that the Southern Democrat and strongly pro-slavery candidate, John Breckinridge, received 6,368 votes in Maine — a relatively small number, but an indication of some sentiment that favored slavery's continuation.[9]

The strong support by the majority in Maine for the fight to preserve the Union was also of interest, given coastal Maine's continued reliance on the shipping industry. Many ships from Maine were involved in the cotton trade, and cotton was not being shipped from the South to New England, and the Union blockade of Southern ports further restricted the shipping of cotton to Europe. In addition, in the 1850s and early '60s, many Maine towns had economies that were tied to cotton mills and many immigrants to Maine had come to work in those mills. As we shall see later, there remained a strong minority in Maine who opposed the Civil War, feared the freeing of slaves, and wanted to negotiate a compromise settlement with the Confederacy. Nevertheless, support for the Civil War was strong enough for Maine to send a higher proportion of its population to fight than any other state of the Union.[10]

Louisiana, a state of great importance to the story of the 22nd Maine, had, of course, a very different history leading up to the Civil War. The area that would become the state of Louisiana had been territory owned by Spain and, from 1800, by France. Its population was largely of French ancestry, with thousands of African slaves imported to work on the farming plantations. A further influx of French colonists took place in the 1760s when French Catholics from Nova Scotia, Canada — people known as "Acadians"— were pressured to renounce Catholicism or leave Canada after the British victory in the so-called French and Indian Wars. And, during the early 1800s, many "free people of color" (persons of African ancestry who were not slaves), as well as whites with slaves immigrated to Louisiana to escape a revolution in Haiti.

During the presidency of Thomas Jefferson, the Louisiana Purchase made this region and its people a part of the United States, more than doubling the size of the country. This acquisition of new land was opposed by many in the Federalist Party, and, as mentioned above, was a reason why some in New England were talking of secession and the formation of a Northern Confederacy. After the Louisiana Purchase, the area was divided in the District of Louisiana and the Territory of Orleans. It was this Territory of Orleans that formed essentially what is now the state of Louisiana.

Louisiana, in the years after its acquisition by the United States, had a large free black population, a substantial number of free mixed race people, as well as many of European descent and a large number of African slaves. This unusual mixture of social conditions between races, while offering some opportunities for some blacks, could also prove volatile. Tensions between slaves and their masters turned violent in 1811 during what is called the "German Coast Uprising." The German Coast, so named because it was initially settled largely by German immigrants, is on the east bank of the Mississippi, near New Orleans. A group of about 15 slaves rose against their owner at the Andre plantation, wounded the owner and killed his son. After this group left their plantation and began a march toward New Orleans, they were joined by slaves from other plantations along the way. At one of these plantations, another white planter, Francois Trepangnier, was killed. Panic spread among the white population, which by some estimates were outnumbered by black slaves 5 to 1. At its largest, the rebellious slaves perhaps numbered as many as 500, but most estimates would put the figure as closer to 200 to 250. As they moved toward New Orleans the slaves burned three plantation houses to the ground and damaged two others. Under the leadership of local militia companies, whites of the area hunted down those suspected of taking part in the rebellion, and at least 95 slaves were killed or executed after a trial. Not long after this slave rebellion, the largest to take place on American soil, Louisiana joined the Union on April 30, 1812. Fear of an uprising of slaves was still a concern at the time of the Civil War.[11]

The importance of the new state of Louisiana was, to a large degree, due to the importance of the Mississippi River to the expanding United States. This made New Orleans into a large, cosmopolitan city with shipping from all over the world visiting its port to export produce brought down the river and to bring imports, primarily from Europe, to be taken up river to new towns and cities. By 1840, New Orleans was the third largest city in the United States, and in that year had the largest slave market in the country. Although the ban on importing slaves from outside the United States was sometimes broken, most slaves of that period were the offspring of slaves already in this country. And many slaves were literally "sold down river" to plantations or slave markets in the Deep South.

By the end of the 1850s much of Louisiana had a plantation based economy, with cotton and sugar cane being the principal crops. Great wealth was gained by many from slave labor and from the slave markets. And, although Louisiana had a substantial population of free blacks, some of whom were middle class, well educated, and property owners, most of those 18,000 or so free blacks lived in or near New Orleans. For most of the state, the black population was made up of the over 330,000 slaves that comprised nearly half of the state's entire population.

With an economy based largely on slave labor, and fears of interference with that labor force, many in the South were considering leaving the Union. In January of 1861, Louisiana delegates to a convention in Baton Rouge voted 113 to 17 in favor of secession. And, in the presidential election of 1860, the most clearly pro-slavery and pro-secession candidate, John C. Breckinridge, won a majority of the votes in Louisiana.[12]

However, a closer look gives an interesting, and perhaps contradictory, perspective on the amount of pro-secession feeling in the state. In that election, Abraham Lincoln, the Republican candidate, did not appear on the ballot in many southern states, including Louisiana. Of the remaining candidates, John C. Breckinridge of Kentucky, the U.S. vice president at that time, held, as stated above, the most clearly pro-slavery position. In addition, his supporters came from the most clearly pro-slavery element of the Democratic Party and were seen as largely pro-secession. It was, in fact, that question of slavery that caused the Democratic Party to split into separate Northern and Southern parties. Breckinridge became the presidential candidate of the pro-slavery Southern Democrats — urged to accept the nomination by Jefferson Davis. Breckinridge had been a major in the Kentucky Volunteers during the Mexican-American War, and as a member of Congress in 1854 he had strongly supported the Kansas-Nebraska Act, which repealed the limitations on the spread of slavery that had been a part of the Missouri Compromise. He had argued that the federal government did not have the right to interfere with slavery anywhere — in any state or territory. In the 1856 election, when he ran as vice presidential candidate with James Buchanan, some in the South thought he showed a lack of commitment to the pro-slavery position. He described himself at that time, perhaps as a way of attracting northern voters, as not being pro-slavery but a defender of the rights of the people of individual states to make their own laws.[13]

In that 1860 presidential campaign, the Northern Democrats, seen by the Southern Democrats as not sufficiently supporting the rights of slave owners, had nominated Stephen Douglas. Douglas had been the U.S. senator who had proposed the Kansas-Nebraska Act, but had in the years after that been an opponent of the spread of slavery. During the campaign of 1860, he had not only spoken out against secession, but had done so in the South.

The third candidate on the ballot in Louisiana was John Bell (a former Whig and U.S. senator from Tennessee), who ran as the candidate of the Constitutional Union Party — a mix of former Whigs and Know-nothings. Bell had opposed the Kansas-Nebraska Act and had further opposed the "Lecompton Constitution" (a proposed pro-slavery constitution for the state of Kansas). He also ran on a platform that advocated compromise to save the Union, and was clearly opposing secession.

The results of the election in Louisiana showed Breckinridge winning with 22,681 votes (45 percent). However, John Bell, an obvious opponent of the spread of slavery and an equally obvious opponent of secession, was a close second with 20,204 votes (40 percent). Stephen Douglas was third in Louisiana with 7,625 votes (15 percent). Combined, the two anti-secession candidates had a majority of the votes in that 1860 election.

Four days after the national election, with the results showing the victory of Abraham Lincoln, the candidate whose name had not even appeared on the ballot of southern states, including Louisiana, a large crowd met in New Orleans to form the "Minute Men of New Orleans." Their purpose was to "help protect the right of any Southern state to secede from the Union." Similar groups were formed for the same purpose, meetings were held around the state to discuss the rights of Louisiana and the other Southern States, and prominent ministers began to preach in favor of secession.[14]

In January 1861, Louisiana militia had forced the surrender of the U.S. arsenal in Baton Rouge and thereby captured a substantial store of guns and ammunition. Also in January, a detachment of Louisiana militia had taken possession of the two United States forts — Fort Jackson and Fort St. Philip — that guarded the entrance to the Mississippi River. In that same month, Louisiana left the Union, and on March 4, delegates meeting in New Orleans ratified the constitution of the Confederate States. By the middle of 1861, there were over 16,000 men from Louisiana under arms and prepared to fight for their state and for the Confederacy. Many in the Confederacy, as well as the Union, anticipated a quick victory for their armies and a short war.[15]

And so, at the time of the American Civil War, these were the situations in the two states that will be featured in this story. The politics and feelings of the citizens of these states can be seen, at the opening of that war, in the context of their histories concerning slavery, the slave trade, shipping, the cotton trade, states' rights, and secession.

2

The Raising of a Maine Regiment

In the summer of 1862, new regiments were being formed to take a place in the Union Army. The idea of a 90 day war was far in the past, and as he had done following the Union's defeat at the First Battle of Bull Run in the summer of 1861, President Lincoln once again issued a call for new troops. This time, with the frustration of the Seven Days' Battles of July 1862, which ended General George B. McClellan's Peninsula Campaign, another 300,000 volunteers were being sought to fill the ranks of the Union Army.[1]

The process by which regiments were raised was not well established at the start of the war, and was far from smooth when this new call went out — the need for more men was putting considerable pressure on states and towns to meet quotas in a variety of ways. (This process is addressed in some detail in Appendix A.)

With all of the confusion, conflict, and concern surrounding the raising of the early regiments, and carrying on to some degree into the summer of 1862, the 22nd Maine can be seen as typical of the 9 month regiments raised that August and early September. The 22nd Maine and the other regiments, whether established for 3 years or 9 months' service, retained the regional nature of regiments raised earlier. Regiments were still typically raised within one geographic area of the state, sometimes one county, and companies were raised from even smaller areas — perhaps one town — so that men would find themselves serving and fighting beside their relatives and neighbors.

In the 22nd Maine's case, it was originally called the "Penobscot Regiment" since most of its men came from that county. However, as the regiment was being formed, its Company D and Company F were made up largely of men from "Downeast" Maine's Washington County, while Company G's men came mostly from Northern Maine's Aroostock County. This caused some problems when regimental officers were being selected and regional jealousies came to the fore. These concerns were typified by a letter from Lyman Bailey, one of those from Washington County, to Governor Israel Washburn complaining that, since his company had been combined with others mostly from Penobscot County, it appeared to him that men from his own county were not being selected as officers. One assumes that he was referring to regimental officers, since the company officers, captain and lieutenants, were in fact from the same locale as the men in their companies. Whether his letter was a factor, we don't know, but the writer was selected to be quartermaster of the 22nd Maine.

Since regiments for the Union Army were raised by the individual states, the choice of officers was a matter that was decided at the state level. As more and more men were called to serve in the Union Army, the numbers of officers needed quickly went beyond the numbers who had military qualifications. The adjutant general's reports indicate that the enrolled militia companies should simply elect their officers, but those officers were not guaranteed a commission when the members of the militia were enlisted and mustered into U.S. service. The officers for those regiments and the companies within them were appointed by the governor and received commissions as the result of recommendations, or from political considerations, or as a reward for raising needed men. The process by which the 22nd Maine's officers gained their positions is typical, and the Maine State Archives contains a great many letters which demonstrate the various efforts to obtain an officer's commission.

On July 17, 1862 Hannibal Hamlin, vice president of the U.S. and a Maine native, wrote to Maine's Governor Washburn to say the Joseph E. Joy of Hampden Corners "who has had some military experience, and who in my judgment will make a good Lieut., desires some enlistment papers to see what he can do, and on the understanding that he will have a Lieutenantcy if he raises the requisite number of men." Hamlin asked that the papers be forwarded to Joy.

Joseph Joy also wrote from Hampden Corner to the governor on August 11, 1862: "Dear Sir being or wishing to recruit some men for the last call of the President if there is a Lieut. berth for me — you will remember the Vice President wrote you on the 24th of July but I was too late to recruit for that Call. Yours, etc. Joseph E. Joy."[2]

We don't know where things went wrong, but perhaps Joseph Joy was not able to raise the "requisite number," but even with the recommendation of the vice president, he became not a lieutenant but a corporal in Com-

2. The Raising of a Maine Regiment

pany A, 22nd Maine. He was promoted to sergeant in 1863, but as we shall see, died of wounds in June of that year.

Turner Waterhouse of Newport had better luck, in part because the request made on his behalf was not granted. He was recommended to the governor by John Benson of Bucksport, Maine, as a young man who "wants an opportunity to do the work necessary to get a Lieutenancy in the 18th Regt. I think he can secure some volunteers for that regt. He is a sound reliable man and worthy of what he wishes to obtain." Whether or not Waterhouse recruited for the 18th Maine, he in fact became captain of Company K, 22nd Maine, and survived the war. He was perhaps fortunate that his original request for a commission in the 18th Maine did not materialize.[3]

The 18th Maine Infantry was converted into the 1st Maine Heavy Artillery and, although they had a rather uneventful couple of years in the defenses of Washington, when General U.S. Grant needed more men for his Overland Campaign in the spring of 1864, they were converted back to infantry. Within days of this conversion, they found themselves in battle against veteran Confederate soldiers of General John B. Gordon's division of General Richard Ewell's corps. In their first action as infantry they lost 476 men killed or wounded. Later, when ordered to charge a heavily defended Confederate position at Petersburg, the 1st Maine Heavies suffered 632 more casualties. And although the 1st Maine Heavies, at the time of their transfer to General Grant as infantry, were greater in numbers than a typical infantry regiment, their losses were nonetheless the highest of any Union regiment in the Civil War.[4]

Another captain in the 22nd Maine was Company E's Henry L. Wood of Dexter. Among the letters of recommendation we find these relating to Wood:

Dexter, Aug. 12, 1862
Bro. Hodsdon [Adjutant General John Hodsdon]

Henry L. Wood of Dexter, a man right in all respects, will be presented for a lieutenant's commission. He is a naturalized Englishman, but a thorough Yankee in heart. We will give him a most ample voucher for his patriotism....

Resp'ly yours, Josiah Crosby[5]

Dexter, 18 Aug. 1862
Bro Hodsdon,

Mr. Henry L. Wood of Dexter, of whom I wrote you a few days since, goes to Augusta [today?] in company with Mr. Horton. Now if you can do anything towards giving him the position desired do it; and you will never regret it. He is every way worth it and we are very desirous of gratifying him, and believe that the Model Republic will receive no detriment thereby. Push him along.

Yours truly, Josiah Crosby[6]

Dexter, 18 Aug. 1862
Bro. Washburn,

We are much interested in securing a position for Mr. Henry L. Wood of Dexter in one of the companies to be raised under the last call for 9 mos. men, believing Mr. Wood every way worthy of it. You will confer a great favor on me and many others by bringing about such an arrangement if possible. As Mr. Horton will have a personal interview with you and understands the whole matter it is unnecessary for me to say more.

Truly yours, Josiah Crosby[7]

Persistence could also apparently pay off for those seeking a commission. In the fall of 1861, Jasper Hutchings, a lawyer from the Bangor area who was then practicing in Northern Maine's Aroostock County, had written to Maine's adjutant general, John Hodsdon, and Governor Israel Washburn asking for an appointment as quartermaster in "a regiment of volunteers [that] is to be raised in this county to be under the command of Col John McClusky." This letter was followed by a letter from a number of leading citizens of Aroostock County endorsing Hutchings' appointment. Another letter, from a Bangor lawyer and probate judge, John Godfrey, also recommended Hutchings and stated, "Mr. Hutchings studies with Pro. Sanborn. He is, however, a reliable Republican — no secession in him." And it added, "I cannot say what his qualifications are for quarter-master, but think he would be faithful, honest, industrious, careful, & reliable." In November of 1861 another letter, from Joseph Bartlett, also recommended Jasper Hutchings' appointment.[8]

The Colonel McClusky mentioned in Hutchings' first letter led the 15th Maine Volunteers, but in spite of these letters, there is no Jasper Hutchings listed in that 3 year regiment. The story continues, however.

In the summer of 1862, new letters appeared, one from 7 members of the Aroostock County bar recommending Jasper Hutchings for a commission, along with a letter of introduction to the governor from Maine's secretary of state, Joseph Hall. Jasper Hutchings was given his commission this time and became 1st lieutenant of Company C, 22nd Maine. Lieutenant Hutchings survived the war and went on to practice law in Bangor. He was perhaps fortunate that he did not win his commission in the 15th Maine, for that regiment suffered even more losses than the 22nd, with

2. The Raising of a Maine Regiment

343 men dying of disease, while 5 died of wounds, compared with the 22nd Maine's total losses of 169 men.[9]

While Godfrey's letter gives an indication of the importance of the political leanings of a prospective officer, this is more clearly stated in a letter to Gov. Washburn from C.H. Norcroft of Charleston, Maine. While recommending Thomas Pekes to be captain of a company, Norcroft stated that "by so doing you would please many of our best Republicans and displease some of our strongest secession sympathizers." Pekes was appointed 2nd lieutenant of Company E, and was later promoted to 1st lieutenant.[10]

Other positions in the 22nd Maine were filled by a variety of means. Josiah Jordan, register of deeds in Dover, Maine, had written regarding the choice of surgeons to examine soldiers for the draft. The doctor who was recommended by Jordan, John W. Cook, became the assistant surgeon for the 22nd Maine. In a letter to Governor Washburn on August 30, 1862, Jordan himself requested a position:

> Dover, Maine, Aug. 30, 1862
> Gov. Washburn,
>
> I wish for a place in the army as surgeon or ass't surgeon. I have had an experience in an extensive practice medical and surgical from 1838 to 1857, and relinquished my practice to Dr. Freeland S. Holmes. Most of the time since then I have been reg'r of deeds for Piscataquis County, but failing of a re-nomination, in consequence of a difference in religious views between me and the Calvinist Baptists to whom I once belonged, I am at liberty to go into practice again, but not in this place as I am barred by agreement with Dr. Holmes. Under the circumstance, an appointment would be a favor. If you will mention the endorses which may be required — or any pre-requisites to an appointment, I shall be grateful for the favor. If you would prefer to see me at Augusta or elsewhere, I will promptly comply with the suggestion.
>
> Are the appointments all made in the reg'ts raised or to be raised?
>
> Your Ob't Sev't Josiah Jordan[11]

Josiah Jordan got his wish and became the surgeon of the 22nd Maine.

Reading some letters, such as those relating to Joseph Joy, can be tinged with sadness, as we now know what happened to the writers. Henry Crosby of Hampden, Maine, wrote to the governor stating that he believed he could obtain sufficient volunteers to form a company and asked the procedure once the required number was raised. At the time he wrote the governor about his hopes to enter the military, Crosby was superintendent of a paper mill in his home town, was 39 years old and had married Hannah Emerson in 1859. Crosby did become captain of Company A, 22nd Maine, was wounded in the night assault of June 11, 1863, and died of wounds on June 12.[12]

And then there is a letter from Edward Hanson, a 42 year old married man from Bangor, who informed the governor that he had enlisted to do his part "in putting down the rebellion." He then stated quite bluntly that his friends thought he should be given "some position that will pay better than a private's." Unfortunately, Hanson, who remained a private in the 22nd Maine's Company B, was sick at Newport News in late 1862 and died in the hospital there on May 10, 1863.[13]

The case of the 22nd Maine's Colonel Simon Jerrard gives little evidence as to why he was selected to be colonel of a regiment. At the time of the Civil War he was the chairman of the town of Palmyra's board of selectmen and was a well to do farmer in that town. In early September of 1862, just before the 9 month regiments were called to meet at their rendezvous sites around the state, he wrote to Adjutant General Hodsdon:

West Levant, Sept 4, 1862
Dear Sir,

I write to inform you that the town of Levant has determined to enlist its quota of men under the call of the president for nine months service and will probably complete such enlistment by the 9th Inst. or before.

The towns of Levant, Kenduskeag, Corinth, Garland and Plymouth desire to unite their respective quotas in one company and have made arrangements to that end, subject to your approval.

Very Respectfully, S. G. Jerrard, Chairman, Selectmen of Levant[14]

No other letters from Jerrard have surfaced relating to military matters prior to the regiment's formation, nor letters from others offering recommendations for Jerrard.

Olonzo G. Putnam became the 22nd Maine's lieutenant colonel and took command of the regiment at the Battle of Irish Bend, and again under difficult circumstances toward the end of the regiment's service. Putnam had written to Governor Washburn in May of 1862 asking for papers to enlist men.[15] He apparently did very well at his recruiting duties, for we find the following letter written to Maine's adjutant general:

Aug. 27, 1862
Adjutant General J. L. Hodsdon

The enlistment papers sent to us with your circular of the 19th instant were placed in the hands of Capt. O. G. Putnam, who has enlisted the quota of men required by our town since Monday morning being two days only.

Respectfully Yours,
Josiah Spaulding, by order of Selectmen of Dover[16]

2. The Raising of a Maine Regiment 23

Putnam is also given the following recommendation:

> Foxcroft, Sept. 3, 1862
>
> Permit me to introduce to your acquaintance and favor, Mr. O. G. Putnam of Dover who has been instrumental in enlisting some fifty or sixty men under the call for the state militia. Mr. Putnam is an active energetic reliable man upon whose sentiments and representations [you] may implicitly rely. Any favor you can grant him will [be] duly appreciated by him &
>
> Very Truly your ob't Serv't,
> John H. Rice
>
> P.S. Should Mr. Putnam desire to see the governor you will oblige me by giving him an introduction.[17]

In the 1862 Maine adjutant general's report, there are several pages dedicated to listing the qualifications of regimental officers. While some of those men had some military experience, many had none. Examples include:

> Colonel Thomas A. Roberts of the Seventeenth Regiment was one of the most valued citizens of Portland, and acquired a reputation as a disciplinarian while in command of the "Mechanic Blues," one of the best of the uniformed militia organizations in the State.[18]
>
> The Eighteenth Regiment was fortunate in obtaining as its colonel, Major Daniel Chaplin of the Second [Maine Regiment], who entered service at the organization of that veteran regiment, and who could bring to the discharge of his new and responsible duties the experience thus acquired.[19]

And, in a regiment well known to many:

> First Lieutenant Adelbert Ames, formerly of Rockland, and who had acquired a high reputation for energy, skill and bravery during the present conflict, was appointed colonel of the Twentieth Regiment. He was graduated from the Military Academy at West Point, and at the time of his appointment was a member of the corps of Topographical Engineers, by voluntary transfer from the Second Regiment United States Artillery. Joshua L. Chamberlain of Brewer, professor of modern languages at Bowdoin College at Brunswick, a gentleman of the highest moral, intellectual and literary worth, was appointed lieutenant colonel, and Captain Charles D. Gilmore of Bangor of Company C, Seventh Regiment, who served with marked distinction and ability in the Peninsular campaign, was appointed major.[20]

One must wonder why Joshua Chamberlain, who was actually offered the colonelcy and turned it down, was given higher command responsibility than Charles Gilmore, the veteran soldier of the 7th Maine. Perhaps the status as "gentleman of the highest moral, intellectual and literary worth" was considered of greater importance. It is also quite possible that there was a hope or assumption that Professor Chamberlain might bring more Bowdoin men with him to the army.[21]

The sentence given to the 22nd Maine's colonel states, "Colonel Simon G. Jerrard of the Twenty-second, though not widely known, is esteemed by his friends and townsmen as a gentleman of energy, capacity and the strictest integrity." The 22nd's second and third in command are described in this way: "Lieutenant Colonel Putman and Major Brackett, will not, it is believed, disappoint the flattering hopes of their constituents."[22] And so, we still must guess at the reasons for these commissions as the 22nd's field officers.

3

Francis Ireland and the Boys from Dexter

To fill the ranks of the Union Army that summer of 1862, the small town of Dexter, Maine, was doing its part and had already sent men to fight for the Union. Dexter was known, if known at all, for its woolen mills. These mills were built along the East Branch of the Sebasticook River, which falls 142 feet in less than a mile and, with a series of dams, provided ample water power.

Even with its mills, Dexter in 1862 was a rural town with a population under 3,000; it was not located on a railroad line, or on the coast, or on a major river. It was a town you were not likely to go through on your way to somewhere else, and, unless you lived or worked there, probably thought little about — a nice, typical working town in Maine.[1]

That summer, Francis Ireland was working in a Dexter woolen mill and had just turned 19. Although he had been preparing for college, he instead enlisted in one of the new regiments, against his parents' wishes. Francis was joining with other local men in volunteering for a company being raised by Dexter's Henry Wood, a transplanted Englishman who had come to Dexter to work in the woolen trade. This company would be part of a regiment being organized by Simon Jerrard from the nearby small town of Levant, who would become its colonel. Prior to this military service, Jerrard had been involved, with his father, in the lumber business and was serving as chairman of Levant's selectmen. The regiment was known temporarily as the "Penobscot Regiment," since its members came primarily from Penobscot County, but soon was designated the 22nd Maine Volunteer Infantry.

The regiment was raised for a 9 month term of service, and its new recruits were assembling that September of 1862 in Bangor, the county

Top: Main Street, Dexter in the 1860s (Dexter Historical Society). *Above:* Abbott Woolen Mill, ca. 1860 (Dexter Historical Society).

3. Francis Ireland and the Boys from Dexter

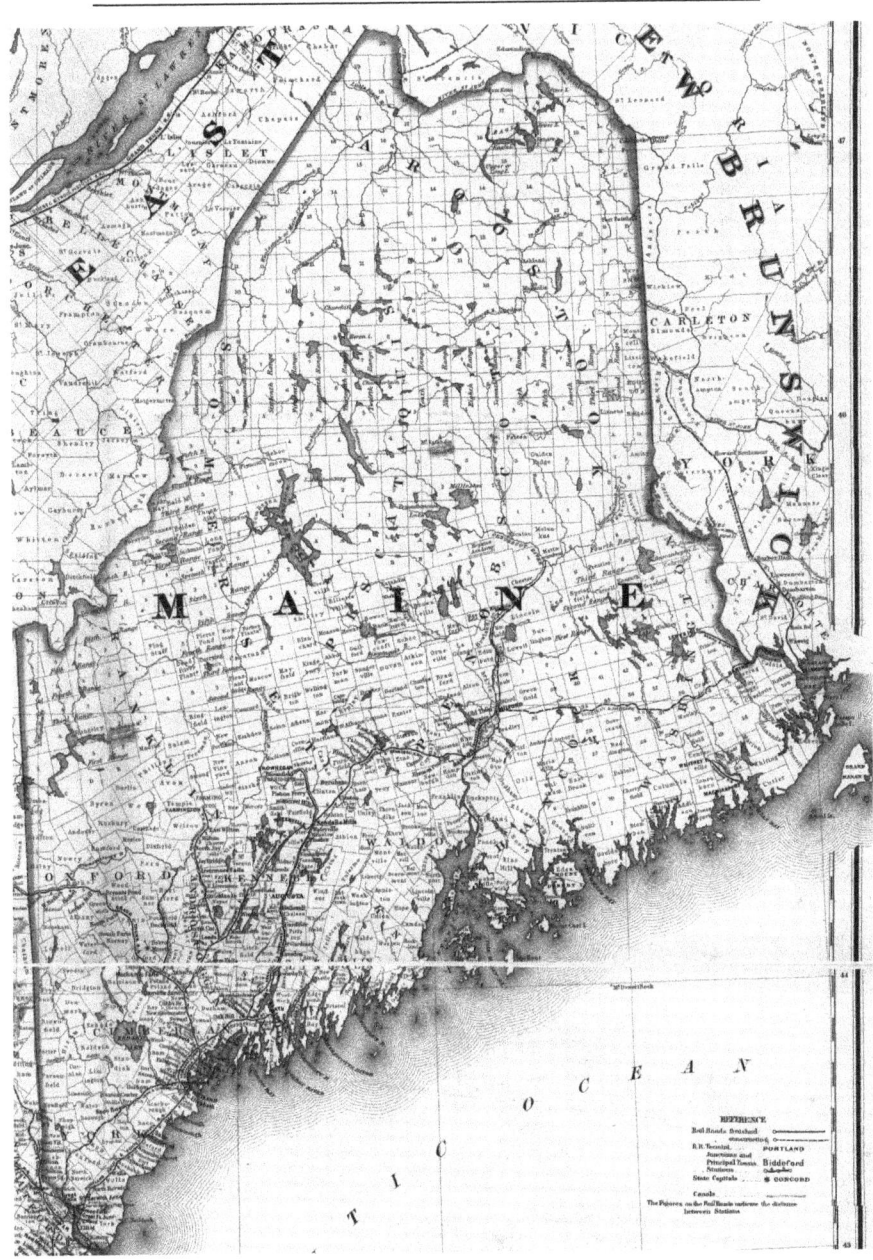

Maine, 1860 (see page 28 for detail) (Library of Congress).

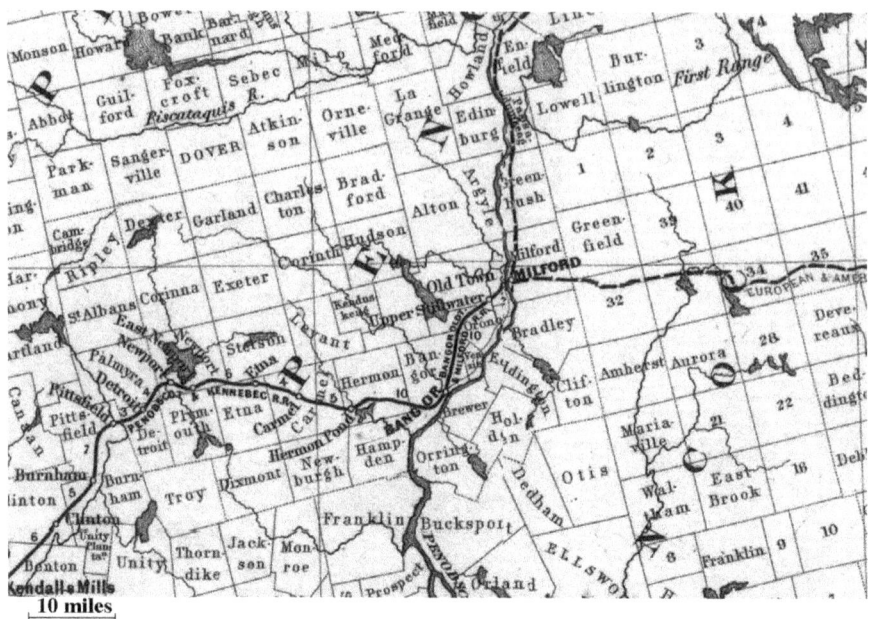

South central Maine, 1860: Bangor is shown at the approximate center, while Dexter and surrounding towns are toward the northwest. While this railroad map does not include roads, it does show the relative positions of many towns mentioned in the text (Library of Congress).

seat, to be mustered in and fitted out. Francis and other Dexter boys were assigned to Company E, commanded by their neighbor, the newly commissioned Captain Henry Wood.[2]

For many young men of that era and that town, a trip to Bangor was in itself a bit of an adventure, and it is unlikely that Francis had ever traveled much more than those 25 or so miles. Bangor of the 1860s was a thriving city with a population of over 16,000. Ships from around the world traveled up the Penobscot River to Bangor at the head of the tidal water to be loaded with the logs which were run down that river every spring, or with lumber that was cut from those logs. Bangor's busy waterfront, its rail junction, its various stores, its many impressive homes, its Irish slums, as well as its ale houses and bawdy houses, would present quite a different level of excitement from that offered in Dexter.[3]

Back in Dexter, Francis' father, John Ireland, worked as a cloth finisher in the woolen mill, one of the more highly skilled jobs. Also at home were Francis' mother, Martha, his two younger brothers, Eben and

Top: A portion of downtown Bangor in the mid–1800s (Bangor Public Library).
Above: The Bangor waterfront in the mid–1800s (Bangor Public Library).

Olin, and his baby sister Flora. Once Francis made the decision to enlist, his parents' letters indicate both support and concern for him. Francis almost always addressed his letters and their salutations to his father, but often specifically requested that his mother be asked or told certain things. Although sometimes signing his letters "Frank," more often he closed his letters with more apparent formality, typical of that era, "from your son, Francis A. Ireland."

By September 27, 1862, Francis Ireland's new life in the Union Army had begun, and he wrote home from the recruits' rendezvous at Camp Pope in Bangor. His letter shows the eagerness with which he was entering upon his military adventure, although this was coupled with a desire that the adventure not last past the agreed upon 9 months. A number of the regiments raised that summer offered a 9 month term of enlistment, and for many young men this presented a more attractive option than enlisting for 2 or 3 years, as had been the case in earlier regiments. The state of Maine raised 8 new regiments that summer for 9 months of service. After all, many of the young men from Maine, including some of those who worked in Dexter's woolen mills, were farm boys whose help at home would be needed the next summer.

> Dear Father,
>
> As I am at leisure today I will write after dinner and let you know how we get along. ... There are but about 12 or 15 hundred soldiers here. When it was decided that we should not be mustered in last week a great many got furloughs to go home. They say we shall be mustered in next week but they said just so last Sunday. The boys are getting very uneasy and they are not much to blame either. The trouble is they want to be mustered in and be sure that our 9 months is not going to run all through next summer.

The conditions in their camp are apparently agreeable, as he continues: "We shall not find so good fare in any respect after we leave here as we do now. We are in a healthy and pleasant location and have the best of food of the kind pork and beans, warm brown bread, white bread and hard bread, beef steak fried once a day or oftener, and soup now and then, also corned beef in any quantity, tea and coffee, and molasses by the wholesale."

The "Boys" were, however, not above expressing their displeasure, as they did with two of the sutlers who sold goods to the soldiers. "Last Thursday night about ½ past 9 the soldiers (about 300) tore one all out everything that there was in the building and stove the crockery into splinters, it belonged to H.L. and R.C. Boyd, they were rather high on prices and the boys were rather saucy for 3 or 4 days before, and it turned out as it did." Yet, Francis and his friends appear to be pleased with their overall situation, their officers, and the attention the new soldiers were receiving. He continues his September 27 letter:

> It is quite a sight or will be when we get uniformed to come to Camp Pope and see the companies out. There are a great many people here every day — coaches, hacks, omnibuses, &c &c &c — a great business. Our reg't officers are first rate men, none of your stuck up dandies with brass buttons, perhaps you know them. Col. Gerard [Simon Jerrard], of Levant, and Lieut. Col. Putnam, of Dover, and Maj. Brackett, of Palmyra. There is a great rush for the office of chaplain, adjutant, surgeon, &c. They will be appointed soon.

After naming the two contenders for the surgeon's position — Drs. Benson and Jordan, Francis goes on to thank his folks for some honey, apples, and tarts they had sent, and then goes on, "Milkmen do a great business here. Milk is 6 cts. per quart and very good, most of it. We "Sojurs" have a dish of brown bread and milk just when we choose." He closes with: "Write soon and write all of the news. I don't get much of any here. ... Our address is "Co. E, Penobscot Reg't, Camp Pope, Bangor. Me. "Care of Capt H.L. Wood"... Write soon. From, Francis A. Ireland."[4] In his closing of this letter, Francis states a theme that was continued in most of his letters — his desire to have frequent news from home.

The question of the term of enlistment and the date on which the men's 9 months' service began was addressed in a letter to Maine Governor Israel Washburn around this same time by H.T. Batchelder — presumed to be Hiram T. Batchelder, sergeant of the 22nd Maine's Company B. In that letter he asks if the 9 months will commence from September 10, the date of enlistment, or from the date of muster, and he adds, "The answer to this will make quiet many minds." For the men of the 9 month regiments, this was an important issue. Nine months starting with September 10 would have the men home early the following June. We may assume that an answer was not given, since this question was raised many more times over the next months.[5]

From Francis' next letter, dated Sept 29, we learn that the men, although still eager to be issued uniforms, had to be satisfied for the time being with drawing their undergarments from the quartermaster. Francis enjoys the play on words of having "nothing to draw but drawers." We then learn of another disruption to military discipline.

> There are a lot of rum shops here or was yesterday, and some of the men got poisoned with the "rot gut" and last night one man was thought to be dying,

which set the men all on fire to rip them out, — the officers made no objections seeing it was no use to resist half a regiment, — and at about 9 o'clock last night it being all understood they all run the guard out to the road about 60 rods then went to the place where the man got the Stuff a large two story house and called them out, — they [said they] knew nothing about it. The boys came back and attacked one of 6 or 8 [rum shops] that stand at the end of our road and tore it all out, everything there was in it, found a little liquor but not the rot gut, — they went back to the first place and about 25 men went into the house while the rest surrounded it and the man caved in and delivered up a lot of kegs, ½ barrels and bottles and jugs which they stove all to bits and burned the liquor. It was a mob but the officers did not say a word for they were glad of it. A hard set of boys here.[6]

On October 5, still at Camp Pope and with some impatience showing, Francis wrote to explain the delay in mustering the new regiment. From the group of 1200 to 1500 that Francis mentioned in his Sept. 27 letter, the recruits gathered in Bangor had grown to approximately 3,000. It appears that those intended to fill the diminished ranks of older regiments were the first to be mustered. Francis wrote: "The recruiting officers have enlisted over 500 for old regiments which has caused a great deal of trouble and delay in forming the companies."[7]

This statement is an interesting reflection of the way regiments were formed. With professional soldiers in short supply, a man might gain an officer's commission as a lieutenant or even captain if he obtained the papers to recruit a group of men for a new regiment, and regimental officers for these new regiments were often chosen by rewarding political reliability rather than military experience. (For a more detailed look at the way regiments were raised, the rationale for 9 month regiments, the squabbles between towns to fill quotas, and the politics of the selection of officers, see Appendix A.)

Francis then continues his September 29 letter,

Then after they [the men for the "old" regiments] were formed, we had two regiments and a battalion of about 400 men. Well it has been "muster in tomorrow" from morning till night: and next week certain for the last 3 weeks until nobody credits or will believe it until we hold up our hand and take the oath for certainty. A part of our uniforms and equipments came onto the grounds last night, and Adjutant Flagg [Frank G. Flagg of Hampden, Maine] told me this morning that we should be uniformed and equipped this week ... and I think very likely we shall be mustered in also.

The second regiment that Francis refers to above and which would be mustered at Bangor at that time was the 26th Maine Infantry, and the men of the 22nd would meet these fellow soldiers again, far from Maine.[8]

With uniforms and equipment about to be issued, many of the men had already made plans to have them altered or various adjustments made. Among those was Francis' friend and cousin, Charles W. Farrar of Dexter, who also served in Company E. In many letters, Francis writes about "Charles" or "Charlie" and unless otherwise indicated, it is to Charlie Farrar that he refers.[9] He writes:

> "Charlie is going [to get a furlough] when he gets his uniform to get it fixed up &c, he wants me to go and as I want some pockets in my uniform, blouse lined, and blanket bound on the ends &c ... I must have them fixed and as folks work for pay here I can't get it done here as cheap as I might go home, all of the Dexter boys will come as soon as we can get a furlough."

Aside from getting uniforms "fixed up," it seems very likely the boys also wanted to show off their new uniforms and military status to the folks at home.

And then, starting with the regiment's chaplain, Francis goes on to reassure his family that not all in the regiment are a "hard set of boys." He says, "Our Chap. is Dr. J.K. Lincoln of this city a young preacher [who] was ordained this week. He appears like a nice man. ... Tell Alice and the rest of the mill girls that this is a grand place for them to pick out a man for there are men and boys of all trades, ages, weight, size, height, and disposition ... they are very good looking and generally behave pretty well taken as a body of men.[10]

The Ireland family had strong ties to the Methodist Church in Dexter, and so the character of the regiment's chaplain would be important to Francis and his family. John K. Lincoln graduated from the Bangor Theological Seminary that summer and was ordained September 30. And Francis may have thought that his previous descriptions of breaches of military discipline might have overly distressed his parents.[11]

4

Leaving Maine

There was a strong inducement to recruit for a new regiment and become an officer, rather than recruiting for existing regiments whose officers were already in place. This also gave a strong local character to most companies, as the men of each company tended to be from a specific town or a group of nearby small towns. Like Private Francis Ireland and Captain Henry Wood, Company E came, for the most part, from Dexter and other small towns in that area. In fact, 32 of the company's 89 men at the time of their muster came from Dexter, with most of the others coming from nearby Corinna, Hudson, and Charleston. However, one group of about a dozen men came from small towns farther north, such as Lincoln, Lee, Springfield, and Macwahoc. It seems that this latter group of men was led by W. Prince Hersey, who had been a sergeant in the town militia in Lincoln. Hersey was rewarded for his efforts by being named 1st lieutenant of Company E.[1]

As the regiment prepared for their mustering into the Union Army, the 10 companies of the 22nd Maine, their captains, and the general geographic areas from which they drew the majority of their men were as follows.

- Company A, Captain Henry Crosby of Hampden, towns just west and southwest of Bangor, such as Hampden, Hermon, Corinna, Carmel, and Newburg.
- Company B, Captain James Williams of Bangor, Bangor and some small towns north, northeast and southeast of Bangor, such as Holden, Dedham, Veazie, Glenburn, Hudson, and Lagrange.
- Company C, Captain George Bolton of Orrington, Brewer and small towns south and east of Brewer, such as Orrington, Eddington, Amherst, Aurora, and Waite Plantation (close to the Canadian border).

- Company D, Captain Charles Union of Addison, from the coast of Maine's "Downeast" Washington County, including towns such as Addison, Harrington, Columbia, Jonesport, and Cherryfield.
- Company E, Captain Henry Wood of Dexter, Dexter and surrounding small towns, but with a group from farther north and east (see above).
- Company F, Captain William Taylor of Calais, from inland Washington County including the towns of Calais, Robinson, Alexander, Crawford, Baring, Cooper, and Meddybemps.
- Company G, Captain Aziel Putnam of Houlton, from northern Maine's Aroostook County including the towns of Houlton, Hodgdon, Fort Fairfield, Danforth, Monticello, Linneus, and Bridgewater. Also, for some reason, several men from Belfast, on the Penobscot Bay, also enlisted in this company.
- Company H, Captain Isaac Case of Kenduskeag, small towns just northwest of Bangor such as Kenduskeag, Corinth, Garland, Exeter, Levant, Plymouth, and Stetson.
- Company I, Captain Archibald Lambert of Dover, towns northwest of Bangor such as Dover, Foxcroft, Guilford, Sangerville, Atkinson, and Sebec.
- Company K, Captain Turner Whitehouse of Newport, Newport and other towns west of Bangor such as Palmyra, Etna, Exeter, Hartland, St Albans, and Dixmont.[2]

The soldiers of the 22nd Maine were finally mustered into the Union Army on October 10, 1862, almost a month after being ordered to Bangor in the second week of September. On October 19, Francis wrote to his father with news of the regiment's impending departure from the state and his attempts to get details tidied up before they left.

Dear Father;

We have received marching orders to leave Tuesday morning, but we may not get ready to leave so soon. Shall leave this week certain. If my mittens are done and you get a chance to send them direct to camp Monday P.M. be sure and send them. If not, wait till you get Tuesday's paper or a letter from me, which will inform you whether we have left or not....

We do not know our destination. Some say it is Washington, New Orleans, *Texas* &c. I think however that we shall go to Washington first at any rate, should not be at all surprised if we left there for one of the last two places or some other place in that direction. We may not get our shoes before we leave here, shall not get our arms until we get to New York or Washington. Be sure and write by the first mail. ... I am on guard today as usual. Must close this soon to send it to the city to night.

Be sure and write,
Francis A. Ireland[3]

On October 21, the 22nd Maine left the state and made its way by rail and steamship to Washington, D.C., arriving there on the 24th. For the young men of the regiment, this trip must have seemed the beginning of a great adventure. Their passage through Portland, Maine's largest city, and Boston would have awed many from rural Maine. And it is interesting to read in Francis' next letter — of October 25 — that after arriving in Boston the regiment "marched about a mile and a half and took another train for Norwich, Conn." (Even today, train travelers from Maine through Boston must get themselves from that city's North Station to its South Station to continue toward Connecticut or New York, although few march.)

Francis goes on in this October 25 letter to give his father further details of their journey, and the general tone of excitement is clear. This letter is written from Washington, D.C. on stationery bearing the 22nd Maine's letterhead.

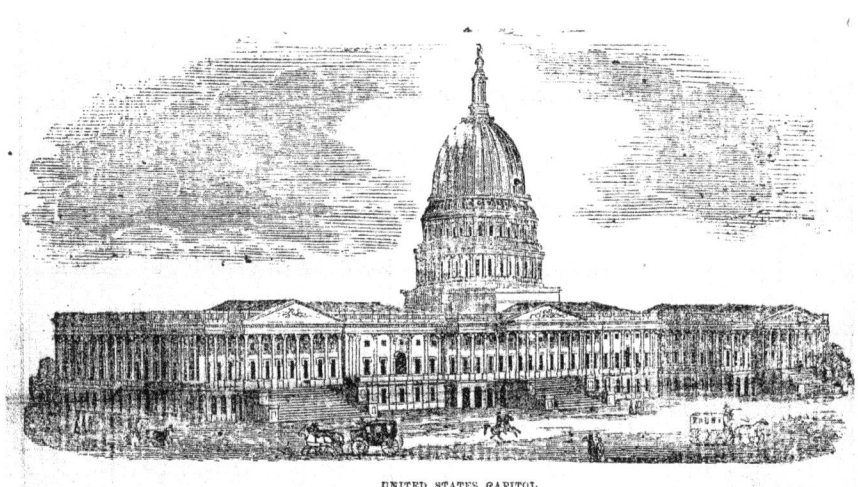

Letterhead of the 22nd Maine's stationery.

4. Leaving Maine

The steamship *City of New York*. (Samuel W. Stanton, *American Steam Vessels*, New York: Smith and Stanton, 1895).

> [At Norwich, the regiment] went onboard the splendid steamer "City of New York" for Jersey City N. J. The wind was pretty high in the river (Connecticut, [Connecticut] it was) but when we got in to Long Island Sound the waves rolled splendid I tell you. The boys went up on deck as soon as we started to look at the sights on the river and sound as we passed along they began to "heave up Jonah" at a good rate. They were a sorry looking set I tell you, heaving as though they had taken a quart of lobelia [a plant known to induce vomiting]. I and Charles never had a touch of it. I never felt better in my life. I must turn from my subject and close so to get this in to the mail. I have been up to the capital this morn ... we got here last night I will write tomorrow or next day
>
> Good bye,
> Frank
>
> direct [mail to] 22d Me. Regt. Co. E M.V.
> Washington, D.C.
> Care Capt. Henry L. Wood
> Write immediately. I close all in a "hub bub."[4]

And with all Francis has seen over those few days — including the nation's capital — it is easy to understand his closing comment.

Upon their arrival in Washington, the regiment was sent to Arlington Heights and temporarily assigned to the 3rd Brigade, Casey's Division, Reserved Army Corps, commanded by Colonel Francis Fessenden of the 25th Maine. Colonel Fessenden was the son of U.S. senator William P. Fessenden from Maine.[5]

Another perspective on the 22nd Maine's journey to Washington comes from a letter written by Company H's Captain, Isaac W. Case.

> Our journey to Washington was a very tiresome one, taking three days and nights, with no stops for rest till we got to Baltimore — & not much chance

The capitol in August 1862: "Great War Meeting." In this drawing, the dome is unfinished, as it was when Francis Ireland visited in late October (*Harper's Weekly*, August 23, 1862).

for rest there, as we slept on the plank platform of the depot, with a roof over us but all open at the sides. It was a cold night & had we not been pretty well worn out we should not have got much sleep. We got to Washington Friday night, Oct. 24th, slept again on a floor & the next day marched across the "long bridge" into Virginia to a spot about five miles from Washington called Camp Seward, which we reached just at dark Saturday night. We had not tents,

4. Leaving Maine

& lay down in our blankets with a cold north wind blowing over & through us. The next morning it began to rain with the wind blowing strongly from the north east, and our only shelter from the storm consisted of tents made of blankets stretched on poles. These gave us little protection from the rain, & we were all wet from head to foot.

Some of the men complained bitterly, but most of my men rather enjoyed the fun. I never felt better in my life, and did all in my power to keep up the spirits of the boys. The rain continued all day, & till noon Monday. Our tents arrived about dark Tuesday night, & we pitched a part of them over the wet ground, built up roaring fires & slept — as much as we could! Some of the men took cold, but most of them bore the hardship well.[6]

In a letter written on October 31, Francis' father, John Ireland, gives the general news and weather from Dexter and news of the mill. After telling his son what reports of the regiment have appeared in the local newspapers, and offering a tip for sending letters home, Mr. Ireland gives Francis some basic advice.

My Dear Son:

We received your letter last evening and were glad to hear of your good luck in going from Maine to Washington. We had not heard anything of the 22d Regt. since the announcement in the paper of its arrival in New York. You and Charles were very fortunate in not being sea-sick, for it gave you a much better chance for observation. ... I see by the papers that several of the new reg'ts from Maine were stopped in New York, and report says that they are to form part of a southern expedition under Gen. Banks.

We want you to write often — write when convenient. By the way, I believe there is an arrangement of the Post Office department, by which soldiers can send letters without prepaying postage, if they are marked "Soldier's Letter," Washington had one from George thus marked and stamped "3 cts. due" and hence paid at the office when received. You can ascertain by enquiring of your capt., or some one that would be likely to know. If it is so, you had better avail yourself of the privilege, so as to save your change. I had rather pay postage on all you send if I can do so. With this I send a Daily Courier [the *Bangor Daily Whig and Courier*] which may be interesting to you.

Be careful of your health: do not expose yourself unnecessarily: but shrink from no duty. If unwell and not able to do duty be not afraid to tell your commander or those having authority in the premises.

Yours, Affectionately,
J.P. Ireland[7]

The reports that John Ireland had seen concerning General Banks' expedition proved to be true. The 22nd was to be a part of the 19th Corps, the Department of the Gulf, under Major General Nathaniel Prentis Banks. The newspapers had apparently gotten advance knowledge of events, since it was about a week after John Ireland's letter that General Banks received his orders to succeed General Benjamin Franklin Butler as commander of the Department of the Gulf. Headquartered in New Orleans, this department encompassed all the Union troops and federally held areas in the Mississippi Gulf states. When General Banks took command in December 1862, he was presented with the following objectives: "The freedom of the Mississippi; an expedition to Jackson and Marion [Mississippi] after the fall of Vicksburg and Port Hudson; and the occupation of the Red River country as a protection for Louisiana and Arkansas and a basis for future operations against Texas."[8]

Nathaniel Banks had come from a relatively poor family in Waltham, Massachusetts, and had, as a boy, worked in a cotton mill. This experience was the basis for his later nickname "Bobbin Boy," which was used as a derisive term by his detractors. After studying law and being admitted to the bar, he entered politics in his mid 20s. After serving in the Massachusetts Assembly, he was elected to the U.S. House of Representatives in 1853. Having been at various times a member of the Free Soil Party, the Democratic Party, and the Know-nothings, he became a Republican in 1855 and was chosen speaker of the House. Resigning from Congress in 1856, he was elected governor of Massachusetts. Leaving that position in 1861, he succeeded George B. McClellan (later to be major general, U.S. Army) as president of the Illinois Central Railroad. With no military experience, but with considerable political power, he was commissioned in May of 1861 as major general of volunteers. First assigned as head of the Department of Annapolis, he later led the Department of the Shenandoah, and in March of 1862

General Nathaniel Banks (Library of Congress).

was briefly given command of the 5th Corps, Army of the Potomac. After a reorganization of the army he commanded the 2nd Corps, Army of Virginia, and in September of 1862 was given the job of overseeing the defense of Washington.[9]

While an obvious goal of Banks' expedition would be the opening of the Mississippi and the elimination of a major supply route for the Confederacy through Texas, the plan for an expedition into the lower Mississippi River and Texas had strong support, for other reasons, from Massachusetts Governor John Andrew. Andrew, a solidly abolitionist Republican, hoped that Texas and western Louisiana, freed of Confederate control, would become a first step toward total emancipation and, on a somewhat more pragmatic level, a source of much needed raw material for Massachusetts' cotton mills. In promoting this expedition, Governor Andrew also strongly urged that his predecessor as governor of Massachusetts, Nathaniel Banks, be put in command.[10]

With their trip south with General Banks just ahead, the 22nd Maine spent their week or so in Arlington drilling and performing guard duty. They left their Arlington camp on November 3 and traveled to Washington, where they expected to board transport vessels. Instead, they were taken by two small steamboats to Alexandria, Virginia, just a few miles down the Potomac, to wait for the steamship that was to take them on the next part of their journey.[11]

On November 4, Francis wrote from Alexandria to tell his family the latest regarding their preparations to move south.

Dear Father:

Here we are. Just left the steamers that have brought us down from Washington. I have looked in vain for letter for 2 or 3 days and as we are to leave for parts unknown tonight or tomorrow, I improve this last chance for I don't know how long! to write again. The 22d, 25th, 26th, 27th Me. Reg'ts were camped together, or near each other on Arlington Heights Va. and have been under marching orders for a number of days past. Our reg't struck tents and commenced leaving the grounds for Washington last night with 5 cos. of the 26th Reg't for Washington. I was one who stayed on the grounds all night and came down with the baggage this morning. It is expected that the 27th with the other 5 cos. of the 26th is going with us. You will ask where are we going? nobody knows! not even the colonel, but all suppose that we are going down South whether to Texas, S. Carolina, Georgia or where we don't know. It is said that we are to have 30 days' rations aboard of the vessel, also that we cannot write (after we get there) and get an answer in 2 months, but these are flying reports. I hear that we are to camp here tonight as it is impossible to get the vessel ready for us to day.

Once again, we see that Francis and his comrades are left to guess their destination from the rumors that surround them.

The other Maine regiments that Francis listed, the 25th, 26th, and 27th, were also serving 9 month enlistments. The 26th Maine, which had been mustered in Bangor at the same time as the 22nd, was, like the 22nd, being sent to General Banks' Department of the Gulf. The 25th and 27th, however, would spend their time of service in the defenses of Washington, losing their 20 or so casualties to disease alone.[12] Francis goes on to give an indication of the living conditions during the move to Alexandria.

> Charlie mentioned my being lame in his letter and for fear that you will be worried about me, I will explain. When we moved into Va. from Washington Sat [urday] I had rather a bad cold, and Sunday it rained like blazes and we had not a rag of a tent in the reg't — the boys took their blankets and made some tents, open on the front — and the back sides running to the ground and built fires in front which was quite a shelter but the men and all of the officers got completely soaked. The tents came just-at-night Sunday. The mud was "kinder deep" and only a few of the squads put up their tents. We put ours up [and] got through the night nicely altho it rained and blowed all night. My cold settled in my legs above my knees — they swelled some and made me quite lame. A great many of the men in the regt took an awful cold which made some sickness, altho it was only temporary. The doctors took charge of them and they are all getting along very well. I have not been on duty yet, but my legs are about as limber as ever; I consider myself better off than a great many of the men, am in tip top Spirit about our trip down South only I feel like all of the rest awful curious to know where we are going![13]

Not everyone in the 22nd Maine was, it appears, in as good spirits as was Francis. The father of Company A's George Knowles complained bitterly in a letter to Maine's Governor Washburn about the regiment's lack of adequate protection from the elements and the nature of the food his son was given. The writer, Elkanah Knowles, also complains about a change in the regiment's commissary sergeant — a change that also has a family connection for Knowles.

> To His Excellently I. Washburn, Gov. of Maine
> You with others who advised this calling out of the nine months men, we would inquire why they were suffered to leave the state in this season of the year before receiving all their clothes and no rubber blankets hurried through to Washington there in sight of the capital to stand out two days and knights [sic] in a cold northeast rain storm, nothing but the Heavens to cover them in that storm. I had a dear son, reared tenderly and in delicate health suffered through this storm, also a brother, lieutenant of Company A 22nd Maine, who writes that he is sick at that they are all drifting towards the hospital. My

son writes that he has had nothing to eat but wheat brick & tin cup of tea, except what they bought, he carried about nine dollars with him he supposed would last till he received some from this state or the general government. He writes he has spent most all for something to eat, the thought of his sufferings wrings my very heart, when I consented that he should serve his country I supposed he would be properly cared for, think of it, you who have dear children, I forgot to say in the time before he wrote they had meat once I believe when he wrote he had been in Washington 3 or 4 days.

I would inquire if the colonel had a wright [sic] to remove commissary sergeant after sworn in to U.S. without any cause but to put in a favorite whom the soldiers disliked. The young man that was removed was John Westly Knowles a nephew of mine, both honest and capable. I hope you will see that our troops are properly cared for.

Yours most respectfully, Elkanah Knowles, Hampden, Maine[14]

The writer's nephew, John W. Knowles, was indeed returned to the ranks as a private. His son, George Knowles, a corporal in 1862, was also returned to the ranks as a private in 1863. And presumably not by mere coincidence, at about this same time that this letter was written, Elkanah Knowles' younger brother, Thomas J. Knowles, resigned as Company A's 1st lieutenant. It should also come as no surprise that, when the national draft of 1863 came, Elkanah Knowles' eldest son, Elkanah Jr., hired a substitute to take his place.[15]

But now, continuing his letter on Wednesday morning, November 5, Francis adds

We camped here last night. Expect to leave today. I am as smart as ever this morn. I want you to send me the Tribune and Courier (weekly if you can get it) regularly as we can't get a bit of war news in the Army. You can write to me and direct it to Washington and I shall be likely to get it. It will do no hurt if I don't, but write. I may get a letter to day from you if we don't leave too early. I will write as soon as we land at our stopping place. Shall send for some stamps then. Would write more but have no time.

From,
Frank

Good Bye for the Present[16]

The importance of newspapers and the lack of news about the war were themes that Francis restated several times. We can, perhaps, imagine the sense of isolation that these young soldiers felt, far from home and cut off from the news of the day. This is coupled with the irony of being at the "seat of war" and not knowing what was happening all around them. As before, the "Courier" is no doubt the *Bangor Daily Whig and Courier*, while the Tribune may be the *New York Tribune*, since there was no Maine newspaper with "Tribune" in its title at that time.

5

New Camps, New Sights

On November 5, the regiment embarked on the steamship *S.R. Spaulding* and moved down the Potomac River and the Chesapeake Bay, reaching their destination at Fortress Monroe on the 7th. According to Colonel Jerrard, the *Spaulding*, although "one of the best transports in the government service ... was not properly fitted for the conveyance of soldiers." Only 7 companies could be quartered below decks, leaving 3 companies to remain on deck and exposed to the elements, resulting in "a most uncomfortable passage" for many of the men during "a most relentless storm of sleet and wind." The colonel went on to say that "the soldiers were late from comfortable homes and had not yet been inured to the privations and exposures inseparably connected with the life of a soldier. And not withstanding the efforts of the officers on their behalf there was considerable suffering."[1]

Perhaps as a reminder to himself for a future letter home, Francis Ireland wrote a short note on the back of his father's Oct. 31 letter:"Left Alexandria Thursday morn and started down the Potomac, went on deck early for observation, past Fort Washington on the Md. side. The land on that shore is very level and pretty, a little more rough on the V'r side."[2]

Arriving at Fortress Monroe, near the tip of Virginia's Yorktown Peninsula, on November 7, the 22nd Maine was the first regiment of General Banks' Expedition to reach this rendezvous. Although deep in Confederate Virginia at the mouth of the James River, Fortress Monroe and the area surrounding it remained in Union hands throughout the Civil War. Cut off from the Union by land, it was nevertheless accessible by sea, and, with the Union stronghold at Newport News just 5 miles to the west, provided a base for Union operations in that area.

Not allowed to land at the fort itself, the regiment proceeded to Newport News, "where comfortable barracks were found for the soldiers." Col-

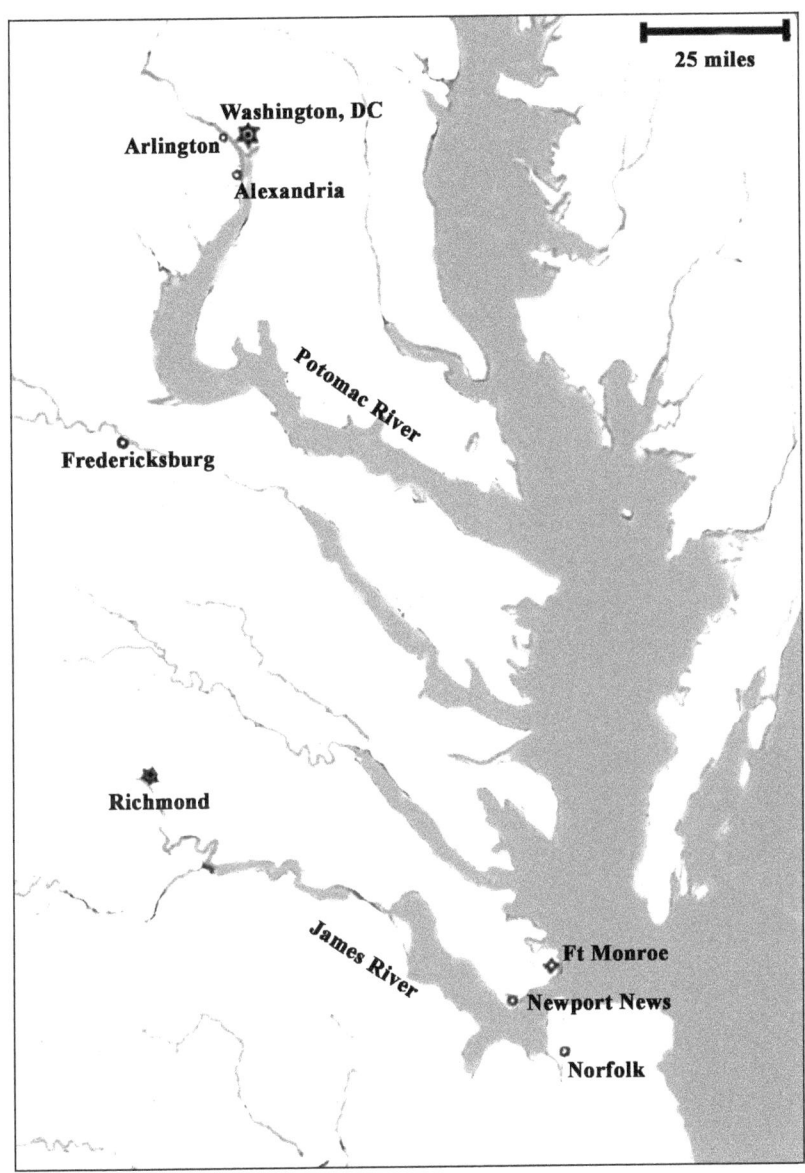

Map adapted from Plate 135-A: *The Official Military Atlas of the Civil War.*

onel Jerrard also noted that at this camp the regiment "enjoyed opportunities for drill which we had not found elsewhere." The colonel also writes that while at Newport News, "the resignations of 1st Lieut. [Thomas J.] Knowles and 2nd Lt. [James P.] Ireland [both of Co. A] were tendered and accepted and 1st Sgt. Geo. E. Brown and Sgt. [Gipson] Patten were

The steamship *S.R. Spaulding* (*American Steam Vessels* by Edward Ward Stanton).

Moat and seaward side of Fortress Monroe (*Harper's Weekly*, June 29, 1861).

promoted to fill the vacancies." What the colonel omits is that Sgt. Hiram Batchelder was originally promoted along with Sgt. Brown, but Batchelder's resignation in December resulted in Sgt. Patten's promotion to 2nd lieutenant. It is interesting, of course, that officers could simply resign if they chose to do so — a luxury not afforded to other ranks.[3]

Union troops arriving at Newport News (*Harper's Weekly*, June 29, 1861).

For the 22nd Maine's arrival at Newport News, Company H's Captain Isaac Case gives us this following perspective. Having spent a night at Alexandria, Captain Case says the regiment

> transferred tents & baggage on board steamer S.R. Spaulding, in which we came down the Potomac to Fortress Monroe, arriving about midnight Thursday, Nov. 6th. On Saturday we steamed up to this place [Newport News], about eight miles from the fort and took possession of a part of the empty barracks standing here.
> These were occupied last summer by sick & wounded soldiers from McClellan's army. At one time it is said there were from two to three thousand of these. Many of the poor fellows now lie in the grave yard on the bank of the river a few rods from camp. The graves are marked with a neat headstone of wood with the name, company & regiment of the occupant. There are a few Maine soldiers buried here, but most of the graves are those of N.Y., Pa, & Western soldiers.[4]

On November 14, Francis also wrote home from Newport News. He seemed in good spirits and eager to give his parents his account of the regiment's trip, their current situation and brigade assignment.

> Dear Father and Mother:
> Here I am this beautiful evening of the 'Sunny South' in the building used as our 'Eating House' at the table with perhaps some 75 others trying to write home. ... We are here yet, don't know when we shall leave. [The] steamship

has gone down to Fortress Monroe to have some temporary bunks put in for our accommodation. We may stop a number of weeks and may leave in two days.[5]

The ongoing uncertainty of the regiment's ultimate destination is echoed in Captain Case's letter to his sister: "We do not know how long we are waiting here [Newport News], but probably not very long as it seems probable that we are to go South. ... The steamer that brought us [here] lies at Fort Monroe with our tents and a large amount of stores on board. I care little for myself where we are sent, but hope it will be where we can do something towards bringing this wicked war to a close."[6]

Francis Ireland's November 14 letter continues, "A great many troops have come in here since I wrote last. They have landed and pitched tents at this place altho there are some on their vessels in the river. Gen. Corcoran is here with the most of his brigade including the old 69th of Bull Run notoriety. I have not seen the Gen. yet but I shall I guess, as he is inside of our guard quite often on business."

The 22nd Maine was temporarily assigned to General Corcoran's brigade. Brigadier General Michael Corcoran had quite a colorful and difficult career. Born in Ireland, he immigrated to New York in 1849. As colonel of the 69th New York, made up almost entirely of other Irishmen, he first gained notoriety in 1861 when the Prince of Wales, the later King Edward VII of England, visited New York. At the parade in honor of the Prince's visit, Colonel Corcoran refused to order his regiment to take part, was arrested for disobedience and ordered to appear before a court-martial. However, at the outset of the Civil War, the charges were dropped and the 69th New York, with Colonel Corcoran in command, was among the first regiments to enter the service of the United States.

On July 21, 1861, at the First Battle of Bull Run, Colonel Corcoran was captured by the Confederates and sent to a prison in Richmond. When he was offered his release on condition that he swore not to engage in hostilities against the Confederacy again, he refused, but he was finally released as part of prisoner exchange in mid–August 1862. Upon his return and promotion to brigadier general, he immediately began to raise new regiments for the Union Army. In November of 1862 he, with the 6 regiments of his newly raised brigade—"Corcoran's Legion" or the "Irish Legion"—stopped at Newport News for a month before moving to Suffolk, Virginia.[7]

While the 22nd Maine was with Corcoran's brigade, Francis apparently saw a considerable difference between the country boys from Maine and these young Irishmen from New York City. Given the smaller average stature of men of the mid–1800s (the majority of soldiers in the Civil War were between 5 foot 5 inches and 5 foot 9 inches tall) the enlistment records show that a good many of the men from Maine were above the average height. Francis, at 5 foot 9, was at the top end of this average range, and his view of these young city lads may have been influenced by this fact.[8]

Continuing his November 14 letter, he writes: "He has got a host of 'babies' in one or two of his N. York Reg'ts that are not weaned! It is a pitiful fact that there are many boys there that can't be over 14 years old, and 90 or 100 lbs. in weight. Some of them are smaller than their knapsacks!"

Brigadier General Michael Corcoran (Library of Congress).

And, as with soldiers in general, food is a topic of great interest. Francis clearly likes much of what he is finding, but has no hesitation in reporting the aspects of army food that are less than desirable. All in all, he takes a fairly philosophical view of conditions.

> We like here first rate, have had splendid weather since Sunday, and quite warm, and one thing! Oysters are plenty at 8 cts. a pint; and such oysters! Fat, large, and delicious: I must say I never saw such large nice ones in Maine, never! We get them, put vinegar and pepper on them, and down they go; slip nice I tell you. The negroes get them by boat loads near here. As to rations we

have seen all kinds. We fare well as a general thing but we have seen hard ships I tell you. I have gone without dinner and supper since I got here, that is since we got into Virginia, because I couldn't eat the rations that were furnished me. For what reasons I will tell. Today for instance, we had a box of hard bread as it happened (somebody must get it). ... In my share I found live animals of the insect tribe. Also it tasted very musty and I threw it away, couldn't go it; we had a mess of salt beef cooked the other day that was hurt so that not one of the companies touched it; now I'm going to make a statement. You never would believe such stories. You may or not now as you think best. At Camp Chase on Arlington Heights we had some beef opened, cooked, and served out at meal times. The men said it was horse beef, carried some bones to the surgeon and he said they came out of such an animal. The beef was referred to the inspector who said it was horse beef and returned "from whence it came." We did not fare very well on the S.R. Spaulding but it couldn't be avoided. This is the bad side of the picture. Some grumble awfully at these things but I most always can see that they are unavoidable. Now as a general thing we fare first rate. We get hard bread most of it very good baked beans that can't be got at home and stewed beans rice and molasses, fried pork and potatoes, fresh beef, (sometimes) (we get it here*)* and salt beef which is most likely to be poor. In fact we fare as well as I expected to if not better.

His description of the area around the regiment's camp at Newport News includes his first encounter with former slaves.

This is a pretty place that we are living in now. That is not the buildings but the country. We are snug to James River. There is a few yards of beach a little higher than the river composed of whitish sand, then there is a bank covered thinly with pitch pine and from this bank it runs back to a mile perfectly level (this is an old camping ground) then there is another ridge of pine, a good chance for wood. Thousands of these nice trees have been cut down since the war commenced. There are a great many negroes here, "contrabands." I wish I could send a picture of about 50 I saw when we first came here. They came out and stood near the stand of the drummers and fifers to hear the music. When we were out on battalion drill they were of all ages, sizes, shapes, and colors that you ever saw almost. They were a comical sight I can tell you. ... It is near roll call and I must leave for tonight.[9]

Captain Isaac Case had this to say about these ex-slaves:

This place had been a "contraband station" for some time past, & there are thousands of darkies here now, of all ages and all shades of color. It would amuse the children at home could they take a look at the crowds of picaninnies clustered around the sunny sides of the cabin of a morning. Some of them are clothed in coats & trousers a world too wide, the coats reaching to their heels, while some have hardly rags enough to cover them. They are all, or nearly all, fed by government. Many of the able bodied men are away at work on fortifications, and and have wages for their labor. I don't know how much better off

5. New Camps, New Sights

"Contraband" camp on the Yorktown Peninsula (Library of Congress).

they are now than when under their masters, but they are free & will never return to slavery. They are said to be very religious in their way, and are quite strict in their observance of the Sabbath.[10]

Speaking of freed slaves as "contrabands" began in May of 1861 when General Benjamin Butler, then at Fortress Monroe, made the decision not to return runaway slaves to the South, but to consider them as contraband which would be confiscated from their former owners. This gained Fortress Monroe the nickname "Freedom's Fortress," as large numbers of slaves sought and received sanctuary there. An act of Congress, concurring with General Butler's reasoning, followed in July of 1861.[11]

The next day, November 15, Francis wrote to tell of seeing the USS *Monitor*. Months after its famous duel in March, 1862 with the CSS *Virginia* (Merrimack), the marks of that battle and the ship's subsequent duty on the James River near Richmond could still be seen on the Union's first ironclad warship. Just over a month after Francis wrote this letter, the *Monitor* met its end in rough seas off Cape Hatteras.

> Here I am again at my pen and ink. The Monitor is here near the wharf. I went down to see her the other day. She looks just as I expected from what I

Turret of the USS *Monitor* showing battle damage (Library of Congress).

had read about her. I saw her at a little distance as she is not snug to the shore. I saw the dent made by the ball fired from the Merrimac, also the one fired from Fort Darling near Richmond. They were on the cheese box, so called. There are a number of the best of our gun boats here in the river. I have heard the Monitor fire her guns several times. They roar like good fellows and echo over the country like a monster. She looks as innocent as a sail boat but when she speaks it is terrible! It would be useless for me to attempt to describe her as you have read all about it. There are several monster steamships here and more at Fortress Monroe loaded with troops. Nobody knows positively where we are going, but I think from what I see and hear that we are going with Banks to Texas. The boys like the idea, only it will take so long to get a mail back and forth, this is the only objection that they have anyway. The wreck of the Congress and Cumberland lie out here in the river with a portion of them sticking out of water. Some of the boys of the reg't got some wood from the Cumberland to make rings to send home. Also they got some sheet copper from off the Congress. I tried to get a piece to send home but couldn't. They stopped them from going out there.[12]

Captain Case had a similar impression of the view of the *Monitor* and other ships:

5. New Camps, New Sights 53

This is the scene of the famous battle between the Merrimack & Monitor. The wreck of the Congress lies but a few rods from where I am writing, visible at low water, and the Cumberland lies about a mile higher up the river, just where she went down, her masts & spars standing above the water, & a remnant of her flag still flying from the masthead. The little Monitor has come up river since we arrived, & lies at anchor just above us, while further out in the stream lie the Ironsides & Galena, both iron clad, all of these keeping steam up night & day, waiting, it is said, for the coming of the "Merrimack No. 2." If she comes down she will have a warm reception.[13]

The USS *Congress* and *Cumberland* were the wooden Union warships destroyed by the ironclad CSS *Virginia* on March 8 of that year, the day before its battle with the *Monitor*.

Francis Ireland continues his November 15 letter with what he hopes is good news: "I hear today that we are to have some new guns. I hope so, for these aren't worth 2 cents."

The 22nd Maine had originally been issued older .69-caliber smoothbore Springfield muskets, converted from flintlock to percussion cap. These weapons, while capable of doing great damage at close quarters, often firing the notorious "buck and ball"—one large slug and a quantity of buckshot—were not effective at any distance, and were in fact obsolete. On November 15 Colonel Jerrard had written to General Ripley at the Ord-

The sinking of the *Cumberland* by the ironclad *Merrimack* off Newport News, Virginia, March 8, 1862 (Library of Congress).

nance Department in Washington stating that the converted flintlocks were suited only for drilling and that they had been accepted only with the "express understanding that they should be exchanged for more effective arms on reaching Washington." A few days after this letter, Captain Henry Crosby of the 22nd Maine's Company A was sent into Washington to see what could be done. After unraveling considerable red tape, the regiment was promised, although not issued at that time, new rifled muskets. Francis was apparently well aware of the older weapons' limitations.[14]

The effectiveness of the regiment's arms was not the only matter worrying Francis. He continues his November 15 letter by expressing his considerable frustration with the current state of the Union's war effort and his disgust at the election of Fernando Wood to the U.S. Congress.

> We got another mail today. I got a letter from Uncle Ben in it. He wonders why [the] govt. don't make some forward movement with their great army. So do I. This war never will close until some foreign power steps in and settles it. Never! For both parties will fight until they have exhausted all their resources, and both ruined forever. When them Woods from New York get into Congress there will be a row of some sort — certain. When I heard that they were elected I was at Alexandria. It is the worst news (taken with the other elections) that I had heard for some time. I wish they were all out here with the Rebels where they belong, justly.[15]

Francis was not alone in his fear of a long, frustrating, wasteful struggle and his despair of Union victory. Other than halting General Lee's invasion of the North at Antietam in September of 1862, the Union Army had suffered greatly in a series of disastrous defeats in major battles from the first Battle of Bull Run in July of 1861 through McClellan's retreat from the Peninsula in July of 1862, and the second Battle of Bull Run that August. Even Union victories, such as Shiloh, in the spring of 1862 had come at a terrible cost in casualties. And although the Antietam battle can be seen, in hindsight, as a significant turning point in the war, that engagement had ended without a decisive Union victory, and certainly Francis and others did not view it as a "forward movement" by the Union Army. Francis also appeared to share the concern of many that either Britain or France would intervene and force the North to accept a Southern Confederacy.[16]

Fernando Wood, while mayor of New York City had, in January of 1861, proposed that his city should secede from the Union. Wood had since then become a leader of the "Copperhead" movement. The Copperheads, also known as Peace Democrats, although a minority in the North as a whole, were a reasonably strong political force in some areas, and favored an immediate negotiated settlement of the war. In 1862, many of these Democrats became outspoken in their opposition to the emancipation of slaves and to the Emancipation Proclamation of that September. Often using rhetoric aimed at the working classes, their speeches and editorials attempted to create a fear of freed slaves taking jobs from white workers and prayed on simple racial bigotry. Fernando Wood was elected to the U.S. Congress in November 1862, where he served along with a substantial number of other newly elected Democrats and his younger brother Benjamin. These men were in strong opposition to President Lincoln's policies.[17]

Leaving the worrisome politics of the war behind, Francis then closes on a more homey note. "I suppose you have plenty of cold weather by this time in Maine. We have awful cold nights and quite warm days. I don't expect to see much snow if we go to Texas. There, I have written a picked up mess and must close. Write once a week *certain* and I shall when I get a chance."[18]

6

The 22nd Settles in to Camp Life

More than 2 weeks later, on November 24, Francis wrote again from Newport News. He took a moment to discuss the weather and to tell of his problems in orienting himself in a distant land.

Dear Father and Mother,

After I closed my last letter I thought of several things that I did not write and as I have a chance I might as well be writing as loafing out in the sun. Here I am squat down on the ground with a small soap box for a writing desk on the east side of our barracks. The sun is quite warm. I can hardly realize that it is the last of November, although I had to walk my beat pretty brisk on guard last night to keep my feet and hands warm. It was as cold last night as it has been since we came here. For news I will say that the 26th Reg't came here a few days ago and have camped a little east of us or rather as it seems to me and many of the boys directly north. ... As regards the points of compass I have been completely turned round ever since we left Washington.[1]

Francis next makes a brief reference to the funeral of a soldier, a man from the 128th New York. Francis had not yet experienced the death of a member of his regiment, and he apparently was moved by this death of a man previously unknown to him, as he attended the burial and thought it worth mentioning to his parents.

Sickness, however, was beginning to take its toll on the 22nd. Francis was apparently unaware that Company G's Private Harrison Howe had died in Baltimore on October 30, and Company D's Sergeant David Wass had died, also in Baltimore, on November 16. And, before arriving at Newport News, the regiment had left 22 sick men behind in Bangor, Washington, and Alexandria. When numbers were compiled, at the end of November, for the adjutant general's report of 1862, at least 20 more men were listed as sick, with many of these ill enough to require hospitalization at Newport News and Fortress Monroe. This number, of course, includes only those who were actually in hospital or listed as sick on the date when the report was created, and would not include others who had been hospitalized but had returned to the regiment, or those who had been sick at the regiment's camp but had recovered sufficiently to return to duty. For the men of the 22nd Maine, most of whom came from very rural settings and were without previous exposure to many illnesses, disease would claim a great toll. This was especially true of these Northern regiments sent to the Deep South. For a look at the comparison of deaths by sickness vs. battle wounds in various Maine regiments and in various theaters of operation, see Appendix B.[2]

Continuing his November 24 letter, Francis gives a wonderfully detailed account of the routine into which the 22nd Maine had settled.

> I will give you a little description of the way we live here as regards getting up, going to bed etc etc — At daybreak (about ½ past 6) the drums are beaten and we have to "turn out" to roll call which comes directly afterward. They beat again at 7 for breakfast — at ½ past 7 they beat the surgeons call for the sick men to fall in from each company and pass examination, receive prescriptions, excuses at the surgeons quarters, and the sickest ones assigned to the hospital. At ½ past 8 they beat again for guard mounting, a performance that I will not stop to describe here. Suffice it to say that it is getting the new guard ready and giving them instructions etc and putting them on in place of the old one of the day before. At 9 o'clock they beat again for company drill which lasts till 11 o'clock at least. At 12 they beat for dinner. At 2 o'clock they beat for battalion drill, which lasts till 4 o'clock. Then comes "dress parade" immediately after we get marched in and form in battalion line. This takes about all the time till 5 and then comes supper. At ½ past 8 they beat the roll call and then we can turn in as soon as the roll is called. At 9 the retreat is beaten when all soldiers' lights must be out and all are supposed to be abed which closes the day. We have 4 roll calls a day, 2 at drill hours and one morning and night. If a soldier is absent without good reasons he is put on knapsack drill in front of the colonel's quarters for 4 hours. This is a peculiar drill! The knapsacks are filled with sand to the weight of 40 lbs., are strapped on to the back and the guilty ones have a post assigned them which they have to walk steady for 4 hours, part of the time on the double quick. The orderly sergeant of Co. I came here to a bank just before I began to write on this subject and filled 3 [knapsacks] with sand and gave them to the men and marched them to their post for their 4 hours' fatigue duty. I guess the 40 lbs. will be heavy at the end of 4 hours.

In this fairly lengthy November 24 letter, Francis once again states that the regiment is anticipating new muskets very soon, and then reports on the various rumors that circulate through the camp regarding their destination.

As to our going to Texas! It looks queer that Gen. Banks is filling out such a monstrous expedition to go to Texas only! Such a lot of men, gunboats, transports, etc! Now we get all kinds of stories here and among them is this. That this is all going up James River to Richmond, and that Texas is only a ruse to keep it from the public. It may be so, but I hope not. For I had rather go to Texas than to stay in Va. this winter anyhow! Some of our men believe this story but I hope we shall know soon.[3]

General Banks was indeed creating a "monstrous" force for his expedition. The 19th Corps, which was created for this purpose, consisted of well over 40,000 men. Much of this force, however, was made up of new regiments and untested soldiers. Forty of its 65 infantry regiments had been created in the fall of 1862. And 22 of these new regiments were mustered, as was the 22nd Maine, for a 9 month term of service. General Banks' orders did include plans for operations in Texas, and one major reason for bringing the Mississippi River under Union control was to cut off the supplies coming through Texas and across the Mississippi to the eastern Confederate States.[4]

Continuing his letter, Francis relates what must have been a truly novel experience for this young man: a conversation he had with a newly freed slave — still technically a "contraband," since September's Emancipation Proclamation did not go into effect until January 1, 1863.

> By the way I must give you a conversation I had with quite an intelligent negro that was in here from a neighboring plantation the other day. Says I to the darky after asking him where he lived etc. How many slaves has your master got? Ans. He had 40 before he went away! Ques. Where has he gone and when did he go? Ans. To Richmond 2 years ago! Ques. What did he go there for? Ans. For protection! Ques. Why don't you go with the contrabands and leave your master entirely? Because we live well, are our own masters, raise what we want, and have the whole plantation to ourselves! Ques. What will you do when he comes back, run away or let him hold you as his property? Ans. Oh well! Uncle Sam is going to settle that question for us! I talked with him some time in this way. He seemed contented as long as they could control the plantation themselves and reap the benefits of it. He seemed to think that by the time his master got back that Uncle Sam would fix it so that he would have no claim on him! Those slaves have got a good chance with a large plantation to use "free gratis" just as they choose....
>
> Fred Hart has got his discharge and left here for home today noon. His health is pretty fair for him now. But he is not fit for a soldier. Say nothing about this out — round until you hear of it from some other source as he don't want his folks to know when he is coming.[5]

Alfred Hart had been born in England, immigrated to Maine and worked in a Dexter woolen mill. As Francis indicates, Fred had trouble with his health — rheumatism and heart disease — that made him unfit to be a soldier. Indeed, in addition to the men listed as sick by the end of November, 1862, another 4 were discharged and sent home — 2 listed as "discharged for disability." Two others, presumably also in some way unfit, were simply listed as "sent home" and "discharged."[6]

Francis closes his letter, "We drawed our dress coats the other day. They are pretty good ones. I got two papers yesterday from you. Write soon and often. From your son, Francis A. Ireland." In a P.S. to this letter, Francis asked his parents to send him a "strong fine comb" and then gave his thoughts on the approaching Thanksgiving Day: "Hope you have a good time Thanksgiving. We boys shall think of it — I'll bet!"[7]

Francis wrote to his family again from Newport News on Thanksgiving Day, November 27. He started with the news that their much anticipated new rifles had arrived.

> Dear Father and Mother
>
> I received your letter of the 23d today noon, also the papers. Today is a sort of a holiday with us although we have been very busy this forenoon drawing our new guns. They have come at last after a great deal of talk and bluster! about them. They are very good looking and are called Austrian rifles. We have not tried them yet but they are said to be very good rifles.[8]

He refers to the Lorenz Austrian rifled musket, a weapon purchased, as the name implies, from the Austrian government. The basic pattern of the rifle had been developed in 1854 by Josef Lorenz, a Viennese gunsmith, and had been modified in 1861. Both the Union and Confederacy bought substantial numbers of this musket — the Confederacy apparently buying mostly the 1854 model from existing stocks, while the Union bought the 1861 model. The musket was originally made in .54-caliber, but many of those used by the Union Army, including those issued to the 22nd Maine, were re-bored to use the standard .58-caliber ammunition. The Union's purchases were perhaps in part motivated by a desire to eliminate the supply of weapons that the Confederacy would otherwise acquire. With the U.S. government purchasing almost 227,000 and the Confederacy purchasing about 100,000, the Austrian rifle was second only to the British Enfield rifled musket in the numbers imported during the Civil War.[9]

Francis went on in his letter to explain that the regiment had expected to leave before this, but had been delayed. He then stated, "I have enjoyed myself first rate here and like [it] well but am anxious to be off, for fear they will keep us in the army of the Potomac which would be a nasty job."

The Army of the Potomac, under General George McClellan, had experienced frustration and defeat during the Peninsula Campaign of that summer of 1862, with over 15,000 Union casualties. More Army of the Potomac casualties occurred when elements were sent to support General John Pope's Army of Virginia and suffered losses during the Union defeat at Second Bull Run in late August. General McClellan, in stopping General Robert E. Lee's invasion of the North at Antietam, had done so at the cost of over 12,000 more Army of the Potomac casualties. Reports of these engagements must have had a sobering effect on the new recruits.[10]

Francis goes on to report the way the regiment would be spending Thanksgiving Day, a very different sort of day from that back in Maine. Although not an annual national holiday until President Lincoln's proclamation of 1863, the holiday was firmly established in Maine and many other states as a time for families and communities to gather and give thanks. In spite of the differences, Francis seems pleased enough with the prospects that his day will offer.[11]

> I haven't had my Thanksgiving dinner but expect to get a pretty good supper. We had a lot of fat left on hand in our Co. and the boys thought they would have some doughnuts if nothing more, and we got 50 lbs. of nice flour and some salerutus [baking soda] and brought them to the cook and he and 3 or 4 others have been frying doughnuts this 2 hours and ain't half thro yet. We shall have about ½ a peck apiece I guess by the looks. I can smell them now from the cookroom in the eating house. I guess I can make out a very good supper as I got a haversack full of ginger cakes and some cheese (I got them to carry to sea however) besides a canteen of molasses. We had services here today the same as if we were in Maine. Our chaplain is a first-rate fellow is liked very well by the men.[12]

The Reverend John Lincoln had apparently succeeded in bringing at least a fond remembrance of home to that Thanksgiving Day. The importance of the regiment's religious life is also mentioned in Captain Isaac Case's letter of November 16.

> We have some very interesting meetings in the regiment now. We have one sermon on the Sabbath, & two prayer meetings a week. Last Sabbath evening there were some twenty soldiers came forward & asked for the prayers of Christians, and on Tuesday eve. several more. Some are indulging a hope of forgiven sins, & many seem anxious to become Christians. Pray for us that our regiment may be blessed with a great outpouring of the Heavenly Spirit.[13]

Francis Ireland continues his Thanksgiving Day letter a bit later that day.

> 6½ o'clock P.M. Well we have been to supper and had a very good one of doughnuts and cheese. We have enough left for breakfast. We have had quite

6. The 22nd Settles in to Camp Life

an interesting time in the reg't since I left off writing. We went out on dress parade and were marched to the parade ground & after a number of moves we were formed into a hollow square which brought the men all facing outward. We "about faced" and in the square was all the officers, [musicians?] etc. We then had a surprise (no surprise to the men as they got it up). The orderly sergeant of Co. A stepped forward and in behalf of the soldiers of the reg't presented Adjutant Flagg with a splendid sword and sash (cost $98.00) for his never failing interest for the men etc. and a token of their love and respect for him as an officer. After this he (the adjutant) proposed three cheers for the colonel for his efforts procuring our guns, & then the col. proposed three for the adjutant and line officers of the reg't. Cheers were then given for the rank and file of the reg't — also by motion of Capt. Williams of Bangor [James Williams, captain of Company B] three were given for the girls left behind. We gave rousing cheers every time.[14]

And the men would have a chance to try their new rifles.

This afternoon we had an order from the colonel which changes the drill in the A.M. to a practice at "target shooting" the best shots to be reported to the colonel every day, who they were that made them, the distance of the target etc. We shall all try our best with our rifles, of course. ... I think we may leave here before I get another letter, but you must write just the same, and I shall get the more when we do get the mail. I must close to get this in to the mornings mail, so good night.

From your son,
Francis A. Ireland[15]

Charlie Farrar wrote home to his family at about this same time. After telling his parents that the weather is fine and "the birds sing sweetly on the shore," he goes on to say that he, too, is impressed with the new rifles. He is pleased that they are lighter than the previous muskets and reports that they will shoot 900 yards. The regiment had been practicing with targets at 100 yards, and Charlie reports that "the first we tried them we most all overshot." We can assume the men were shooting as they would have with the old smoothbore muskets and aiming higher than would be needed for these new, rifled, weapons. But Charlie also writes, "I hit the target yestiday." He also lets the folks know that two other Dexter men, William Hall and Jonas Hutchinson, had been the best shots so far. In a note to his mother he also remarks, "I am bound to be a good rifle man if practice will do it and if I have to go into battle I can take my mark," but continues, "I hope I shall never see a battle." Perhaps an unusually candid statement from a volunteer soldier, but perhaps not an unusual sentiment.[16]

Charlie's late November letter also gives a good look at the conditions in the camp at Newport News. He tells his folks that "5 or 6 died since we left Maine" but that "none of them in our company" and "our company is very healthy now," although "I believe there is about 30 [from the regiment] in the hospital" and "some are pretty sick." The "comfortable barracks" that Colonel Jerrard had reported finding upon the regiment's arrival at Newport News are, Charlie says, much like staying "at home in the shed." He describes how the men put their rubber blankets on the floor with their overcoats on them and use their knapsacks for pillows. He and two others then sleep 3 together so that there are 3 blankets over them. When the men are sleeping in their tents, Charlie says that they get "meder" (meadow) grass to put under their blankets and "we lay as well as I ever did on a fether bed." Charlie also says that they have heard that there has been "another draft in Maine" to enlist more soldiers for the Union, and he wonders if that is true. And, as with Francis Ireland, Charlie asks his parents to write "all the news" and lets his mother know, "I am bound to be a good boy as I can. That is so shure."[17]

A letter written that same Thanksgiving Day by Francis' father, John Ireland, gives an indication that Francis wants even more and "newsier" letters from home. After explaining that he has had a bad cold, the elder Ireland wrote a rather lengthy letter to satisfy Francis' request.

> You seem to think I don't write much news, and that you write more interesting letters than I. Well, as to news, I have told all I knew of. I intend to keep you informed of passing events. As to your letters they are very interesting to us, and some of your friends that have seen them speak highly of them. I copy all your letters into a book I have for that purpose, but I am now more than two letters behind hand. I have had so much writing to do, and having been unwell besides that I find myself thus behind. But never mind, I'll catch up again soon.[18]

He then goes on to give a substantial sampling of the news of the town. In his attempts to write more of the happenings in Dexter, John Ireland seems frequently to recite a fairly grim list of those who have died: "I heard of the death of old Nat Goodwin, the soap man. He had been sick about 3 weeks with typhoid fever. So the old "Apostle" has got through and will no more disturb religious people or any body else. ... Levi C. Morgan will stop on the Twombly farm this winter. By the way, by the death of that entire family, the whole of that estate falls to John's child."

Nate Goodwin, who apparently worked in one of the town's soap works, must have been more than just a colorful and eccentric character. The town's expenses for 1862 include Nate's "insane hospital care."[19]

6. The 22nd Settles in to Camp Life

For family matters, John Ireland mentions, "Your mother wants to know if you have forgotten Flora, says you do not speak of her. She will repeat a great many words after us. Her mother says if 'tis pleasant out New Year's day, she will have her picture taken, and will send one to you. ... Eben has gone into the hen business; has traded his gun for hens and will winter about a dozen."

Ireland also proposes a remedy for the bad water the soldiers encounter. "You speak of the bad water you have to drink. I send you some tartaric acid, with which you can make, at any time, a pleasant and healthy drink. Sweeten a tumbler or so of water with sugar as you would to make lemonade, and then sour it with the acid to your liking; 'twill require but little acid, and this you can keep about you, ready at any time."[20] Tartaric acid, a natural acid derived from fruit, is still used as a food flavoring and in cream of tartar. It does not appear to have any medicinal properties.

By November of 1862 state governors were sometimes finding it difficult to fill their enlistment quotas from volunteers alone, and were resorting to a sort of local draft. In Maine, the selectmen of the various towns were empowered to choose men to meet their required numbers if needed. The Confederate government had instituted a draft in April of 1862, but it was not until the spring of 1863 that the Union created a national draft. Under this federal draft, however, many professions were exempt, and a man could hire a substitute, or avoid service by paying a $300 commutation fee.[21]

In answer to Charlie Farrar's question about a draft in Dexter, John Ireland states, "There is to be no drafting as Charlie wrote. An order was issued requiring draft to fill towns' quotas if not otherwise filled by a certain time. It was said that there were 2 wanting to fill our [Dexter's] quota, I hear they have been furnished."

The letter closes with a request from Francis' mother and offers of financial help.

> There, if I had not supposed you could read any thing I write, I should not dare send this, for I can hardly sit up to write. ... [He had complained earlier in this letter of a bad cold.]
>
> Your mother says when your hair is long enough, to send her a lock, that she can put into a hair wreath. You, of course will be prudent with your money, but don't do without any thing that you actually need, for if you are likely to get short of money before another payment, let me know it and I will send some.
>
> Must close and sign here, J.P. Ireland[22]

7

Heading South
Banks' Expedition Sails for New Orleans and the Lower Mississippi

On December 2, Colonel Jerrard received orders to have the 22nd Maine board ship "and join the extensive fleet that had assembled at Fortress Monroe preparatory to starting on some unknown expedition."[1]

In Francis' next letter he tells of the regiments' departure after almost a month at Newport News. Having boarded their ship, they were anchored and waiting for other elements of the convoy to assemble and it was one more day before they actually got under way. The letter is written "on board Steamship S.R. Spaulding off Fortress Monroe Dec 3rd."

Dear Father:

> Here we are again on board ship. We left Newport News at 8 o'clock yesterday morning and got here at a little past 9. Dropped anchor and remain here in the same position at present. We are waiting for the fleet from New York which was due here last night I believe. There are about 8 or 10 large steamships within almost a stone's throw of us loaded with troops and a number of gun boats. It was busy here yesterday, troops loading and unloading, steam tugs going to and fro with dispatches, orders, etc. We are close to the fortress. If it had been fair today we should have gone on shore to drill but did not as it is raining. We are somewhat more comfortable on board than before. Shall get along very well I guess. I cannot stop to write much about what I see etc. as I write to let you know where we are. We may leave today and may stop several days. Will let you know when we leave if I find out before we start. ... By the way I heard the captain of the boat say that his opinion was that we were going to Charleston, S.C. There is a host of troops going to some one or more places *certain*.[2]

Then follows a complete change of theme while Francis responds to a part of his father's latest letter, sent from Dexter just 6 days earlier. "I hope you will have Flora's picture taken as I should like to have it. Hope you will get over your cold soon. As the mail is coming on board in a little while I will wait and see if I have anything in it." Stating that he was checking the mail may have been intended as a not too subtle hint for his parents. He goes on,

> 2 o'clock P.M. Mail has come and no letter for me. I have been on deck for a while to see if I could get any sign of the fleet. It is time that they were here. I counted in sight this afternoon over 72 of all kinds of craft — some 10 are river steamers used to run as mail boats and for passengers to and from the fort — about the same of sea or outside steamships loaded with troops, a few gunboats, a lot of small steam tugs, sort of "errand boys" from one place or vessel to another, and lots of sloops and schooners etc. I should think that they were nearly all in the government service for one thing and another. I can see the great "Lincoln gun" in front of the fortress that you have heard so much about. My health is tip top now. Hope we shall have a healthy voyage.[3]

The "Lincoln gun" referred to is still on display at Fortress Monroe. It is a huge, 49,000 pound "Rodman" gun firing a 15 inch diameter projectile — a style developed by Thomas J. Rodman. His experiments, started when he had been a young lieutenant in 1844, led to the casting of much larger iron cannon than had previously been thought possible.[4]

Francis then talks about the health of his regiment, relates a curious accident, and closes this letter.

> Our Co. left 5 at the hospital at Newport News. We have been very lucky as to deaths in the regiment — since we left Bangor (5 weeks) there has been 5 died, 3 out of one Co. (Co. D.). By the way a fellow on guard yesterday night shot off his two fingers next his thumb. He was standing with his right hand on the muzzle of his gun, was rubbing his leg with one foot, and when he put it down it caught on the lock and off it went! It was opposite our barracks, the report of the rifle and his calling for the corporal of the guard waked me up. He hollared like a good fellow until the corporal relieved his post. Careless fellow! Don't think you can read this very well. It is written way down on the lower deck and is rather dark. Must close now.
>
> Later. We sail tonight is the present orders. Good bye for a while. Write.
>
> From your son,
> Francis A. Ireland[5]

In his next letter to Francis, written on December 7, John Ireland starts by letting Francis know that the family had received his November 27, Thanksgiving Day, letter after only 10 days in transit from Newport News. Telling of the progress of his cold, the worst he had ever had, Ireland

The "Lincoln gun," a 15 inch Rodman gun at Fortress Monroe (Library of Congress).

goes on to tell his son some of the latest news of the town — listing who has died and mentioning 3 local men who have been recently discharged from the army. Captain Isaac Haskell and Lieutenant Edward Fifield, both of Company D, 20th Maine, had resigned their commissions on November 20 and come home. Private John Crocker had been sick for some time and was discharged November 22. Two other men from Dexter had also recently returned home, or were expected soon. The mention of these men's return from the army may seem a bit tactless when writing during the holiday season to a son still far from home, but judging from Francis' letters, it did not appear to be a problem.[6]

After telling that a large party from Dexter had taken the 20 mile round trip sleigh ride to the town of Newport, John Ireland then relates two bits of news that had apparently caused a stir in Dexter.

> Landes and Weeks arrested for stealing were let off by paying about 80 dollars apiece. Persons can do almost anything in Dexter and get clean by paying a small sum. [Many of that time would not consider $80 a "small sum."]

> A little incident took place on the evening before Thanksgiving which I will mention. Our temperance people are on ... Hersey's track watching his liquor business. Friday before Thanksgiving, Goff ... returned from Bangor and twas know by some that he brought up liquor for Hersey. It was determined to make a search in his stable, etc. Thanksgiving morning and take all that could be found, but in the early part of the evening, Lo! and Behold! a 10 gall. keg of liquor, which was doubtless intended for Hersey, disappeared from Goff's woodshed! I guess it was put where it wont do hurt. At any rate, 'tis said they were pretty dry at Hersey's Thanksgiving day.[7]

Justus Hersey ran a livery stable in Dexter and apparently did a bit of a side trade in liquor. From this and other references to strong drink by John Ireland and by Francis, we may assume that the Irelands' religious beliefs included temperance. They were Methodists.[8]

John Ireland then tells Francis what news or rumors of the war are reaching Dexter: "There is much speculation with the people as to where you are going. It appears that Burnside is preparing for an attack on Richmond, and it is thought by many that you are to form part of a force that is to approach by way of the James River. This, however, is mere conjecture."[9]

General Ambrose Burnside had succeeded General McClellan as commander of the Army of the Potomac early in November, and was indeed planning an advance, a plan that ended with the costly Union defeat at Fredericksburg, Virginia. An advance toward Richmond via the James River from Newport News would have seemed a sensible part of a plan to attack the Confederate capital from two directions. However, when he wrote this letter, John Ireland was not aware that the 22nd Maine and a large Union force had left Newport News and were heading south.[10]

The elder Ireland ends with a comparison of weather conditions:"I see by today's paper that there was 4 inches of snow in Virginia. ... There was about 18 inches fell here. No more at this time. From your father, J.P. Ireland."[11]

As the ships transporting General Banks' forces left the area of Fortress Monroe and headed down the coast on December 4, 1862, Colonel Jerrard was given sealed orders "relating to our destination which were not to be opened unless [our ship] became unavoidably separated from the fleet." And that did, indeed, happen: "The weather [at the time of departure] was fair and we proceeded without event until when off Hatteras ... we experienced one of those terrible gales to frequent that coast. The fleet was scattered and on the following morn, not a sail was in sight. We continued on our course ... without falling in with any part of the fleet, when I opened my orders and found our destination to be Ship Island."

The colonel then directed the captain of the *Spaulding* to make for Ship Island, just east of New Orleans, and the entrance to the Mississippi, where they were to rejoin the rest of the fleet. The 22nd Maine arrived at Ship Island on December 12, "12 hours in advance of any other transports of the fleet."[12.]

Shortly after the 22nd Maine's visit, Ship Island witnessed another encounter involving troops from Maine that did not go smoothly. One of the controversial decisions made by General Butler in New Orleans was to take "men of color," including former slaves, into the Union Army. This led to the establishing of Native Guard units made up of black soldiers, and moreover, while field grade officers were white, the line officers — captains and lieutenants — were black. With the organization of the 1st Louisiana Native Guard in September of 1862, so many ex-slaves came to join up that three more regiments were formed in the next few months — the 2nd Regiment in October, the 3rd Regiment in November, and the 4th Regiment in February of 1863. (I use the term "black" soldiers for convenience, but in reality, the Native Guard regiments were made up of men of purely African descent along with men of mixed race heritage — all of whom were considered "men of color" at that time.)[13]

In January of 1863, the 2nd Regiment of the Native Guard was sent to garrison Ship Island along with 2 companies of the 13th Maine. This mixture of black and white troops did not go well, and as a result of racial disputes and high tension, General Banks withdrew the companies of the 13th Maine and left the 2nd Louisiana Native Guard to garrison the island.[14]

To return to late 1862, the 22nd Maine, with other elements of Banks' expedition, left Ship Island on December 13, arriving at New Orleans on the 15th. New Orleans, with an 1860 population of over 160,000, was the largest city in what would become the Confederacy, and had been heavily involved in the slave trade. As the Civil War began, New Orleans was the commercial center of the Deep South, a center for the export of cotton and tobacco, a banking center, and the home of a U.S. mint. The taking of that mint by the Confederacy resulted in the production of a considerable quantity of coinage for the Confederate war effort. With its commercial importance, its importance as a center for importing supplies for the Confederacy, and its importance as a Confederate Naval base, New Orleans became a target for Union forces early in the War.[15]

Captain David Farragut's fleet began naval operations against Confederate positions on the lower Mississippi on April 16, 1861, and on April 24, had fought its way past the Confederate Forts Jackson and St. Philip, which guarded the Mississippi below New Orleans. On April 28 these forts surrendered and Union land forces were able to occupy New Orleans without further military action.[16]

It was during the first months of the Union occupation of New Orleans that the Union commander there, General Benjamin Butler, was given the nickname "Beast" Butler. His well known order that any women of New Orleans who insulted Union troops would be treated as a "woman of the town plying her trade" outraged many Southern sympathizers, but did stop such actions by the women as emptying their chamber pots onto Union soldiers. Another action that caused anger in the South was the execution, in June 1861, of a Confederate supporter, William Mumford, who had torn down the U.S. flag flying over New Orleans' City Hall. This execution provided a propaganda opportunity for Jefferson Davis, and the Confederate president took full advantage of that opportunity. In a proclamation dated December 23, 1862, he described the execution of Mumford as murder, and went on to state:

I, Jefferson Davis, President of the Confederate States of America, and in their name, do pronounce and declare the said Benjamin F. Butler to be a felon, deserving capital punishment. I do order that he be no longer considered or treated simply as a public enemy of the Confederate States of America, but as an outlaw and common enemy of mankind, and in the event of his capture the officer in command of the capturing force do cause him to be immediately executed by hanging. ... All commissioned officers in the command of said Benjamin F. Butler be declared not entitled to be considered as soldiers engaged in honorable warfare, but as robbers and criminals deserving death; and that they and each of them, whenever captured, reserved for execution.[17]

These accusations of murder, the announcement of threats toward women, and other actions imposed under martial law, coupled with accusations of looting by Federal troops, created a difficult situation for President Lincoln. It had been hoped that southern Louisiana could be seen as a model of how occupied areas of the Confederacy could return peacefully to Union control. The controversy surrounding General Butler led to his removal as commander of the Department of the Gulf, and the appointment of General Banks as his replacement.[18]

Writing home on December 18, Francis tells of his travels and

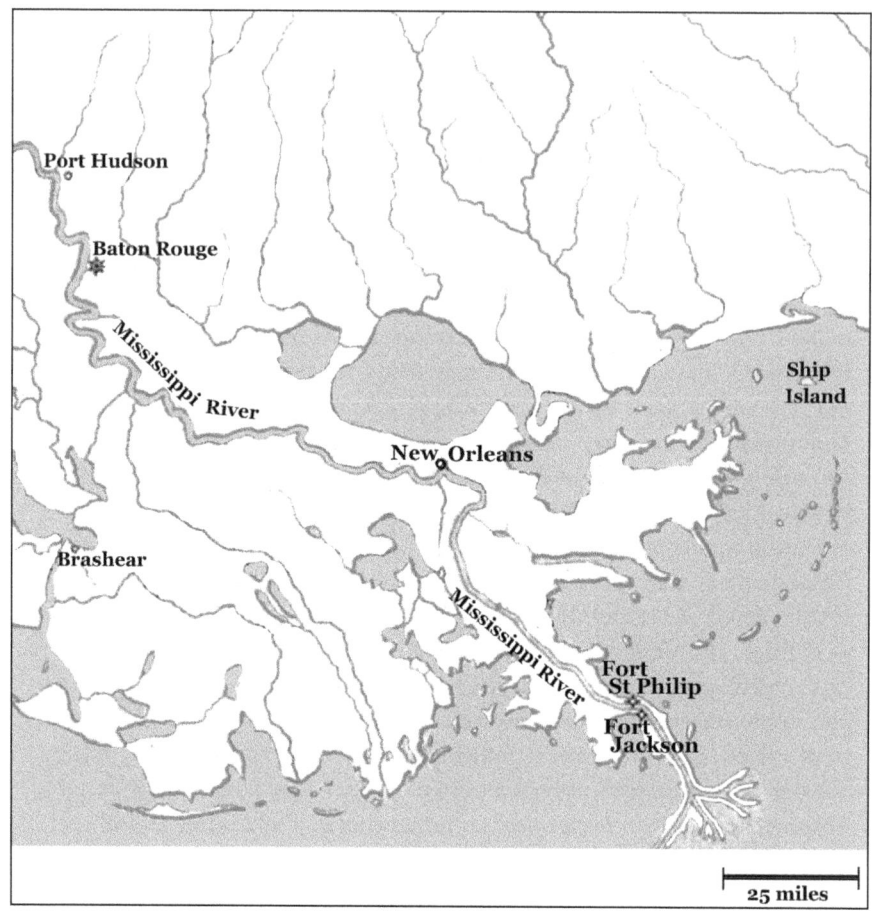

Map adapted from Plate 135-A: *The Official Military Atlas of the Civil War.*

describes sights very new to a young man from rural Maine. His excitement at being on the Mississippi seems quite clear.

> We anchored about 12 o'clock Saturday night out side of the bar in the mouth of the Mississippi to wait for a pilot to guide us up. They made their appearance at daylight and we started again up the pass. We found the water very muddy and the pass very narrow, in many places just like the inlet at home. It is a large bog as far as the eye can reach with streams running all through it. Nothing grows but a tall coarse grass and a few bushes. We came to a few houses now and then that were occupied by the pilots. They are very low and must be unhealthy in summer. We left all passes behind and came into the main river in the afternoon. Most of the land near the mouth is taken up in rice

plantations that are mostly below the level of the river. No one living here except the negroes that work the plantations. Later in the P.M. we came to Fort Jackson and St. Philip on opposite sides of the river that hold the passage up the river to New Orleans. They are fine looking forts made of bricks. Fort Jackson is a very strong one and would "pepper" vessels in good shape attempting to run by. (One thing the river was altogether different in width from what I expected to find it, being no wider all the way up to New Orleans than the "Dexter Pond" from the Island directly across to the other shore [with a few exceptions].) The 31st Mass. Regt. is at Fort Jackson and a part of the 13th Me. at St. Philip. They came out as we passed and cheered us while their band played "Hail Columbia." As we got up the river the sugar plantations and orange groves begin to be very plenty although the land was very low and wild in places not cultivated. Oranges are just ripe now and the trees looked splendid hanging full of them. It made the boys want to jump ashore no mistake. It was about as pretty [a] sight as is to be seen.[19]

The forts and orange groves apparently made quite an impression on the Maine soldiers. Company H's Captain Isaac Case, writing as before, to his sister, commented,

> This day's sail was full of interest to us Down Easters, as the scenery was both new and strange to our eyes. Early in the afternoon we passed Forts Jackson and St. Philip, standing on either side of the river where it appeared to be not more than half a mile wide. And how any vessel less vulnerable than the Monitor could pass them & keep afloat seemed to me impossible. But we knew that through the skill and energy of Farragut & Butler the thing was done, which gave the Union arms possession of New Orleans....
> These Yankee eyes were first delighted with a sight of orange orchards, the trees literally loaded with their golden fruit. The boys were almost crazy at the sight, and would have given the boots off their feet for the privilege of going ashore for a few minutes, but they were compelled to hold on for a few hours, assured that the fruit was plentiful and cheap at New Orleans, as they found it to be the next day, and had a chance to eat their fill.[20]

Continuing with Francis Ireland's December 18 letter, we read more of the sights and experiences as the regiment approached New Orleans. "Just above Fort Jackson we passed the wreck or remains of the Rebel ram Manassas just in the place she was burnt." The CSS *Manassas* was an ironclad ram, built originally as a river towboat. Refitted with 1.5 inch iron plates and armed with a 32 pounder cannon and an iron ram, it was said to resemble a floating cigar. As Admiral David Farragut's Union fleet worked its way into the Mississippi River past Forts Jackson and St. Philip, in late April 1862, the *Manassas* came under heavy fire from the USS *Mississippi* and was run aground, set on fire, and abandoned by its crew.[21]

Francis' December 18 letter continues.

Wreck of the CSS *Manassas* (National Archives).

Just at night we stopped at a place and passed an examination or rather were boarded and had our hospital record examined to see if we had any contagious disorder on board. Two of our transports were stopped here and not allowed to go up to the city as one (a part of the 26th Me.) had the small pox and another the ship fever [typhoid fever, which was also known as camp fever]. At ¼ to 9 we anchored just below the city of New Orleans at last. ... Monday morning we started up the river a short distance about half way up the city which brought us right abreast of it. You very well know how the city is built as it is below the level of the river. There are a great many splendid buildings here but the city has a deserted look for the most part.[22]

A second view of New Orleans is given in Captain Case's February letter to his sister:

> Our stay at New Orleans was short, and only the officers were allowed to land. I went ashore twice & traversed some of the business streets, but things looked dull and lifeless — in no way like New Orleans as I had heard & read about. The streets were clean, however, thanks to General Butler, though [but?] a little of its usual business is now done. Here its advantages for trade remain, & when this unholy rebellion shall close, it will regain its former prosperity.[23]

7. Heading South

Francis Ireland's December 18 letter, after mentioning seeing a French and a British man-of-war at New Orleans, along with Union warships, goes on,

> The transports that were at Ship Island with us were here, at night we sailed up about a mile to get coal. The wharves up here were burnt most all down when the city was taken and cotton, rice, etc. burnt with them. The great cotton store houses along here are all deserted. We got oranges in great abundance here as there were bushels of them for sale at 3 and 4 for 5 cents and 1.50 per bbl. Apples 2.00 per bbl! It was nothing but oranges for the next two days on the boat. The companies were treated with a barrel apiece by their officers also.[24]

8

The Reoccupation of Baton Rouge

On December 16 in New Orleans, Colonel Jerrard later wrote, "I was ordered to report to Gen. Grover who had been placed in command of a force for the capture and occupation of Baton Rouge, then held by a small rebel force." (In the February, 1864 rough draft of his report to Maine's adjutant general, Colonel Jerrard wrote that Baton Rouge was then held by "a considerable Rebel force.") That afternoon, General Cuvier Grover's troops, including the 22nd Maine, started by steamboat up the Mississippi to recapture and occupy Baton Rouge. The term "recapture" might be more accurate, since the Union Army had first occupied Baton Rouge in May of 1862, after capturing New Orleans. Confederate General John Breckenridge attacked Baton Rouge on August 5, and although he pushed the Union troops to the river bank, he was not successful in taking the city. However, a week later, the Union commander at New Orleans, General Benjamin Butler, ordered Baton Rouge evacuated.[1]

In Francis Ireland's letter of December 18 he writes of the regiment's journey up the Mississippi and includes a description of some plantations.

> Tuesday the transport started at noon for Baton Rouge, with three good gunboats in case of need. We passed many sugar plantations on the river between New Orleans and this place. I liked the appearance of things first rate, the plantations looked thrifty and neat and the residence of the planters on nearly every one (although smaller as a general rule than houses of the wealthy in the North) were very tasty and splendid with beautiful trees all around them. The houses of the negroes were a short distance from this in rows and neatly whitewashed. I saw one place with 4 rows of 12 each, enough to put 40 or 50 families of 10 or 12 each into. Then a short distance from these was the "sugar works" large buildings with tall chimneys.[2]

8. The Reoccupation of Baton Rouge

Arriving at Baton Rouge at daybreak, December 17, and whatever the actual number of Confederate forces might have been, the regiment landed without opposition. Colonel Jerrard wrote that "the gunboats, of which the rebels always stand in reasonable fear, prevented them [the rebels] from offering that resistance to the landing of the troops which we had reason to expect. After shells from the Essex entirely demoralized them," the Confederate forces withdrew and, again according to Colonel Jerrard, "The 22nd was the first regiment ordered to land and occupy the works."[3]

The regiment's proximity to the enemy and the uncertainty of the situation in the city is demonstrated as Francis continues his December 18 letter.

> Our rifles were inspected and 40 rounds of cartridges dealt out to us this P.M. We arrived near the city of Baton Rouge near daylight yesterday morning. I will here state for explanation that we had no force in the city and the Rebels held the city in one sense of the word, but the gunboats in the river here kept them from getting any force here or building entrenchments. There was a small force of cavalry here yesterday when we got here. At about daylight the vessels, about 8 or 10, came up off the city and began to unload the troops. While we were coming on shore the gunboats shelled the woods and our present camp ground to drive back whatever force there might be here. One of the regiments marched in and raised the flag on the State House. After doing this the rest on shore gave three cheers for the flag on the State House of Louisiana, and then we formed into line and loaded ready for what there might be up the bank on the edge of the city on almost the same ground where the 14th [Maine] had their battle.[4]

The 14th Maine Infantry, a 3 year regiment, had fought in the August 5 battle that had taken Baton Rouge, suffering 119 casualties (killed, wounded, or missing).[5]

General Cuvier Grover (Library of Congress).

The Recapture of Baton Rouge, Louisiana on December 17, 1862 — Federal troops under General Grover drive off the Confederates and occupy the city. The gunboat *Essex* is near the shore at right (U.S. Naval Historical Center).

Francis continues, "We marched up to the grounds and each company was given its place to guard inside of the entrenchments that had been thrown up around the grounds when our troops held the place before. We had two companies sent out as pickets for the rest of the day. We put up our tents in the afternoon and slept on our arms with orders to turn out at ¼ past 4 and stand ready for action till further orders."[6]

Although the Union forces landed unopposed, Captain Case, writing about 2 months later, apparently felt that the newspaper reports of the landings did not give a fair picture of the event: "I never thought due credit was given to the prominent part played by the 22nd in the capture of the city, but the truth of history will one day be vindicated."[7] There was concern that the Union troops in Baton Rouge would be attacked by a superior force of Confederates reported to be in the vicinity, and the Union troops were "kept constantly under arms" for several days as a result.[8]

8. The Reoccupation of Baton Rouge

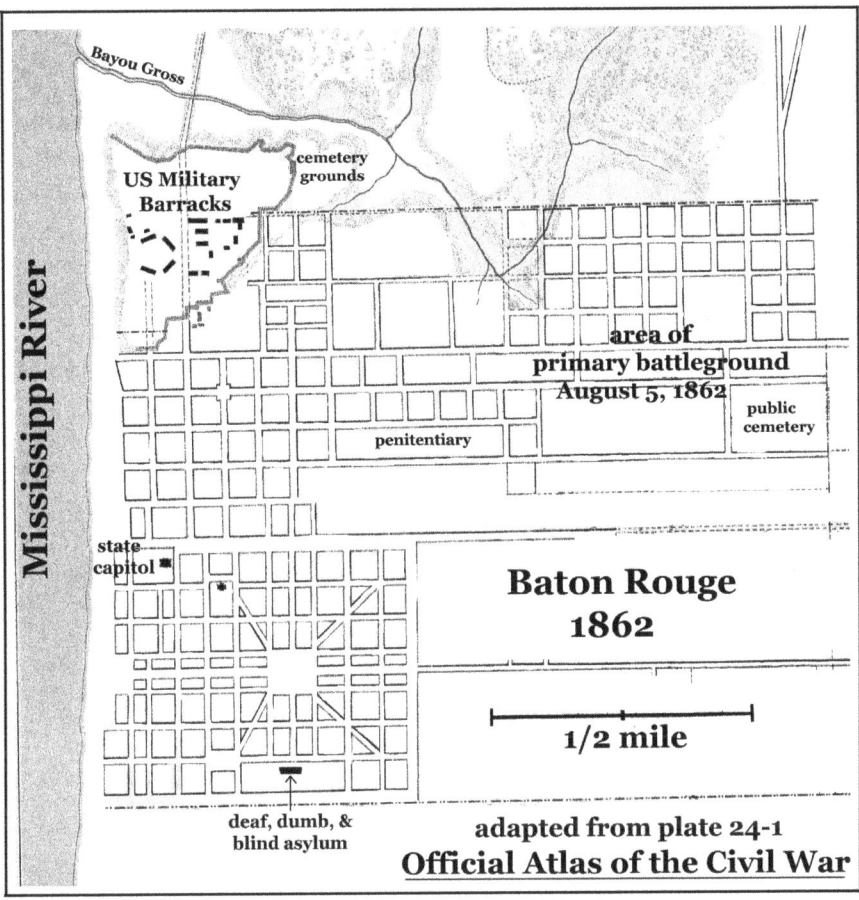

Map of Baton Rouge, 1862; adapted from plate 24–1, *The Official Military Atlas of the Civil War*.

Continuing with Francis Ireland's December 18 letter, we read more of the 22nd's first day at Baton Rouge:

> The pickets captured about half a dozen men and about 20 horses yesterday that were strolling about in the woods near here. We are a little out of the city and I guess none of the force have been into the business part of the city yet. I heard the railroad whistle today. I suppose the rebels run it. We are camped near some state or county buildings I guess. They're public buildings of some sort and were very nice ones but some of the glass is broke out and the buildings otherwise mutilated. I forgot to say that our pickets shot one man that run when the guard halted him yesterday.[9]

In that last sentence, was Francis attempting to appear nonchalant and hardened to the realities of war, or had he actually forgotten? I suspect the former case.

After a few days of worrying about the possibility of a Rebel attack, Jerrard wrote, "Reinforcements soon arrived sufficient to relieve Gen. Grover of any fear of a successful attack after which the regiment settled down to the usual routine of garrison duty."[10]

Francis continues by telling how mail is often misdirected and making his usual request that his father write often. He adds, "Eben could do well out to New Orleans with his hens, as eggs were brought to the boat at the low price of 1.00 per dozen or 10 cts. apiece. Some of the people here are said to be half starved. Flour is $60.00 per bbl. and scarce at that." After letting his mother know he'll send her the requested lock of his hair, he goes on to mention the possibility of contact with the enemy.

> I suppose these troops are sent here preparing to an attack on Vicksburg. Give my respects to all hands and tell them I am smart and anxious to see a brush with the rebels. We may before morning, as it is said they have a force about 12 miles from here. We had been at work strengthening our entrenchments today and we have had several pieces of artillery set on them already. I will close here, and I want you to copy my letters before you show them and correct mistakes, etc. You will direct in future to me at —
>
> New Orleans, Louisiana
> Co. E, 22nd Maine Regiment, etc.
>
> From your son,
> Francis A. Ireland[11]

In the last paragraph of this letter, Francis' comment about being anxious to see a brush with the rebels is in sharp contrast to Charlie Farrar's letter in which he tells his mother he hopes never to see a battle. Francis' sentiment may be, at least in part, due to the fact that John Ireland is copying his son's letters and showing them around town.

As Christmas of 1862 approached, Francis and his comrades found themselves in a situation that few of them could have imagined in previous years. Still at Baton Rouge, he began a letter on December 24, this time opening "Dear Father and Mother" and giving the details of a recent picket duty, guarding approaches to the city.

> I am in tip top health with the exception of a little cold I got out on picket duty the other day but that is what every man, almost, has got since we came here. The day after I wrote last our company was sent out with 3 or 4 Cos. from other reg'ts here on picket duty. We were sent over in the south side of the city and each company divided into two platoons, one under charge of the

capt. and 2nd lieut. and the other with the 1st lieut., and sent in different directions out in the woods at the corners of the roads etc. Our platoon was stationed near the corners of two or three roads coming in to the city. Twelve men were then sent out a little ways and stationed three on a post to stand there for 24 hours. The rest of us with the capt. and 2nd lieut. were left in a central place between these as a reserve in case of an alarm, and as a sort of headquarters for the pickets to bring their prisoners and whatever negroes come into our lines. We took 32 negroes, a four mule team, and some other things that they brought with them. They began to come in the first day after we got here. When we came here flour was $60.00 per bbl., Beef 75 cts. a lb. and none to be had at that, only now and then. Their living has been corn bread and sweet potatoes.[12]

In an exchange with some of these runaway slaves, Francis gets their ideas as to the progress of the war. "Some of them are quite intelligent. I talked with several the night we were out about the war etc. and they seem to know about how things were going. They represent the rebels as sick of the war, starving to death, etc., which I know to be about so far as the few that are left in Baton Rouge are concerned." He goes on to describe assistance to residents left at an asylum near their camp, and to report on the way escaped slaves are put to work.

Our station that I mentioned above was near a large asylum for the deaf, dumb, and blind of the state. It is a splendid structure, about the nicest I ever saw. There are but a few pupils here now and I guess that in these times they have to support themselves the best they can. The lady teachers sent out to buy some hard bread. We gave them what we had to spare. I suppose it looked good to them as they didn't get any flour. Some of the families sent sweet potatoes and corn bread to exchange. We have got our negroes to work on our earthworks which will save us a great deal. They must earn their living if we take them in and keep them from their masters.

After a visit to the 12th Maine's camp (a 3 year regiment sent with General Butler's 1862 expedition to Louisiana), and a chance to chat with some other boys from Dexter, Francis saw more of the battlefield where the 14th Maine had fought. "On our way we went onto the grounds where the 14th Maine was engaged [in] the battle here. A part of it was a Catholic cemetery the place that the rebels retreated into. The marks of the shell and ball are to be seen very plain. I saw a tomb made of brick that had a hole in the side where a cannon ball went through it. It had broken the coffin all to pieces. Everything is just about as it was left after the Battle."

He then paid a visit to the Louisiana State House.

Deaf, dumb, and blind asylum in Baton Rouge (G.H. Suydam Photograph Album, Mss. 1394, Louisiana and Lower Mississippi Valley Collections, Louisiana State University Libraries, Baton Rouge).

>We came back and spent about 3 hours looking at the State House and the ruins of its contents. I wish you could go thro it. It is a building finished in magnificent style especially inside. As to its contents, in the different office rooms are papers, charts, maps, official documents etc. strewed in every direction on the floor, in the cases and everywhere under foot. Everything of value that could be carried off is gone, everything out of the cabinets except for a few rocks and some iron ore. In the library rooms there are cart-loads of books (mostly reports) on the floors. There are a great many on the shelves bound in sheep that have not been disturbed as they were either too large to bring away or of no value except in a state library. By the way this sheet of paper I got there. It is just like my other, but I write on it just for the curiosity of it. I also got the last message of the last governor of this state. The furniture is most all destroyed. There is a great deal of wood work inside that is carved and wrought out beautifully, especially in the Senate Room and Representative Hall. In there we had the pleasure of sitting in the chairs of the pres. of the Senate and speaker of the House, which we found very comfortable if they were in a rebel state! The grounds are very prettily laid out altho they have been some neglected for some time.

Francis goes on to describe the condition of the city in general and the place where the 22nd is encamped.

8. The Reoccupation of Baton Rouge

This is or was a very pretty city but when the battle was here the north part of the city was pretty well burnt up. This is just below us. I can count the ruins of over 40 buildings while I am sitting in my tent door now. The rest of the city would have been in good condition had the owners stayed here instead of running off as they did when the place was taken last summer. Their property is not in the best shape, while that of those that remain here is undisturbed. Our camp is at or on the grounds of the former U.S. Military Depot. There are a lot of large brick buildings on them for magazines, barracks, and arsenal, and other military purposes. It is a pretty location and I hope we shall remain here. The rebels have not disturbed us and I don't think they will.[13]

Captain Case gives his view of Baton Rouge in this way: "I shall not attempt to describe the city, except to say that it is regularly laid out, has many fine buildings, both public and private, chiefly of brick, but like nearly all Southern cities, fine houses & wretched hovels stand in close proximity on almost any street."[14]

Francis Ireland's December 24 letter next relates a rumor that he and the others have heard of a recent battle, most likely a garbled account of the Battle of Fredericksburg, which had been fought about 2 weeks earlier, on December 13 and 14. "We have heard the story this way and that for a week that Richmond was taken. We did not credit it at first but begin to believe it is so for it comes pretty direct, and the troops are coming in here pretty fast." The rumor that Richmond had fallen was, of course, wildly inaccurate. Perhaps the arrival of more and more Federal troops in Louisiana convinced the men there that Virginia must be under Union control.

Francis next tells of these regiments and batteries that are gathering near the 22nd's camp, and estimates that 12,000 to 15,000 Union troops are at Baton Rouge. He then goes on to speculate as to why so many new troops are arriving and wonders about his regiment's possible role in the upcoming campaign. "We can't make out ... where we are going (if we are to leave here) much better than if we were at home reading the papers. The only Rebel force of any account near here is at Port or Fort Hudson about 25 miles above here. It is well fortified and is held by a pretty large force." Francis then speculates that, considering their placement, his regiment may be left to defend Baton Rouge while the newly arriving troops will form a Union expedition against Port Hudson.

After a brief description of the latest weather: "It is just about like fine June weather at home, with cold nights," he goes on, "I like here first rate as it is a pretty place and said to be the most healthy in the state. Only one thing that is any way objectionable. That is we are so far from news and it takes so long to get a mail. I am getting very anxious to hear from home. It is said we shall get a mail in a few days and I hope we shall for I want to see a "Daily Whig" [*Bangor Daily Whig and Courier*] and get the news."

His overall favorable opinion of the area is underlined by his commenting, "This is a splendid country and a Maine farmer could make himself rich with a little labor on a few acres of this soil in a few years. It is rich and easily tilled." He then tells of souvenirs he is sending home. "I will send you some copies of the governor's message just before the war broke out. I got them at the State House, also a piece of copper from the roof of the State House and some leaves from the trees on the grounds. They are of no consequence but I send them for the fun of it."

Continuing his letter on Christmas day, Francis makes only a passing comment about what must have been a very different holiday indeed. With a morning free from drill the only apparent concession to the day, Francis gives his usual daily schedule.

> I wish you a merry Christmas! altho I can't make it seem so to me. It is so different from any Christmas I ever saw before, as it is supposed to be. We don't have any drill this A.M. I will give you a detail of a days business here.
>
> | | | | |
> |---|---|---|---|
> | Drums Beat at | 5 o'clock A.M. | | roll call |
> | " | 6¼ | " | Surgeons call for the sick |
> | " | 7 | " | Breakfast |
> | " | 8 | " | Mounting the guard |
> | " | 9 | " | Drill |
> | " | 10 | " | Recall from drill |
> | " | 11 | " | For drill |
> | " | 12 | " | Recall from drill |
> | " | 12¼ | P.M. | Dinner |
> | " | 1½ | " | Drill |
> | " | 2½ | " | Recall from drill |
> | " | 5 | " | Dress parade |
> | | | | No beat for supper |
> | " | 8 | " | Roll call |
> | " | 8½ | " | Lights out and all abed |
>
> This is the present routine of business now. It may be changed now and then by the general if necessary.

Although most of this long Christmas letter remained newsy and free from sentiment, he closes with even more than the usual wish for contact with home:

> Our boys are very well as a general thing. We have not heard from those we left at New Orleans since we left. I can not think of any thing more of impor-

tance to write. Will write the next mail. I want you to write often. I hope to hear from you soon. Charlie is pretty smart.

Give my respects to the mill girls and tell them I expect a letter the next mail from them. Be sure to get Flora's picture to send to me in your next letter.

From your son,
Francis A. Ireland[15]

9

At Baton Rouge
Balmy Breezes and Deadly Diseases

In his next letter from Baton Rouge, started on December 28, Francis begins with more comments on the weather,

> I suppose it is very likely that you are hovering around the fire at home with snow and ice aplenty out of doors today. While I am sitting with the front of my tent open and am in my shirt sleeves writing as comfortable as if it were the last of May in Maine.[1]
>
> We are all well and hearty, that is the most of us. A number of the men are sick but the Dexter boys are most of them on the gain. Roscoe Haynes had been sick [but] is getting better quite fast. Jacob Whittimore is rather slim at present. We heard from Henry Fitzgerald today that he was getting better fast and would rejoin us again soon.

Francis then states for a second time, "This is a pretty healthy place and the longer we stay the better I like [it]. Hope we shall be lucky enough to stay here some time." That feeling may have been influenced by the warm December days that this young man from Maine found so enjoyable. The facts of the matter turned out to be quite different. Overall, the Union regiments sent to the Gulf suffered greatly from diseases common to that area and aggravated by the lack of sanitary conditions in their camps. Malaria and typhoid were serious killers, while intestinal disorders such as dysentery were responsible for the greatest number of deaths. In addition, many of the soldiers from rural areas found themselves exposed to childhood diseases such as measles or mumps for the first time. In this the men of the 22nd Maine were no exception.[2]

In his February letter to his sister, Captain Case had commented,

9. At Baton Rouge

> Our reg. has suffered greatly from sickness since we came here [Baton Rouge]. More than thirty have died since we left Maine, and at this time more than two hundred are unfit for duty. Three have died from my company — one here and two at the gen. hospital near Fort Monroe, & several others are quite sick here. My own health has been very good for the most of the time, though none of us have anything like the physical energy & strength we have at home. ... I have not been really sick for a day since I entered the service.[3]

Colonel Jerrard's report of this same time period states: "While at Baton Rouge the regiment suffered severely from sickness and death notwithstanding every care and effort to preserve the health of the troops." In a part of his letter to the adjutant general which he crossed out, the colonel had originally stated, "Notwithstanding the most rigid attention to diet and cleanliness, and the skill and unwearied efforts of Drs. Jordan and Huckins, [men of the regiment became] sick and died at a fearful rate." In the rough draft of his report to Maine's adjutant general, Colonel Jerrard stated that the "condition of things soon began to tell seriously on the spirits of the soldiers and the attention of the Genl. commanding was called to the matter." An investigation followed which examined the management of the hospital and camp as well as the habits of the soldiers and found "nothing unusual." It seems that, as we might expect, young men from Maine simply had no previous exposure or immunity to diseases of the Gulf and bayous. Colonel Jerrard reported that it wasn't until the regiment left Baton Rouge and "entered on more active duties that the prevalence of disease and death abated."[4]

Francis Ireland goes on in his December 28 letter,

> A man in Co. D [Private Wentworth Leighton] died in the hospital last night. He is to be buried this afternoon. This Co. (D) has been very unfortunate since we left. They have lost four men since we left Camp Pope and there has been only six died out [of] the Regt. since then.

Wed. Dec. 31

> As I am at leisure again I will write a little more in my letter. After I left off Sunday I went to the funeral that I spoke of. It was a Masonic funeral and was largely attended from other reg'ts. The capt. has just received a letter from New Orleans informing him of the death of Augustus Scales of Dexter. He died last Friday. This is the first man that has died out of our company. He had not been very smart for some time and was taken with fever on our trip to New Orleans.[5]

Apparently Augustus Scales lied about his age in order to enlist, and so died a long way from home. His enlistment card and the adjutant general's report give his age as 18 in October of 1862. However, his gravestone states that he died Dec. 26, 1862, at age 17, and census records confirm this younger age.[6]

And, when writing that Augustus Scales was the first from Company E to die, Francis was apparently unaware that another Dexter boy of his company, Joseph Smith, had died on December 10.[7]

Francis continues, "Roscoe Haynes joined the company again today, has been in the hospital some time here. There are no dangerously sick now

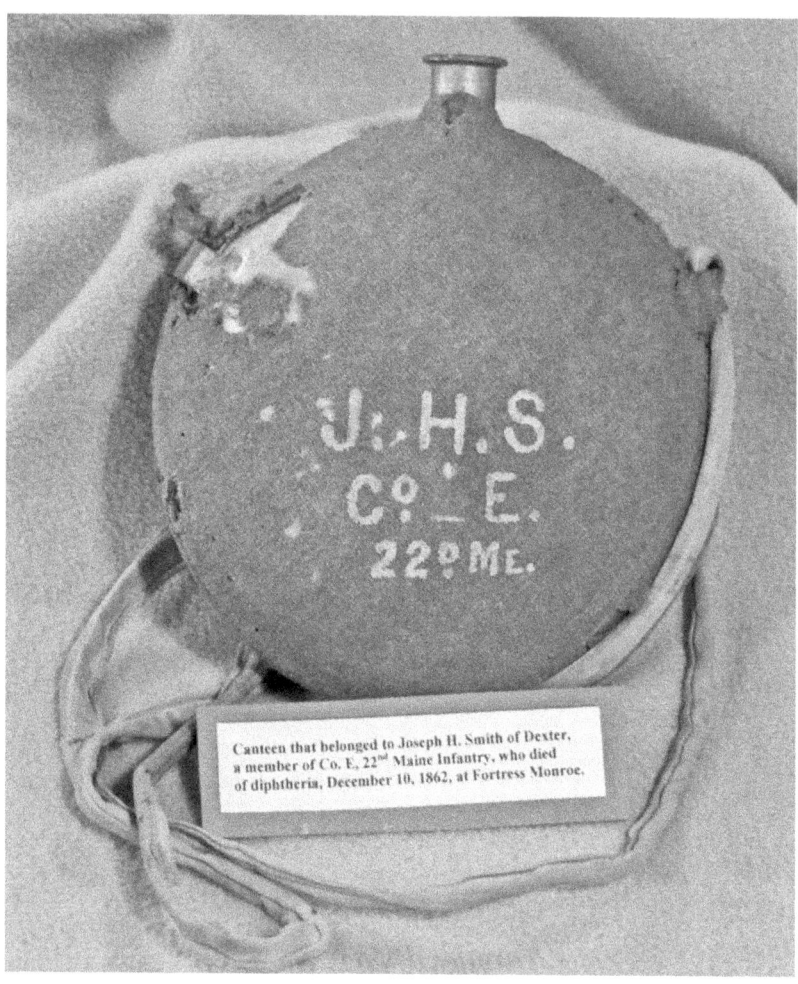

A canteen that belonged to Joseph Smith, Company E, 22nd Maine (Dexter Historical Society).

from our company. We are to be mustered for our pay to day, a performance we go thro the last day of every other month. May not get the money for some time." He then tells of a fire that destroyed the Louisiana State House:

> We have had a great fire here since I wrote last Sunday night. As we were eating our supper the city bells rung for fire and we soon saw the blaze in the direction of the State House, which it soon proved to be. It burnt very brisk for two or three hours and then abated during the night — and I guess they expected to save a part of it. At five in the morning the fire took a new start and burnt the inside all out! leaving only the stone and marble walls and a pile of ruins of what was in the morning a splendid structure which had cost a great many thousands of dollars. I don't know how it caught fire. There was a few cos. of soldiers quartered there and some prisoners in guard. I suppose the Rebels will say we destroyed it when all was done that could be done to save it.[8]

When he continues his letter on January 2, Francis tells of the latest move by his regiment and the brigade they are now a part of.

> I have been very busy for two days just past as we have moved somewhat. We received orders to march yesterday morning and struck our tents ready to leave. At 1 o'clock the regt. left the grounds marched down thro the city to where the 12th Me. is encamped about a mile and a half from their former camp where we pitched our tents and are formed into a brigade composed of the 12th, 22nd Me., 2nd Louisiana, 131st N.Y. & Billy Wilsons Zouaves of New York [6th N.Y.] that you have heard so much about, under the command of Col. Wilson until brig. gen. gets here.[9]

Colonel William Wilson had been a prize fighter as a young man and was associated with the New York City Democratic political machine and in particular with Fernando Wood's Tammany Hall and "Mozart Democrats." In an apparent break with Wood and the Copperhead (Peace Democrats), Wilson raised a regiment of "roughs" from New York City in response to the attacks made against Union soldiers in Baltimore.[10]

Although Francis was there and seems clear about the makeup of this brigade, there seems to be some confusion about the inclusion of the 2nd Louisiana. It was one of a dozen or so Louisiana regiments that fought for the Union, and was organized in New Orleans in late September 1862. Its assignment to Baton Rouge doesn't seem to have taken place until a week or more after this letter was written. Further, Colonel Jerrard's letter to the adjutant general, and the subsequent Maine Adjutant General's Report for 1863 state that at that time, the 22nd Maine was combined with the "6th N.Y., 12th Me., and 131st N.Y., forming the 1st Brigade of Grover's Division [4th Division, 19th Corps], under command of Col. William Wilson, 6th N.Y., but later under Brig. Gen. William Dwight."[11]

The burned shell of Louisiana State House in Baton Rouge (G.H. Suydam Photograph Album, Mss. 1394, Louisiana and Lower Mississippi Valley Collections, Louisana State University Libraries, Baton Rouge).

This organization of these 4 regiments is the same as that given in General Order 599 of December 30, which lists the regiments of the 1st Brigade, 4th Division, as the 6th New York, 12th Maine, 22nd Maine, and 131st New York, and states that the brigade will be commanded by

Brigadier General William Dwight. General Dwight — who like General Banks was from Massachusetts — had been expelled from West Point in 1853 for poor grades, and had gone into the manufacturing business. With the outbreak of the Civil War he had a second chance at a military career. Starting as lieutenant colonel of the 70th New York, he was given command of a brigade and later a division, and eventually became General Banks' chief of staff.[12]

Continuing with Francis' December 28 letter, now being written on January 2, we read of the 22nd Maine's new camp in Baton Rouge. "We are 5 regts all encamped where the battle commenced here last summer on the left side of one of the roads to the city in a

Colonel Billy Willson (*Harper's Weekly*, May 11, 1861).

large, level, and low piece of ground. There are a great many others about ½ a mile back of us on another road. I don't like here near as well as I did at the city. It is or must be very wet in rainy weather and good water is very scarce. We have it hauled to us with mule teams from the Mississippi River about 2 miles."

After telling of his reunion with some men from Dexter in the 12th Maine, Francis once again talks about the men who are sick, and tells of his tent mates.

> We left some of our boys at the hospital in the city, that will probably be with us soon, as the most of them have only got a cold or jaundice or dysentery, some temporary sickness. They are D.H. Remmick, Charlie and Jacob Whittemore, Ithamer Merrill are the Dexter boys. As for myself I am as smart

as ever I was in the world. As to my tent mates, they are the same. They are Sam Morril [Solomon Morrill], Jonas Hutchinson, Isaiah K. Ireland [Francis' cousin] and a Mr. Carpenter of Charleston. He used to live in Monson, and was some acquainted with Grandfather Day [Francis' maternal grandfather, Thomas Day] or at least said he used to sing with him after they were done work. ... He is about 55 years old and a first rate camp mate with 3 boys in the army and then came himself![13]

Apparently an attempt to appear older was not the only reason for lying about one's age. Asa Carpenter listed his age as 44 at the time of his enlistment, but the 1860 census records give his age as 52, which would make Francis' report of 55 accurate. Asa had been a farmer back in Charleston, Maine. In the 22nd Maine, at least 58 men gave their age 40 or over when they enlisted. In Company E, there were 7 men over 40, and while we may think of a drummer-boy as a young lad, Company E's musician, James Crawford, was 43 when he enlisted.[14]

Continuing with the January 2 part of his December 31 letter, Francis goes on to describe some food the regiment has recently acquired: "Our folks are confiscating Rebel property here somewhat — out in the country — such as cotton, molasses, corn, and sugar and livestock. By this means we get a little fresh beef here now and then. I took some cotton out of a bale as the team was passing by here today. I send a bit as a curiosity as it was taken from rebel owners or from their plantations."

And he closes with:

> I also send some locks of my hair as mother wished. They are rather short, but will do till I get home (in about 5 months!) Oh! I tell you if we don't get a mail soon we shall all flummox, for none of us have heard any thing from home for over 4 weeks and

Private Sam Morrill (Dexter Historical Society).

don't know when we shall! I must close as the boys are coming in from drill and will rush into the tent and spoil my writing with their nonsense (I have been digging around the tent this P.M.) Write often etc. If I never get them no matter!

Send Flora's Picture. Good by all.
Francis A. Ireland[15]

In Francis Ireland's next letter, started just 3 days later on January 5, he once again speculates on the plans for the regiment.

Dear Father and Mother;

I will commence another letter as I have time before this afternoon's drill. I am as well as ever, and enjoying myself as well as most any soldier out here.

Drum, fife, and canteen that belonged to James Crawford, 22nd Maine (Dexter Historical Society).

> We are encamped as we were when I wrote last. Don't know how long we shall stay here. There are a great many troops here and around the city (some say 40,000). I don't have any means of knowing — only what I can judge from hearsay, and appearances. There are seven reg'ts and a battery at this one camp where we are, and any quantity more a short distance off. I suppose it is intended to send some of them up river soon, to try their luck at Fort [Port] Hudson.[16]

He goes on to describe encounters with Rebels near the camp.

> The Rebs have not troubled us anywhere yet, only by troubling the outside cavalry pickets (about 8 miles out) now and then. They were out about 10 miles one day and a squad of about 60 of them were fired into by a company of guerillas that were laying in wait for them, wounding several men and horses. One fellow had his horse shot from under him, and seven bullets put into his own body! He was brought to the city and from last accounts was doing well. I don't think that they will attack this place unless they get drove down the river.

And again, he comments on rumors he has heard. "We are in great suspense here to hear from the state of things at Washington. We have rumors of peace and all kinds of stories about a settlement of affairs immediately! Hope to hear soon." Once again Francis mentions the sickness within the regiment, his concern about the care the men receive at the military hospital, and his feelings regarding the doctors and nurses.

> We are having quite a sickly time at present in our regiment. Not many of a dangerous disease, but they are getting acclimated and are having colds, dysentery, etc. I have not been on the list excused on account of sickness since we left Virginia, and if I am as well as I have been since then I shan't be again, for I don't want to see the inside of an Army Hospital, as it would only make a bad matter worse to get into one ... the way they are managed. We have a great many boys in them. If they could have proper care might soon get better even in this climate, but I fear they will never see the good old state of Maine again. The great trouble is not in the ability of physicians or their hospital nurses so much as it is they are not interested from them as they would be if they were at home where their reputation as such would be at stake. To be sure they visit the sick and ask for their wants quite often, but a sick man don't always know when he wants anything, or what he wants, and he will say no, and they pass along to the next patient instead of trying to find out his wants and supplying them. Their pay goes on just the same as if they had done all they could for the men. You need not mention what I have said to those that have friends sick here as might be a cause of unnecessary anxiety to them as I hope the most of us Dexter boys will outride the storm. It was neglect that I had seen of other patients that made me think of this to write, as I always write a thing just as it is. Charlie has got some cold and complained of the Rheuma-

tism yesterday, but is on duty today and I guess it is only a "Louisiana cold." I think that he is about as rugged as he is at home. It is not the toughest of men that are tough out here. We have men that were called tough and could camp out at home, that are ailing with cold etc. while there are many that looked like small potatoes that are as tough as boiled owls. The smallest fellow (and about the youngest) in our company has not seen a sick day since we started! That is the difference.

Continuing on January 6, he describes the weather and a recent thunderstorm, and then writes about Jefferson Richardson, another young man from Dexter who is Company E's wagoner.

> Jeff Richardson is in business and is as big as a brigadier. As we have no teams for him, he is detailed to "boss" 10 mule teams drove by niggers that are used to haul in from the country. There is a boss to every 10 teams to see to the loading and that the niggers are taking care of their teams, etc. These teams are most of them "run in" here by the niggers when they leave their masters, some of them are two abreast, some three, and some with one in the shafts and two on leads.[17]

In this letter, Francis is now referring to "niggers" when in previous letters he used the terms "Negro," "contraband," or in one case, "darky." One can't help but wonder why he has changed his term for these people, and just what the word "nigger" meant in that day to a young man from rural Maine. Whatever he thought the word meant, it seems that he had picked it up during his months in the South.

Indeed, we may wonder just what the term meant to the slaves or freedmen of that day. A newspaper report concerning the welcome General Banks' army received from Louisiana's slave population quotes the slaves as singing, "Massa run away, hi, hi! Nigger bound to say, ho, ho! I think that now de Kingdom come, Dat dis de year ob Jubilo!"[18]

An essay on the African-American Registry Website suggests that slaves who used that term were simply internalizing the negative images of themselves that white society had created, and a recent book by Randall Kennedy on that topic indicates that by the first third of the 19th century the term was used to show contempt for blacks.[19]

In this January 6 letter, Francis goes on to say that he has heard of a recent battle and wonders what happened. He is writing about the battle at Fredericksburg, back in mid–December, and he is apparently unaware of the more recent battle at Stones River (Murfreesboro, Tennessee) which was fought from December 31 to January 2. This letter and others give us an appreciation for how little the men in the Department of the Gulf knew of the war in other areas.

He wrote, "I heard of a great battle near Richmond or Fredericksburg and that our folks met with heavy loss. Was any of the Maine 6th from Dexter lost — anyway? I don't know much more about the state of things at the seat of war than I should if I was in China. Hope to get some papers soon." There were several young men from Dexter in the 6th Maine. Francis would no doubt be pleased to learn, at some point, that none of them were wounded or killed at Fredericksburg.[20]

He closes, saying that he expects many letters from home when the regiment gets its next mail, as he has not gotten a letter since early December, a month earlier.

> I think we ought to have had a mail long ago if the officers had looked out and had it ordered when we got to our stopping place. The latest letters the reg't has received was when we were at Fort Monroe and were dated Thanksgiving Day. By the way if you can send me some good largish sized letter paper and envelopes in my papers or some such cheap way I should like it as it is high out here. Send me a sewing awl in a letter if you can get a small one, such as they are to sew up breaks in leather! I may not get it this two months if I do at all but it may come handy then. Write all the news both at home and abroad. I don't care how much. I can find time enough to read them.
>
> Give my respects to all and a Happy New Year!
>
> From your son,
> Francis A. Ireland
> Co. E 22nd Maine Regt.
> Camp Banks, Baton Rouge, Louisiana[21]

10

More Sickness, Surviving the Cure, Longing for Home

In January, Francis joined the many others of his regiment and corps who had been sick. Saying that he has received a letter from home and had intended to write sooner, he writes on January 24 telling of his health and of medical treatment he had received.

> First — as to my health it seemed to grow worse, and Wed. I went to the surgeon's at the call in the morning and he gave me a rather severe prescription. ... It was this croton oil applied externally to my chest. Also a cough mixture 4 times a day — a very pleasant medicine. They use croton oil a great deal here for internal pain, cough, etc. Mine has operated well for my chest is completely covered with little blisters from the size of a pin head to a kernel of wheat by hundreds. They are rather uncomfortable as they itch and smart like time! and I can't scratch. But I think it is going to be quite a help to me as my cough is a great deal better already. With this exception — my cough — I am as smart as ever and expect to be rid of that soon. I am not on duty now and Doct. Huckins will not mark me for it till I get over the effect of my medicine. By that time in a few days I will be over the cough.[1]

These days croton oil is generally regarded as unsuitable for human use. One source indicates that its use is "now entirely without justification or excuse" and that when applied to the skin it will cause inflammation leading to pustules. One lab that sells croton oil "for research use only" does so with the warnings that gloves and mask should be worn when using it and that care must be taken to prevent exposure. *Dorland's Illustrated Medical Dictionary* lists croton oil as "a drastic purgative and counterirritant, unsafe for human use." However, in *A Modern Herbal,* first published in 1931, and still in print, the author indicates that croton oil may be used in very small amounts as a powerful laxative, or externally as a "counter-irritant" for rheumatism, neuralgia, and bronchitis.[2]

Francis goes on to report on another condition with which the men are suffering. "Our reg't is still suffering with the disorder of this country to a great extent. A great many cases of a bad diarrheas. Charly has had it some time, is getting along well." As mentioned earlier, intestinal disorders such as chronic diarrhea and dysentery, and the dehydration that resulted, were the greatest causes of death in the Union Army.[3]

After telling of a frustrating series of moves that ended with the brigade encamped about a half mile from where they started, Francis goes on to report the arrival of General Banks and additional troops, including a "Negro" regiment.

> Last Thursday we (the brigade) got orders to move and we went about a mile to a new camp ground and we had got our tents up and everyone his grounds clean. We then sat down in the tents to rest a little. Just as the sun was setting what should come round the camp but the aggravating story that we had got to move again the next day back about half a mile towards our camp as we did and came to our present position a little out of the city.
>
> Military begins to look on the offensive here, that is. I guess some of us troops here have got to march for Port Hudson soon, as the troops are coming in here lately pretty fast. A negro reg't arrived here today 1,000 strong. I should like to see them. Gen. Banks arrived here this week. I saw him Thursday as he and his staff were riding round. He looks just as I expected from what I had seen of his portraits. I don't believe he will ride round in "purple and fine linen" and do nothing for his country, but get his pay out of them![4]

On the other hand, Francis has taken a strong disliking to the acting brigade commander, Colonel Wilson of the 6th New York, but thinks he knows the reason for Wilson's behavior.

> Our Act.-Brig. Gen. Wilson I don't like! In fact I shall soon despise him. He is a vulgar and awful profane man and has no patience at all, and he ain't the greatest that ever was in Military tactics, etc. As to his profanity, if we are out on brigade drill and a reg't or its officers commit a blunder (which of course is not uncommon) it seems as if there were not oaths enough in the English language for him to use while talking to them. But then has had to do this in his own reg't as that is the only way you can make an Irishman start!

Francis then tells of the health of a few men from Dexter and indicates that he is looking ahead to the end of his term of service. "Jacob Whittemore and Sam C. Silver are the only Dexter boys in the hospital now. Sumner Brawn came out today. Henry Leighton has not yet started for home. Don't know when he will. Capt. Wood is as fat and hearty as a bear. By the way I suppose our 9 months is half out tomorrow. It seems some time since I enlisted, but it looks short ahead as the weeks slip off pretty fast so long as I am well enough to be in camp."

Continuing on Sunday, January 25, Francis reports on the weather and the food and water available to the regiment.

> One thing, it is pretty darned warm today. Anyhow that is what makes me feel so lazy I suppose. I should like a good sleigh ride today is the common remark among the boys here these warm days. Well I think a good meal of victuals at the table in the right style would suit me as well as anything today, altho our living is the right kind for a man in the army. I shall be a great tea drinker when I get home. Our water here is from the river as usual. If the mud was out of it I should admire it as it is cold enough to make your teeth ache and very good tasting water. But you can't see the bottom of a pint dipper half full of it, it is so riley.

Francis then gives a typical soldier's complaint about the weight of his equipment. Other than their march from Washington to Arlington, all of the regiment's moves of any substantial distance had been made by rail or water, and the prospect of carrying his belongings for many miles is something he hopes to avoid. "If we are called out on a long march (which I hope and trust we never shall be as we have not yet) I shall have to lighten my knapsack by throwing away the things that I can best get along without, for when fully equipped we have a load that is no fun to carry. Whenever I have been on drill or guard duty or anything that required my rifle for the last 5 weeks, I have had no less than 50 round of cartridges in my box. They weigh down when you have to keep them on 24 hours steady I tell you!"

Mentioning that he is still waiting for the promised picture of his sister Flora, he closes with "Keep on writing as usual all the news. ... My respects to all. Tell the girls I will answer their letter soon. Also the sort room. From your son, Francis A. Ireland"[5]

On February 7, still at Baton Rouge, Francis began another letter to his parents. The picture of his little sister has arrived, as have copies of Maine newspapers. The "Whig" is, once again, the *Bangor Daily Whig and Courier*, and the "Gem" is Dexter's weekly newspaper, the *Gem and Gazette*. "Dear parents; I received your letters of the 18th and 20th last night with the picture which was all right. Flora has changed a great deal in her looks, but she looks same in the face as she did when I was at home. I got 11 Whigs and one Gem by the same mail."[6]

He then talks about his recent illness and treatment, reassures his parents that he is now feeling better, and explains his reason for telling them about it in the first place.

> As for myself I am quite smart and on duty again the same as ever. My cough is a great deal better, and the doctor drove the jaundice out of me in two days, almost before it had got fairly on to me. My medicine was croton oil on my chest to take the soreness out of my lungs and a cough mixture for my cough. For the jaundice I took 2 pills a day (they were the real blue pill, calomel) which soon brought me all right. I write these particulars just to let you know how I was, and my treatment so that you will not think that I conceal my sickness from you when I am so, for fear that you will worry needlessly about me. I am all right now however.

The calomel that Francis writes of was a mercury compound, that often did more harm than good, but which was in common use during the Civil War. Side effects of the buildup of mercury in the patient's system could bring on extreme salivation and painful inflammation of the tongue and gums. In some cases, ulcers in the mouth led to a gradual eating away of the bones and tissue of the face, resulting in permanent disfigurement. In the spring of 1863, the Union Army's surgeon general, William Hammond, forbid the use of calomel, but his order was met with considerable resistance from the American Medical Association.[7]

Once again, as we would expect, Francis is wondering where he and his regiment will be sent.

> We are in the same camp as when I wrote last. Don't know when we shall move if we do at all. One brigade left here yesterday to go down river. I suppose they are going to stop at a place between here and New Orleans where we have an insufficient force in case of danger. As to the prospect of moving, I judge from what I see in the papers that Gen. Banks is expected up river, but he is here with quite a large force around him. Whether he will move or not, time will only tell. We have been highly favored so far as to long marches, never having marched over 6 miles at once (from Washington to Arlington Heights) and I hope we shall not see any longer one during the rest of our term of service. The 21st Me. arrived here a few days ago from New York.[8]

The 21st Maine was another 9 month regiment that had been mustered in at the same time as the 22nd. The 21st, after its muster into U.S. service in October in Augusta, Maine, had, when enroute to Washington D.C., been sent instead to New York City. After spending about 3 months there, they were then ordered to Baton Rouge.[9] Francis goes on to describe the conditions in their camp and the frustrations of becoming too comfortable.

> We have been having awful cold weather for a week past, or it seems so to us. The ground froze hard night before last, and the boys slept cold — some of them that did not have chimneys to their tents. I will explain this. We have

10. More Sickness, Surviving the Cure, Longing for Home

most any quantity of brick here, as brickmaking was one of the trades in the penitentiary here and there were a great many in the yards there, also a good many brick houses that were burnt up in the fight here last fall. Well the boys build a chimney with a fireplace in it, snug to the tent in front and have a very nice warm chance but it has got to be a by word here, that as soon as they begin to build chimneys that we are going to move. For every time we have got our tents fixed up in good shape, putting up chimneys etc. we have had to change our camp immediately afterwards! This cold weather will soon be over with and spring soon show itself. It is some like fall weather in Maine here at present.[10]

We then are told about the various Dexter boys who are in the hospital, Francis' current tent mates, and his hope that they will soon be paid.

> Our boys are about as usual. Only three Dexter boys in the hospital. Samuel Silver, Jacob Whitimore [Whittemore], and Mr. Crawford. They are all doing well I believe. Jonas Hutchinson is not very smart just now, but it is only a temporary ill turn, will be all right in a few days I guess. Jonas and Sam Morrill and myself occupy one tent now. We are very well matched and get along nice as a pin! They are very good camp mates. There is some talk of our being paid off. I don't know whether it is all camp talk or a fact. Hope it is so, for the sake of the reg't, for it is strapped from col. to corporal and private! I guess I can think of no more to write. Will wait till tomorrow to finish.

Continuing on the next day, Francis writes briefly of the weather and then goes on to indicate that he would like to be able to hear the local Dexter Methodist preacher. He then repeats the concerns that had already been expressed (and would be raised again) as to the actual date of the regiment's muster out of U.S. service. The soldiers were hoping that their 9 months of service would be counted from their arrival in Bangor in September, rather than their muster date in October.

> I have been to services this fore noon. Should like to step in and hear Elder Knowles this afternoon just for change. But then I must forego all such and the dinner you spoke of till after the 10th of June or July as the case may be if I live. ... We live well, but it is "Army living." The time has passed away fast so far, and it looks short ahead, but the only trouble is I should like to look into the next 4 months as I can into the past. We have had a great deal of dissension ever since we started as to when our term of service ends, the 10th of June or July, and we can't know for certain till the time comes. Sometimes we are positive that it is the 10th of June and then again we are just as sure that we shall have to stay till the 10th of July. Be it as it may I hope I shall have as good luck for the future as in the past in the army. There are 2 reg'ts in our brigade whose time is out in May. They are from N.Y., 2 years men.

Francis seems to be mistaken in this last statement. The 6th New York, Billy Wilson's Zouaves, was indeed due to be mustered out in late May of 1863, although they were not actually mustered out of U.S. service until June 25. The other two New York regiments in the 22nd's brigade, the 91st and 131st, were 3 year regiments whose time of service would not end in 1863.[11]

After saying that he may have his picture taken "if my whiskers were a little longer," and saying that he will send a portion of his pay home when he gets it, he goes on with an interesting combination of thoughts: "How did Isaiah's folks feel about his death? Are there any changes in the help in the mill? Does Harvey say as much about war and enlisting as ever? If he could be in the Army 4 or 5 months and see the 'animal' as he is, he would dry up mighty quick. No more at present. Good Bye, Francis A. Ireland."[12]

It seems that Francis uses the expression "see the 'animal' as he is" to mean seeing the army and army life as it really is. This is similar to the 19th century expression "see the elephant," which meant being confronted with a harsh reality and which came to refer specifically to seeing the realities of the army and to be confronted with the horror of battle.[13]

The Isaiah who had died was Isaiah Ireland, Francis' older cousin and one-time Company E tent mate, the son of Francis' uncle, Shephard Ireland, and his Aunt Chloe. Isaiah was yet another of the young men from Dexter who worked in the woolen mills, and when he died of illness in January 1863, he left behind his wife, Hannah, and 2 young children.[14]

On February 10 Francis wrote a brief note to let his father know that he had been paid and what portion of their money he and Charlie Farrar were sending home.

> Dear Father;
>
> In haste I sit myself to inform you that we were paid off today and our squad's money leaves in the morning's boat by express. I send $20.00 which leaves me $6.00 which if we are paid off in April ought to last me. If not, I will do the next best, as I thought it had better be at home. As the most of the boys kept more Charlie sends $24.00 (he had some on hand). You may not get this until after you get the money, but I write to let you know how much I and Charlie send. We are all right! I am on guard and must hurry back to the guard tent, as I got leave for supper. The troops are all getting paid off here. Write as soon as you get the money and let me know.
>
> It is getting dark and I must close.
>
> Yours as ever,
Francis A. Ireland[15]

10. More Sickness, Surviving the Cure, Longing for Home

On February 13, Francis wrote to tell his folks about the latest action near their encampment, and to give his opinion about General Banks' campaign. He goes on to give his thoughts about General Banks, as well as General Grover, their division commander, and a bit more about Colonel Wilson, still their temporary brigade commander.

> Dear Father;
>
> As I have not much to employ my time this morning, I thought I might as well commence a letter to you, altho I have not much to write about. There has been some considerable firing of artillery, some 20 miles down river for a day or two, and it is said that Paine's Brigade that went down there has had a fight at a place called Indian Village and I guess it is so. We have not moved yet but may before long and may not, just as the luck turns! It is said of Banks' Expedition that it is a failure but as to this the future will disclose. Perhaps the public expected more of him than those in authority. If it was sent here to prevent or as a safeguard against foreign intervention why then his purpose is accomplished in part for we are here ready to resist any such attempts. But I think that he was sent here to help clear the Mississippi but after that repulse at Fredericksburg he was stinted as to the number of his troops, they at Washington thinking they might do more good on the Potomac. At any rate we are here lying idle as far as fighting is concerned. But the future will tell how long we shall be in this position. But the number of troops that are in Banks' dept. ought to be doing something. But then *I* don't care, for our 9 months is going on in spite of fate. It won't wait for slow Generals. But to do justice to Gen. B. I think if he was just here to work then he will do it if it is a possible thing, for you know him to be as active an officer (where he has a chance) as the government has got. Brig. Gen. Grover, acting maj. gen. of this division, is a very smart appearing officer, is about 35 years of age I should think, and he issues good, strict, and wholesome orders for the regulation of his troops, is often to be seen riding thro the camps observing everything, as he is ever on the watch. Polite as an officer should be never failing to return the touch of the cap from the lowest private to the col. At any rate he always returned my salute, if his horse was on the gallop, and I have passed him hosts of times. It is just the way a officer is obliged to do. The Army rules are, that an inferior officer or private must salute the superior officer whenever he meets him and he must return or recognize it or the private can report him if he chooses. Gen. Grover is a native of Bethel Maine I believe.[16]

Their division commander, Brigadier General Cuvier Grover, of whom Francis approves so heartily, was indeed a Maine man, born in the small town of Bethel in 1829, and an 1850 graduate of West Point.[17]

> As to Col. Wilson I have written before. He is a smart officer and talks the officers right up to the mark! Tells them if they keep on the lookout and do their duty, the men will do theirs. His doctrine is that the privates are more perfect thro the army than the officers anyhow. I never heard him scold or

swear at privates for not doing as they should on drill, but if they were not up in time to the orders. How he will (d — m) [Francis wrote the word "swear" above that line] at the officer commanding them. He has his failings as well as the rest of the World, but they consist in his profanity and his propensity to take a drop. It is getting to be near drill time and I must close for the present. We got a mail yesterday. I got 4 papers but no letters. They were delayed on the route somewhere I suppose.

F.A.I.[18]

On February 25, John Ireland began a letter to his son with lots of news from Dexter.

Dear Son;

Yours of Feb. 7th and 8th came to hand last Monday evening and we were very glad to learn by it that you had got over your sick spell and was again at your post of duty.

Eben is at spelling school this evening up to uncle Farrar's district and Olin has gone to the office. Flora is asleep, and your Mother is about her work, so thought it best to begin another letter.[19]

After telling of lectures on spiritualism at the Universalist Church, John Ireland gives some news from the woolen mill and then goes on to tell who has died around town. As he continues his letter 3 days later, we hear of another family member in the Union Army, Francis' uncle, Eben Day, who had been captured by the Confederates.[20]

Saturday evening, 28th

We received a letter today from Aunt Lydia giving us the particulars in regard to Uncle Eben. She had a letter from him dated Jan. 24th. He was in a hospital at Murfiesboro [Murfreesboro], Tenn. On the night of the first day of the battle of Stone River, that terrible battle of several days continuance, by Rosecran's army, while out skirmishing, and lying on the ground he was wounded in the instep and succeeded in getting off a short distance, and got his foot dressed, and then while being removed further, was taken prisoner by the rebels and conveyed to their hospital where he remained for a few weeks and was then paroled and sent to Murfreesboro. He expects to be sent to Columbus, or to be exchanged. He says that he fared well while with the rebels.[21]

The Battle of Stones River (Murfreesboro) was fought between the Union General William Rosecrans's Army of the Cumberland, and Confederate General Braxton Bragg's newly reorganized Army of the Tennessee. The battle was fought over a 3 day period from December 31 into January 2, and ended inconclusively, but with the Union repulse of Confederate attacks and the eventual withdrawal of the Confederate forces, it gave a boost to Union morale. The cost, however, was appalling, with the highest percentage of casualties on both sides of any major battle of the Civil War.[22]

We then learn of the death of one of Dexter's soldiers.

> William Hasseltine [Haseltine] died in Boston last Thursday. His wife and Joseph were with him. His body arrived here today and funeral services are to be held at the Baptist Church tomorrow afternoon.
>
> This is a sad case indeed, and his loss will be felt very much, not only by his family, but in the neighborhood and town. You very well know that he was a very worthy man. I understand he possessed an excellent state of mind in view of the prospect before him.[23]

William Haseltine enlisted in December of 1861 at age 36 and became a corporal in Company C, 13th Maine Infantry. Hospitalized in late 1862 and discharged for disability in January of 1863, he died on his way home, leaving his wife and 4 young children, a sad case indeed.[24]

Continuing his letter the next day, John Ireland reports yet more deaths in town, this time two children who died of diphtheria. And he then goes on to write of William Haseltine's funeral and closes telling Francis that Charlie's parents and younger brother are visiting.

> Afternoon: We have just returned from funeral. The house was full — no other meeting in the place. There was never a more solemn funeral in Dexter, nor one where the sympathies of the people were more generally called forth. Mr. Ringman preached — Mr. Knowles and Lovejoy were in the desk and assisted in the services.
>
> The text was in the 90th Psalm, the words were "So teach us to number our days, that we may apply our hearts unto wisdom."
>
> Uncle Farrar and Aunt Lizzie and Andrew are here to supper with us — I will now close. Give our love to Charlie.
>
> From your Father,
J.P. Ireland[25]

The letters in which Francis writes of illness and deaths within the regiment, and this letter, telling of a soldier's funeral at home, are of particular interest, since the official reports of the regiment only give special attention to the deaths of officers, and even those reports were often quite impersonal. Colonel Jerrard, in his notes for his brief history of the regiment, wrote: "On the 20th of February Lieut. Wm. Prince Hersey of Co. E died of [illegible] chills and his remains are forwarded by the offs. [officers] of the reg't to his friends in Lincoln. He was a nephew of Genl. Hersey of Bangor and a young officer of much promise." In the adjutant general's report, it is written as: "Among the deaths I have to record that

Grave of William Haseltine at the Elm Cemetery, Dexter, Maine. His stone includes: "Died in Boston on his way home" and "I have fought the good fight" (author photograph).

10. More Sickness, Surviving the Cure, Longing for Home

of 1st Lieutenant W. Prince Hersey of Com. E, a young officer of much promise."[26]

To return to Baton Rouge, with the regiment having camped there for almost 3 months, Francis wrote home on March 9 from "Camp New York" and tells his parents that the regiment is finally expecting to move. Starting with a rather matter of fact statement of their preparations to march, the letter ends with thoughts of death and danger.

Dear Father,

I seat myself to just drop a line to let you know that we have been getting ready to march for the past 24 hours and shall probably leave some time tonight or early in the morning. We have not the slightest idea as to where we are going, but it is evident that it is quite a distance and to a place where we shall meet sharp resistance as nearly all the force in Baton Rouge is going which is pretty large, as over 20 regt's arrived here Sat. and Sunday and they are all with the same orders. We are to go in light marching order, only overcoats and blankets to be carried. The rest is packed in boxes. Three minutes after I put my last in the office I heard of the death of Charlie Whittemore. He was buried Sat. and we lost another Sunday. It was Mr. Carpenter that used to tent with us. We shall not carry any tents. I do not fear or dread the coming battle, altho I dread the march some what. I hope and trust that I shall do my share of the deadly work and escape unhurt. If I fall so let it be, as thousands have already. Charlie [Farrar] has just come in and says he won't write tonight. Tell his folks he is well and in good spirits, the same as the rest of us. But I must close. Will write again the first chance I get.

Good bye.
From your son,
Francis A. Ireland[27]

Reporting the death of Charlie Whittemore, Francis apparently did not know that Charlie's brother Jacob, whom Francis reported as sick in the hospital back in early February, had died February 27. When he enlisted, Charlie was 18 and single, while Jacob was 22 and had married Ellen Scott just before joining the army. Ellen lived until 1915 and never remarried. A third Whittemore brother, Franklin, had enlisted as a private in the 17th Maine, fought with them at Fredericksburg, Chancellorsville, Gettysburg and elsewhere, was promoted to corporal and then to first sergeant, and was killed at the Wilderness in May of 1864.[28]

Another letter asking when the 22nd Maine's men might be heading home was sent to Maine's governor, Abner Coburn, at about this time.

Dear Sir,

Many of the friends of volunteer soldiers of [the] 22nd Reg't of Maine are inquiring when the nine months of their service expires who were called into camp on the tenth of Sept. 1862, but who were not mustered into the service in a formal manner until a month after. The government reckoned their pay from the time of enlistment viz. 10th Sept. My only son is capt. of one of the companies in said regt. As much sickness attends them at this time where they are on the Mississippi, we all [are in] a great degree of anxiety to know how long a term they will be held under the provisions of enlistment. My neighbors have requested me to make this inquiry of the executive and if you will have the goodness to inform us we shall deem it a favor.

Very respectfully,
Isaac Case[29]

Captain Isaac W. Case (Isaac W. Case Library, Kenduskeag, Maine).

As with other letters regarding various soldiers whose fate is now known to us, this letter has a special meaning. The writer was a physician from the small town of Kenduskeag, Maine, and Dr. Case's comments about sickness were, of course, accurate. And in a tragic turn of fate, his only son, Isaac W. Case, the captain of Company H whose letters have been quoted earlier, having survived the regiment's battles, died of sickness—"congestive fever"—later that summer on July 2.[30]

11

The First Advance Toward Port Hudson

The 22nd Maine and Grover's Division, as a part of a larger force, left Baton Rouge on March 13 under the command of General Banks. In his adjutant general's report, Colonel Jerrard states that this was done "for the purpose of making a reconnaissance in the rear of Port Hudson." However, in his rough draft for that report, the Colonel wrote that this advance toward Port Hudson was made to distract Confederate attention from Admiral Farragut's attempt to move his fleet up the Mississippi past Port Hudson's guns. This was, in fact, the object of the exercise, although the specifics of the precise intention and the level of success varied somewhat in different reports. On March 15, General Banks reported that his troops were nearing Port Hudson. "I was anxious to get our artillery before nightfall in a favorable position to keep up a fire during the night, with a view of drawing off a portion of the enemy's attention from the fleet," He wrote in his report of March 21, General Banks recorded that the movement of his troops toward Port Hudson "was to make a diversion during the passage of the fleet." In General Banks' much later report of April 6, 1865, he stated, "The army was called upon to make a demonstration against the fortifications at Port Hudson, while the fleet should run the batteries upon the river." In further reports, we shall see General Banks' and Admiral Farragut's assessments of the operation.[1]

The Confederate artillery guarding the river at Port Hudson included cannon firing 24, 32, and 42 pound projectiles, and some river batteries also held 8 inch and 10 inch Columbiads, the latter able to fire a 128 pound shell. This firepower, the high bluffs on which the artillery was placed, and the sharp bend in the river just at the north end of the Confederate defenses would make the fleet's passage a very hazardous maneuver, and a diversion by the infantry might indeed be helpful. In spite of this plan, the 22nd Maine and most of the land force would have to wait for another time to be tested in battle.²

The original timetable called for the fleet to pass Port Hudson in the early morning of March 15, by which time General Banks would have infantry and artillery in position to engage the Confederate defenders from land. On the 14th, General Banks informed Admiral Farragut that his men would be ready to support the fleet that evening. Banks' assurance that he would soon be in position apparently influenced the admiral to start moving his ships upriver earlier than planned in order to take advantage of darkness to lessen the effects of the Port Hudson guns. But, slowed by Confederate cavalry and infantry skirmishers, only a few Union troops

Confederate battery overlooking the Mississippi at Port Hudson (*Review of Reviews*).

were near Port Hudson when General Banks learned that Admiral Farragut was moving upriver from Baton Rouge that evening instead of waiting until the next morning. This change in the timing of the fleet's movement left the Union troops too far distant to be directly involved. In addition, with this earlier advance of the fleet, the Union captains soon learned that the nighttime darkness presented them with serious problems. There was, for example, difficulty in picking out landmarks for navigation and some ships ran aground, while in the confusion some Union vessels narrowly escaped being fired on by their comrades, and many did suffer considerable damage from the Rebel batteries. Of the 7 main ships with which Admiral Farragut attempted to pass Port Hudson, only the first 2 in line, the USS *Albatross*, and his flagship the USS *Hartford*, were successful in moving up past the Confederate position.[3]

Although the land force's involvement was almost nonexistent, General Banks' report of the action, written much later in April of 1865, congratulated the infantry and stated that their objective was "completely accomplished." Although his forces were not in position to attack Port Hudson on the evening or night of March 14, General Banks also stated, "The army reached the rear of the works [of Port Hudson] on the night of the 14th, and made a demonstration as for an attack on the works the next morning." One must suppose that the general's definition of "a demonstration as for an attack" might mean that he had troops near the

USS *Hartford* (U.S. Navy photograph).

enemy who would have attacked had they been called upon to do so. A signal corps officer who witnessed the fleet's attempt to pass Port Hudson, and who communicated with both Admiral Farragut and General Banks, stated that "the [signal] corps and cavalry were the only branches of the army that did anything, as not a gun was fired during the trip." Again reading from General Banks' report of April 1865, he stated that Admiral Farragut achieved his goal and that "naval history scarcely presents a more brilliant act than the passage of these formidable batteries." However, in a report to General Banks shortly after the attempt, Admiral Farragut states, "The failure of my vessels to get by Port Hudson was a sad blow to me." Later in that report, he writes, "My feelings have been most severely exercised in consequence of the disaster at Port Hudson."[4]

With the attempt to bring the fleet past Port Hudson over, on March 16 Union forces had withdrawn from the area of Port Hudson back toward Baton Rouge, the 22nd Maine stopping at Monte Sano Bayou.[5]

An interesting perspective on these events can be read in the reports of General Franklin Gardner, Port Hudson's Confederate commander, writing to his superior, Lieutenant General John Pemberton, and to Major General Richard Taylor, commanding the District of Western Louisiana,

Admiral Farragut (at wheel) on the deck of the USS *Hartford* (U.S. Navy photograph).

11. The First Advance Toward Port Hudson

and General Albert Rust, whose cavalry, infantry, and light artillery brigade was operating outside Port Hudson.

March 12 to Pemberton: "The enemy appears to be advancing slowly on three roads"

March 12 to Rust: "Place your regiment of infantry and one light battery ... on picket" at a place where their advance "can easily be resisted."

March 14 to Pemberton: "The bombardment commenced at 2 P.M. Firing very slow. fleet not in range of my guns. The land forces are advancing."

March 14 to Taylor: "The steamboats have arrived with corn just in time. I shall get them all off tonight. The enemy are now bombarding this place and their land forces have advanced. Their whole fleet of eleven vessels is in sight, but nothing decided is yet shown in their operations. I shall need 17,000 bushels of corn per month for the commissary and 20,000 bushels for quartermaster; also about 1,200,000 pounds of fodder. It is impossible to obtain these supplies elsewhere than from Red River."

March 15 to Pemberton: "We have burned one gunboat in front of Port Hudson. The others have gone back."

March 15, 2 A.M. to Pemberton: "One gunboat passed at 12 P.M. She returned our fire boldly. Don't know if we hit her. Steamboats have started."

March 15 to Pemberton: "Gunboat fight lasted heavily from 11 to 2. All came up within range. *Hartford* and *Monongahela* passed crippled. *Mississippi* burned. *Richmond* disabled and sent back. Our losses very small. Forces by land advanced, but all is quiet this morning." The Union ships that passed upriver from Port Hudson were in fact the *Hartford* and *Albatross*.

March 16 to Pemberton: "The Essex fought at long range. The Hartford passed with the *Monongahela* [*Albatross*] lashed on the far side. The former much damaged, but gone up river. I have ten days' subsistence."

March 16: "The *Essex* did not pass. They say she won't fight. The vessels (*Hartford* and what he took to be the *Monongahela*) are still above. All quiet."

In another dispatch, Gardner had told of a rumor that the lieutenant of the *Essex* had been arrested for treason. There is no record of that happening, and according to the plans for the passage of the fleet, the *Essex* was intended to provide bombardment from down river.[6] His report continues.

March 16 to Pemberton: "It is not safe to send a boat down. The *Hartford* and *Monongahela* [*Albatross*] are up the river. Last reports the land forces had withdrawn. Fleet still in sight just below."

In a more detailed report of March 16, General Gardner gives his losses at Port Hudson as 1 killed and 8 wounded. He also reports that he had "four steamboats unloading until the moment of the fight, and I sent them up the river. They have all escaped, as the *Hartford* was too badly damaged to pursue. I request that you send them back with corn as soon as the enemy passes beyond the Red River, which I suppose will be the case in a day or two."[7]

And indeed, on March 20, four Confederate steamships "were seen to arrive at Port Hudson, said to be from Red River." It appears that Admiral Farragut had taken his two ships that had passed Port Hudson up to Vicksburg, once again leaving the Red River open as a conduit for Confederate supplies. This is difficult to understand in the light of orders and reports which gave as a major reason from bringing the fleet up past Port Hudson "cutting off [Confederate] supplies by the Red River." Reports written by Admiral Farragut, however, indicated the need for him to resupply his ships and his concern that the number of ships he had available to block the Red River would not be sufficient. Having gotten additional ships from Admiral Porter, in command of the Union's Mississippi River Squadron at Vicksburg, Farragut did return to blockade the Red River.[8]

We get a good look at the events of those last few days from the perspective of the 22nd Maine in Francis Ireland's letter of March 19, written "7 miles above Baton Rouge."

Dear Father,

As I have a chance to send a letter to the city this morning I will write a line to let you know where we have been for the past few days. We (Grover's Division) left Baton Rouge Friday P.M. and marched up a mile above here arriving at about 10 o'clock and bivouacked for the night; marched about 8 miles farther next morning (Sat.) Within 5 or 6 miles of Port Hudson. ... As to the attack Sat. night on Port Hudson and the gun boats "running" up by etc., you will probably know as much as I, by the papers. I will mention a few items. About 11 o'clock at night the whole camp was awakened by the report of a big gun, followed by a host of others in the direction of Port Hudson, about 5 miles distant; we could see the shells when they went up in the air and then go up a mile or 2 and then come down on P.H. as we supposed. Soon there was a big light in that direction which soon began to move down river with frequent explosions. When it had got down within 3 miles of Baton Rouge there was a flash that lit up the country for miles. As I was lying on my back in my shelter tent I saw it and soon there rolled up a lurid or red smoke which

11. The First Advance Toward Port Hudson

The caption of this illustration reads: "Bombardment of Port Hudson by Admiral Farragut's Fleet, March 14–15." Given the outcome of the night's action, it might be more appropriately stated the other way around (*Harper's Weekly*, April 18, 1863).

made it lighter still. In about half a minute we got the report which fairly shooked [shook] the ground. It proved to be the gunboat "Mississippi" which had got aground near P. Hudson and they abandoned her and set her on fire to keep her from the rebels. It is said that the pilot ran her aground so that the rebs. might get her and that as soon as he did it the capt. of the boat shot him on the spot. Whether it is so or not, I don't know.[9]

The official record of the end of the USS *Mississippi* does not include a tale of it being run aground on purpose by a traitorous pilot or of its pilot being shot. The ship was a steam and sail powered frigate which had been Admiral Perry's flagship on his historic expedition to Japan in 1853. As Admiral Farragut's fleet was attempting to pass the Rebel fortifications at Port Hudson, and the 22nd Maine was camped some miles from that fortress, the *Mississippi* ran aground on a sand bar, apparently due to the terrible visibility resulting from the dark of night and the smoke of artillery fire. Its captain, Melancton Smith, after tying in vain to refloat his ship, and under devastating enemy fire, ordered it abandoned and set on fire. The ship then slid off the sand bar and drifted some miles down river, blowing up when the 24 tons of gunpowder in the magazine exploded. The vessel's executive officer was George Dewey, later to be known for his Spanish American War exploits in Manila Bay.[10]

Francis' letter of March 19 also speaks of the regiment's withdrawal from the area of Port Hudson.

> Sunday we came back about 9 miles, got wet all thro by marching thro an awful shower and stood or sat as best we could in the water and mud up to our ankles in a great field. But we did not get cold for we kept a good fire of Rebel fence. Monday after noon our brigade started up the road again to the place where we went first as there was a force of 600 Rebs there. We got there about 4 o'clock and about 50 or 60 empty [wagons] with a regiment went down and got about 200 bales of cotton and a lot of forage (corn). They bought the cotton I believe, that is the officers bought it for government. We had been turned in about an hour when we were turned out with orders to march and we marched back here arriving at 1 o'clock at night. We may stop here a little while, but we expect now that we have got into the field to be going here and there all the time.
>
> I must be closing. Charlie has not got time to write and says he is well, which is so with both of us. We stand marching first rate. ... Now we get any amount of fresh pork, beef, live chickens, etc. by just going in the fields and

USS *Mississippi* (G.H. Suydam Photograph Album, Mss. 1394, Louisiana and Lower Mississippi Valley Collections, Louisiana State University Libraries, Baton Rouge).

getting them. It is rebel property you know. But this must suffice till I get another chance.

Yours,
Francis A. Ireland

I suppose you will hear of Sam Silver's death before you get this.[11]

Samuel Silver, another 19 year old who had enlisted from Dexter, died in the hospital on March 10.[12]

When references are made to paying for such things as cotton or corn, the assumption is that the Union officers are paying "loyal" Southerners — those who had sworn an oath of allegiance to the U.S. The Confiscation Act of 1861 not only allowed, but ordered, Union troops to simply confiscate any goods that might otherwise be used for the benefit of the Confederacy or of Confederate troops. This Confiscation Act of 1861 was the congressional bill that followed General Butler's lead in declaring slaves, who were liable to be forced to work for the aid of the Confederacy, to be subject to confiscation. The 1861 act was strengthened in 1862, so that it was no longer necessary to show that the property of Rebels was intended to be used to support the Confederacy. Any property of any officer of the Confederate Army, or any member of the Confederate government, or of the government of the states of the Confederacy, and others acting in a high capacity, could simply be seized.[13]

Richard Irwin, General Banks' assistant adjutant general, also issued General Order 27, which makes it clear that "well-disposed persons" (i.e., loyal to the Union) would be paid for goods taken. And, while forbidding pillage, the order also makes it clear that losses incurred by Confederate sympathizers was their own problem. The order stated:

> Pillage and depredations upon private property are forbidden and must be suppressed. Whatever property is necessary to the support of the army will be taken by the government, and liberal compensation will be made therefore, according to its value, in the country where it is taken, to all well-disposed persons. The loss of property applied to the use of the rebels or destroyed by fire will fall upon the owners and the people. If they ask reparation for their losses, the preservation of their property, or a return to peace, prosperity, and power, let them restore the government of the United States. By command of Major-General Banks.[14]

In addition, both General Butler and General Banks, when Banks took over the Department of the Gulf, had issued strict orders against the theft or plunder of private property by Union soldiers. It was made clear in General Order 29 that "pillage and plunder is an offense made punishable by death by the Articles of War." At least one soldier in the 1st Brigade, a private in the 131st New York, was indeed executed for "quitting his colors to plunder and pillage."[15]

Leaving Monte Sano Bayou on March 20, the 22nd Maine and its brigade "returned to the vicinity of Port Hudson, as a guard to a wagon train engaged in collecting cotton," no doubt the wagons that Francis had mentioned. Colonel Jerrard reported that during these movements the regiment had "its first experience in active service in the field ... although not under fire." And he wrote that "the conduct and general deportment of officers and soldiers gave me great satisfaction." Also, the colonel is pleased to state that there was no straggling or plundering by his men, and none threw away heavier pieces of equipment during their march.[16]

On March 28, John Ireland wrote his son another nice newsy letter.

My Dear Son,

Yours of the 5th inst. and also one of the 9th inst. came to hand Wednesday and Thursday evenings of this week. Charlie's came one night before yours, giving us the same information in regard to moving as yours. We are glad to hear of your good health and spirits with so much sickness. We cannot say that we feel any worse to hear of your advance towards Port Hudson even with the prospect of a battle, than we have while you have remained at Baton Rouge, exposed as you have been to the diseases of the camp. We hear this, this week of Com. Farrigets [Farragut's] success in passing the batteries at Port Hudson, and we are looking every day for an account of Banks' attack by land. O, how anxious we feel for the success of the enterprise; that our cause may triumph, and our men be spared.[17]

It is, of course, worth noting that John Ireland had been reading of Admiral Farragut's "success" in passing Port Hudson. Apparently General Banks' upbeat assessment of the fleet's attempt was the version passed on to the press. Ireland then goes on to tell of local opposition to the war.

The copperheads had a meeting in the town hall to-day; Speakers from Bangor and other places were on the stand and addressed the people. I did not attend. Their meetings are becoming quite frequent; the whole thing is opposition to the government and the war; especially the "conscript act." If this war does not close without more men, I receive some consolation from the thought that some of these seccesh will have to face the music; and one thing is certain, if they offer any resistance to the draft, as some already threaten, they will find themselves prisoners mighty sudden; that's so.[18]

This was not the last Copperhead meeting in Dexter. Another resident, writing a few months later, mentioned that the area's Copperheads were having a large picnic gathering, complete with brass bands. While

11. The First Advance Toward Port Hudson 117

there were certainly some with strong political feelings, the writer indicates that she and her husband were not Copperheads, but attended anyway and the food was good. At the same time, the Republicans of the town had their own meeting, with their own brass band, at the town hall, but there is no mention of food at that event.[19]

Continuing his letter on Sunday morning, the 29th, Ireland tells that two of the town's young soldiers have arrived home and gives his son some advice for the time when he is discharged.

> John Smith and Alonzo Merrill arrived home last week. The former on a discharge and the latter on a furlough of 13 days. A system of furlough has been established in Hooker's department which gives the boys a chance to visit home by turns. [General Joseph Hooker had, at this point, taken over command of the Army of the Potomac.] One thing I want to mention for your benefit and that is when your time is out and you have an opportunity to change rations, you must be very careful in changing your diet; don't dip into other things hastily, for there will be danger of being made sick thereby.

Gravestone of Jacob Whittemore at the Elm Cemetery, Dexter, Maine (author photograph).

For local news John Ireland lets Francis know that his little sister Flora has got a new puppy "a little larger than a good sized rat!" and, "There are 7 ladies baptized by Elder Knowles at noon at the upper dam all by immersion."

Baptism by full immersion in late March in Maine must have tested one's faith and fortitude since the ice goes out of many of Maine's lakes and rivers at about that time of year or a little later. Continuing, the elder Ireland reports a much more sober event.

> We have just returned from the Baptist meeting where the funeral sermon of Jacob and Charlie Whittemore were preached. In a letter that Jacob wrote to his wife some time this winter, he enclosed some verses he had picked up, each verse of which commenced "No night shall be in heaven," and by request of his widow they were sung at the close of the service. The text was "And there shall be no night there."[20]

John Ireland then closes after relating some news from the mill and reporting his own current good health.

12

The Men of the 22nd "See the Animal"

On March 26 the 22nd Maine, with the rest of their division, traveled by steamships to Donaldsonville. From there, they marched to a camp site at Bayou Boeuf, near Brashear City. This movement, and the concentration of other Union forces in the same area, was the beginning of a series of actions by General Banks' 19th Corps that was intended "to get possession of Western Louisiana, then held by a considerable rebel force." This enemy force, Colonel Jerrard wrote, was situated "principally at Fort Bisland on the Bayou Tesch [Teche] and twenty miles from Brashian [Brashear City]" With Colonel Jerrard ill with the measles, Lieutenant Colonel Putnam was in command of the 22nd Maine from March 23 to April 18.[1]

In his letter home written April 4 "In Camp at or near Bayou Bef [Bayou Boeuf], La.," Francis gives us his story of the regiment's latest activities.

> Dear Father;
>
> Here I am 50 miles or more from the place that I wrote my last letter, smart and in good health, but a little tired after all, altho there are many tough men that are foot-sore, lame, and beat out after our march. We left Donaldsonville last Tuesday morning on our march down the road that ran over 30 miles by the side of the canal or as it is called out here Bayou Lafoursche [Lafourche] It is no more or less than a branch of the Mississippi made by building levies on both sides, the surface of the water being higher than the level of the country the year round. We passed through a very pretty country and saw many splendid Plantations on both sides of the bayou. Among the rest was the home and place of Gen. Bragg of the Rebel Army but formerly of the U.S. and is in command at the well known Fort Pickens I believe. We made our march 33 miles in 3 days not marching any after 2 o'clock PM. On the third day we left the Bayou road at the city of Thibodaux [Thibodeaux] and went 3 miles to a railroad station. We remained there till yesterday morning. Our regiment and the

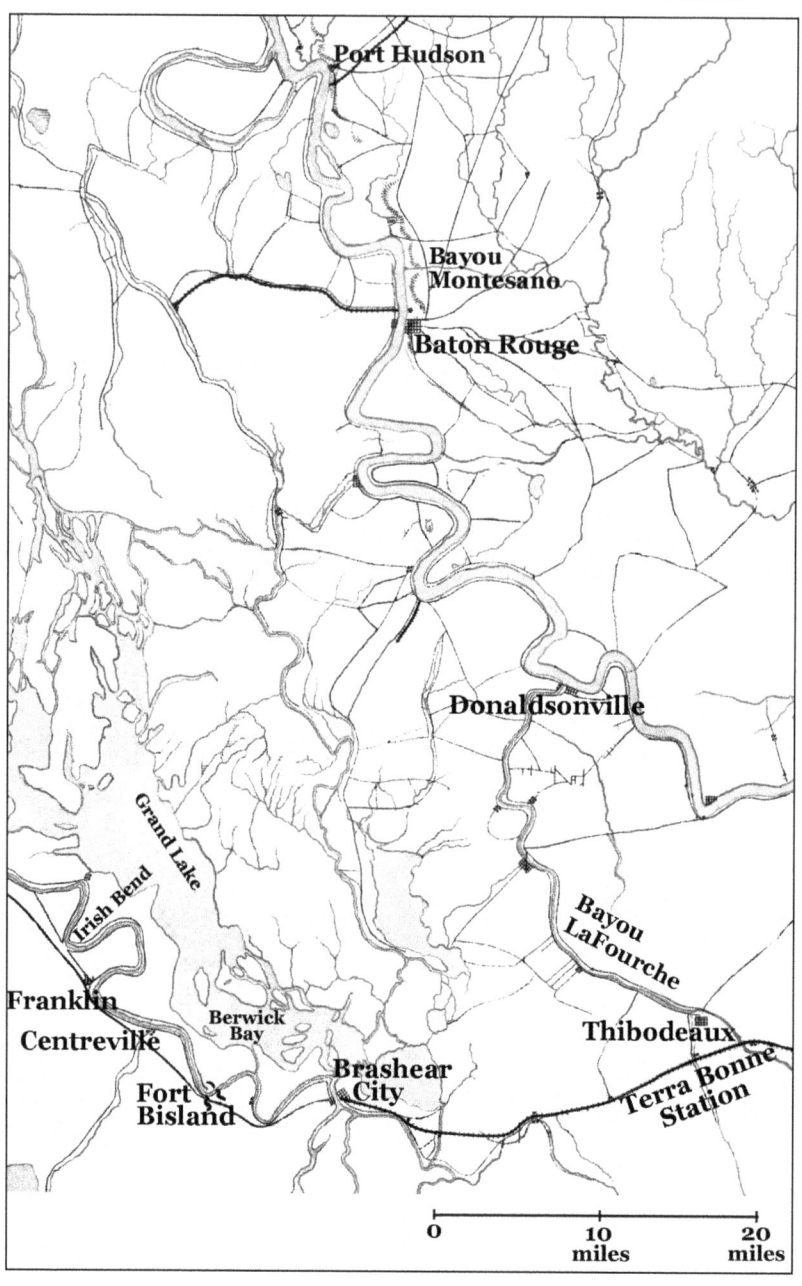

Map adapted from Plate 156, *The Official Military Atlas of the Civil War.*

12. The Men of the 22nd "See the Animal"

91st N.Y. went on board of the cars and came to this place, about 20 miles and 45 from New Orleans by rail. Gen. Weitzel [Brigadier General Godfrey Weitzel] had retreated from Berwicks Bay to this place (8 miles) but went back the night before we arrived here. We shall probably join him in a few days.[2]

While the usual definition of a "bayou" is simply a slow-moving stream that is a tributary of a larger stream or river, Francis is correct in his assessment that, in many places, the course of a bayou is sometimes channeled and enhanced by human activities such as the building of levees.

General Weitzel's division had been in Brashear City, but when he learned that the Confederate gunboats *Queen of the West* and *Webb* were near, he felt that his force was too exposed to possible Confederate attack and withdrew "to the railway bridge over Bayou Boeuf, and took up a position where he was not exposed, as at Brashear, to the risk of being cut off by any sudden movement of the enemy."[3]

Braxton Bragg had been a captain in the U.S. Army and had fought in the Mexican War. He resigned his commission in 1856 and operated his sugar plantation in Thibodeaux, Louisiana, and was given the rank of colonel in the state's militia. At the outset of the Civil War, Bragg was promoted to major general of militia and then transferred to the Confederate Army as a brigadier general and did, for a time, command troops around Pensacola, Florida, including Fort Pickens. He was promoted to major general in September of 1861, and to full general in April of 1862. At the time of Frank Ireland's letter in April of 1863, General Bragg was in command of the Confederate Army of Tennessee.[4]

Francis' April 4 letter continues,

> I wish I had a good small map of this section of the country but we shall not want any a great while longer, as we can or expect to have a chance to purchase [one] in Maine sometime this summer. There are a great many 9 months men to go home before long but they cannot all go at once. I should like to be at home to see the conscripts leave for the war. There was a private in the 91st N.Y. reg't (that is in our brigade) sentenced to be shot this morning at sunrise for disobedience of orders and attempting and threatening the life of an officer of Gen. Dwight's staff, but the order was stayed for the present by Gen. Grover last night. I can write no more now, must go out and see if I can get ripe blackberries enough to make me some sauce for dinner. They will be ripe soon as they are turning red now.

With a good dose of "Downeast" humor, Francis also tells his father in this letter of seeing alligators, and says they are "larger than you find in Maine, I reckon."[5]

In his next letter, later in April, Francis would find no call for humor, for the 22nd Maine was soon to see action against Confederate troops. In the second week of April, General Banks ordered an attack against Confederate forces around Franklin, Louisiana, and in particular against Fort Bisland, southeast of that town and between the towns of Pattersonville and Centerville. Banks' main force was to attack the Confederate troops at Fort Bisland, while Grover's division, which included the 22nd Maine, was to be transported to the west, up Grand Lake. Grover's force would then attack the rear of the Confederate fortifications from the northwest, or trap Confederates retreating in that direction should the attack by the main force of the 19th Corps drive the enemy from Fort Bisland.

The fortifications at Fort Bisland (called Camp Bisland by some) consisted of a line of trenches and breastworks on the banks of the Bayou Teche, with one redoubt, which served as the command center and observation post. Some of these trenches at Bisland — in particular those on the east bank of the Teche, had only been constructed during the two days before the Union attack. The Confederate troops at Bisland were under the command of Major General Richard Taylor (son of U.S. president Zachary Taylor and brother-in-law of the Confederate president, Jefferson Davis), who had been put in overall command of the District of Western Louisiana the previous summer. His force at Bisland had been estimated at around 4,000 troops. The total of Union troops attacking Bisland and Irish Bend was likely to have been at least 4 times that number, with Grover's division alone very probably outnumbering the total Confederate force.[6]

And so, after a few days' rest at Bayou Boeuf, Grover's division, which included the 22nd Maine, marched to Brashear City on April 11 and boarded transport craft — the 22nd being one of the regiments on board the *Clifton*. On the morning April 12, after being delayed by a heavy fog, the division started at around 8 A.M. up the Atchafalaya River and Grand Lake. "Only seven companies of the 22nd regt. accompanied this movement, companies B, G and H, under Major Brackett, were left at Brashear for want of transportation." Due to Colonel Jerrard's continuing illness, the 7 companies of the 22nd that were with Grover's division at this time were led by Lieutenant Colonel Putnam. As Grover's division was making this move, the other divisions of General Banks' 19th Corps were advancing toward Fort Bisland from the east.[7]

General Grover's forces first anchored near Cypress Point on the evening of April 12, but a reconnaissance party determined the road there to be impassable. The transports moved up the shore of Grand Lake, around

12. The Men of the 22nd "See the Animal"

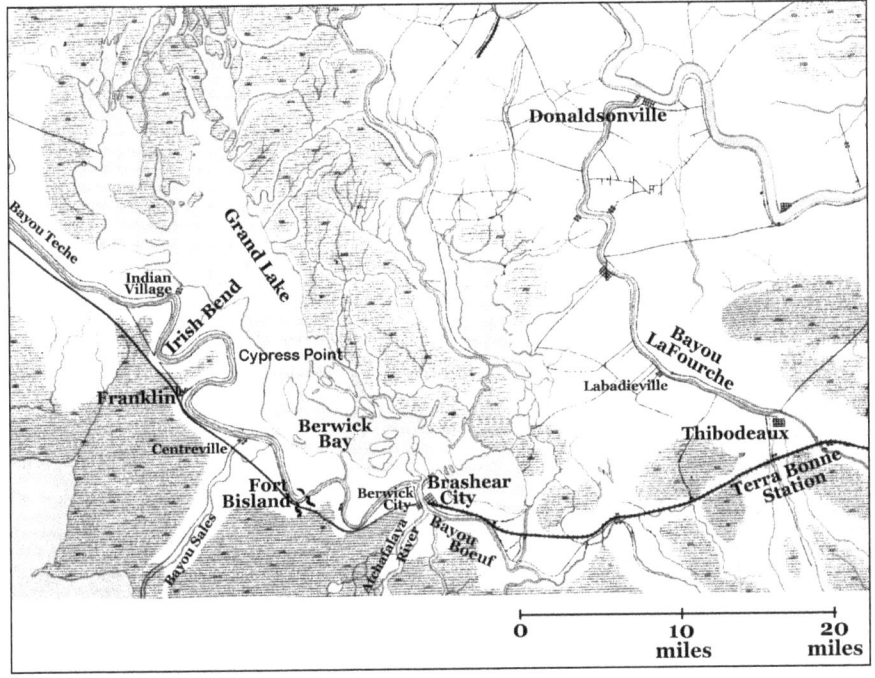

Map adapted from Plate 156, The *Official Military Atlas of the Civil War.*

Miller's Point, and found a suitable landing place just west of that point near Irish Bend of the Bayou Teche. The 1st Brigade of Grover's division, which included the 22nd Maine, was the first to land at this location, about 2½ miles north of Franklin, on the morning of April 13. This advance party met with what was later described as "light opposition," but was, at the time, faced with a body of Confederate troops of unknown size in a wooded area to their front. The 1st Brigade was ordered to clear the force of Confederates from the woods near the landing site — this force was later estimated by General Grover to consist of 300 or 400 Rebel infantry supported by one piece of artillery. The enemy gradually withdrew, and Grover's entire force was landed, but with delays caused by having few small craft with shallow draught to carry soldiers from the larger ships, as well as the horses and artillery pieces, the 100 yards or so from the transports to the shore. As a result of these delays, and Grover's uncertainty regarding the nature of the Confederate forces in front of his division, it was well into the afternoon of the 13th before the entire division was landed and ready to move forward. Grover had sent out an advance party to secure the bridges over the Teche, and while one bridge was burned by the Confederates, at least one other was taken and held by the Union forces. At around 6 P.M. the division began crossing the Bayou Teche by this bridge, just south of their landing site, and went into camp for the night. It was, according to Francis Ireland's letter reporting these events, well into the late night before all of Grover's division was able to cross the Teche.[8]

There are conflicting reports of the nature of the Confederate opposition and the exact location of General Grover's landing place. Colonel Holcomb of the 1st Louisiana Infantry, who was among the first to land, reports 2 artillery pieces, and one report has General Grover's force landing at Indian Village (Charenton). The reports made shortly after the actual event indicate that the division landed slightly east of there and nearer to Miller's Point. This is also the location which is indicated on the period maps available. Reports agree that the road just southeast of Miller's Point at the Porter plantation was not passable.[9]

Meanwhile, Confederate General Taylor, realizing how badly outnumbered his force at Bisland was, had already begun evacuating those fortifications on the night of the 13th, and he, himself, had then come to assess the danger posed by Grover's division north of Franklin at Irish Bend. The larger part of General Banks' force, waiting for Grover to get his division into position before making an all out assault on Bisland, had been advancing very slowly and had been slowed further by skirmishes and artillery exchanges with the Confederates on April 11 and 12. On the night of April 13, General Banks was unaware of the withdrawal of the Confederate troops that he supposed still waited for him at Fort Bisland.

The next morning, April 14, Grover's division moved toward Franklin, intending to proceed toward Fort Bisland, or to block the Confederate retreat through the road at Frankin. In the lead was the 3rd Brigade (25th Connecticut, 26th Maine, 159th New York, 13th Connecticut). This brigade was followed immediately by the 1st Brigade, which was made up of 22nd Maine with the 6th New York, 91st New York, 131st New York, and 1st Louisiana. As they advanced, the leading brigade was fired on by a substantial Rebel force positioned in Nerson's Woods, near the McKerall Plantation, about a mile or so north of Franklin. The Union troops were in a difficult position — the ground over which they were advancing was a muddy sugar cane field cut through with drainage ditches. To their left was the Bayou Teche, while to their right was a swamp. The Confederate troops, in their cover of woods, had considerable advantage. After exchanges of musket and artillery fire, the 3rd Brigade had advanced to within a hundred yards of the woods.[10]

The Confederate troops in Nerson's Woods consisted of Col. W.G. Vincent's 2nd Louisiana Cavalry Regiment, a battalion of Louisiana infantry under Major F.H. Clack, and the 4th Texas, commanded by Col. James Reily. They were supported by 4 artillery pieces. When this force was reinforced by Col. Henry Clay's 28th Louisiana Regiment, bringing their numbers to perhaps 1,000, General Taylor ordered this entire force — still greatly outnumbered — to charge the Union troops. This was done, and with supporting artillery fire from the Rebel gunboat *Diana*, at first seemed to be a success. The leading regiment of Grover's Third Brigade, the 159th New York, suffered the most from the Confederate attack and fell back. General Banks wrote that "in their retreat the New Yorkers swept over the position of the 26th Maine and the 25th Connecticut and carried these already shaken regiments with them, in some natural disorder." General Grover then ordered General Dwight "to deploy the first brigade [which included the 22nd Maine] and take up the broken battle." The 22nd Maine's Colonel Jerrard reported, "At this moment the 1st Brigade was ordered forward and the 22nd regiment took its position in line with the coolness of veterans. The rebels came dashing forward, firing and yelling ["like devils" Colonel Jerrard added in his rough draft of the report], and when but a few yards distant, halted and delivered a volley. Lieut. Col. Putnam, with commendable presence of mind, ordered his men to drop upon the ground, and the leaden shower passed with but a single casualty. The regiment immediately sprang up and the whole line advanced on the enemy who broke and left the field in disorder."[11]

It is assumed that General Taylor's order for the attack on what was actually a greatly superior Union force at Irish Bend had worked just as Taylor had hoped. It was not an attack intended to overwhelm the Union troops, but rather the intention apparently was to make enough of a demonstration of force to cause General Grover to pause or halt his advance. That attack by the Confederates did indeed cause Union General Grover to think he was confronted by a substantial force of the enemy, and after successfully repulsing the Confederate attack on his troops, Grover hesitated to advance and follow up this success, and halted his movement toward Franklin. As a result of this hesitation, he failed to prevent the Confederates from retreating along the direct road from Franklin northwest toward New Iberia, and was unaware until that afternoon that Taylor had in fact withdrawn his forces, not only from Fort Bisland, but

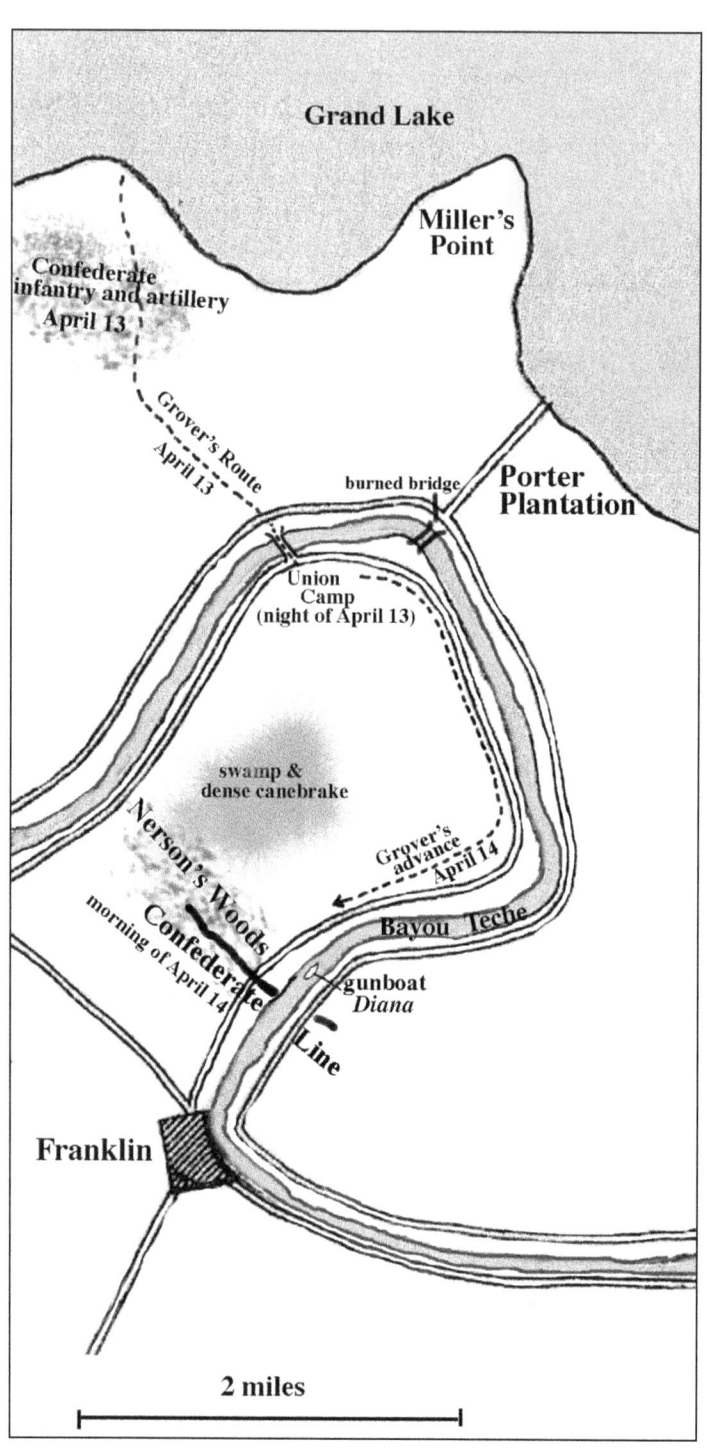

from the area in his (Grover's) front. In doing so, Taylor had avoided both the defeat in battle or the trap and capture that General Banks had envisioned.[12]

This battle, while amounting to little when compared with the larger and more frequently recalled battles fought by the Army of the Potomac, nonetheless made quite an impression on those young men who were under enemy fire for the first time. On April 17, Francis told his parents of this, his first battle — the Battle of Irish Bend on the 14th, which is sometimes included under the larger heading of the Battle of Franklin. It is moving to read, toward the end of the letter, Francis' feelings for the wounded and the dead Confederates.

Dear Father;

My last letter was dated at Brasher City [Brashear City], when we were expecting to march. Well, we went on board the gunboat Clifton the Sat. night after wards and in the morning started up the river (or bayou). I don't know which it is, for I have lost my reckoning as to the geography of this country). We had the 1st La., 5 Cos. of the N.Y. 6th and 7 Cos. of our reg't on board making 22 companies in all besides the force of the boat. We were on Gen. Grover's flag ship. He and staff and Gen. Dwight, ditto, on board. The most of Grover's division was (on the other steamers) with us, about 6 or 8 vessels in all. Our boat went ahead to clear the way if the Rebs attempted to fire into us on the route, but they did not. Monday we dropped anchor early in the morning and made preparations to land, the 1st La. going on shore first. We had to go on to small river boats to land, as the water was too shoal [shallow?] for the large vessels. I have now come to the scene of Conflict. I have said before I was anxious to have a brush with the Rebs, and I have been gratified somewhat as our division whipped them most out-rageously in a 2 day fight last Monday and Tuesday. First let me explain our position from Brasher City. A force larger than ours went up to Franklin by land at the same time that we went up the river. [Francis is apparently referring to the rest of Banks' 19th Corps, which was approaching Bisland, not Franklin itself.] They were to attack the place and we were to be in the rear to cut off their retreat, or bother them the most we could. Our landing place was some 4 or 5 miles from and above Franklin, an opening in the woods that were on the river for a mile back from the river.

Just as the troops began to land a shot came whizzing over the water and struck near one of our steamers. At this the Navy boys began to pour the 9 inch shell and solid shot into the woods double quick time while the first La. landed, the 6th N.Y. and ourselves following. By the time we got on shore the Rebs had retreated up thro the woods into the open field behind a dense hedge

Opposite page: Map adapted from Plate 23–8; "Official Atlas," and map, page 113, *History of the XIX Army Corps.*

of bushes. We (2 or 3 regt's that got on shore first) formed in line of battle and began to advance, having a company of cavalry harassing the rebs and a line of skirmishers behind them and in advance of us.

After we got within about a ¼ or ⅜ths of a mile of them we all laid down the rebs shelling us but not doing any harm. The 6th N.Y. and the cavalry were the only ones engaged besides 2 guns of one of our 3 batteries. The shell from these made the rebs scamper in good style across the Bayou Teche (which was behind them) burning the bridges or trying to. One of them was saved by a Negro putting out the fire. I cannot enumerate the various movements during the after part of the day. Suffice it to say that our batteries followed them across the bayou, giving them "Hail Columbia" in the shape of shell. The whole of our force got onto the field so that we all marched across the bayou and got a chance to turn in on the wet, cold ground (as it had rained some in the first part of the night). By 12 o'clock they had all got across except 2 or 3 reg'ts of us and a battery which in crossing broke down the bridge and we had to wait for it to be fixed so that we could all get across before daylight.

I slept sound as a log not knowing a thing after lying down till I heard Lieut. Col. Putnam calling wake up boys! It was just light enough to see and we started, not having time to eat a mouthful as [one?] brigade had gone [Col. H.W. Birge's 3rd Brigade] and one was waiting for Gen. Dwight [commander of the 22nd Maine's 1st Brigade] to start his. After marching about a mile we could see the brigade that went ahead [the 3rd Brigade] drawn up in line of battle, skirmishers out, reserve laying down, etc.

Just as soon as they began to advance, the rebs poured in upon them with artillery and musketry. At this Gen. Grover sent a part of Nims' Battery [the 2nd Massachusetts Light Artillery] in to the field which made the artillery dry up a little. The firing at this became terrific on both sides and remained so till our brigade took the place of the one that was coming off the field. When we laid down bullets were whizzing and dropping around us. One man in Co. F was wounded just before we laid down, but it was the only one in our rgt. during the battle, as the rebels run into the woods, the 91st N.Y. following them up as skirmishers.

The 3rd Brigade were the only ones engaged and suffered bad, the 26th Me. 25th Connecticut & 159th N.Y. losing the greater part that was lost. They were retreating when our brigade entered the field. And Father! the sight of the wounded coming and being brought off as we advanced was awful! I hardly noticed the bullets or shells until we came to a halt for the groans of dying rebels, and the bloody and wounded boys passing us was all I saw or heard for the time being. The rebs got off a great many of their dead and wounded, but after they retreated I went back over the field and saw 6 or 8 rebels that had been shot instantly, one poor fellow (about my age I should think) had lived just long enough to get out his handkerchief and put it to his head where a bullet had gone into it and he remained in that position after he had breathed his last. I could not help thinking as I looked around at the poor fellows laying in their hearts' blood, that they had friends as well as me, just as dear to them as ours! But I will not dwell on this too long. Thank good fortune our reg't came out far better than anyone expected when we entered the field under such a raking fire! But a fresh force coming out to the field and Nims' Battery pouring death into their ranks at such a rate was more than they could stand under and they fled in confusion, without our reg't firing a gun.

Our loss is said to be 2 or 3 hundred in killed and wounded. We took about 50 prisoners. Just at night we advanced thro woods expecting to find the rebs (by the way they had a gunboat in the bayou that had been shelling the woods to prevent our advance). After we got thro we saw the game, for Lo! Behold! they were gone! and had blown up their gunboat Diana for fear that we should get it, which they took from us some time ago.[13]

The 22nd had come through the battle without serious injury — the *Official Records* (along with Francis Ireland's letter and Colonel Jerrard's report) list one enlisted man wounded. As a whole, the battles at Bisland and Irish Bend had resulted in some success for General Banks. As mentioned earlier, the Confederate commander, General Taylor, realizing that he was greatly outnumbered on both his front and rear, had abandoned the fortifications at Bisland during the night of April 13–14. When General Banks, eventually realizing that the Confederates were on the move, ordered an attack at around 4 A.M. on the 14th, the Rebel garrison had completely withdrawn, leaving only empty trenches behind. This could certainly be seen as a Union victory, of sorts. But, General Banks' hope of defeating Taylor's army in battle or of capturing a substantial part of the Confederate garrison was unfulfilled. General Taylor made no report of casualties, but left 21 dead on the field at Nerson's Woods, and another 35 wounded who were captured. General Grover reports an additional 120 Confederates taken prisoner. Nevertheless, the great majority of General Taylor's force was able to avoid being trapped by General Grover's division and made its way to the northwest, toward New Iberia. In his advance toward Fort Bisland, General Banks had lost approximately 40 men killed and another 184 wounded. At Irish Bend, General Grover had suffered approximately 53 men killed, 270 wounded, and 30 captured or missing.[14]

The drawing depicting the Battle of Irish Bend that later appeared in *Harper's Weekly* was taken "from a sketch by Mr. W.M. Hall, of the Twenty-second Maine Regiment." William Hall, another young man from Dexter, apparently had some artistic ability. In 1877 he did the frescoes for Dexter's town hall, and the 1880 census shows him living in Boston, with occupation listed as "fresco painter."[15]

General Banks, still intent on his mission to clear the area on the western side of the Mississippi of Confederate forces, began a pursuit of

The Battle of Irish Bend, from a sketch by William Hall, 22nd Maine (*Harper's Weekly*, May 16, 1863).

the retreating Confederates while also moving elements of his corps into various towns to establish a Union garrison. Meanwhile, General Taylor was having problems maintaining his force. Many of his troops had apparently had enough of soldiering, were somewhat dispirited by their withdrawal and retreat, and were deserting in substantial numbers and headed for their homes.[16]

13

New Iberia and St. Martinville

A Slave Uprising, an Escort for an Ailing Rebel Officer

On April 15, the day after the battle at Irish Bend, which Francis described in the previous chapter, the 22nd Maine had been ordered to garrison the town of Franklin. Then, on April 25, leaving companies D and I behind under the command of Major John Brackett as a part of the force maintaining the Union presence in Franklin, the rest of the regiment proceeded a few miles northwest to garrison the town of New Iberia. Francis wrote home on April 27 from nearby St. Martinville to tell of his recent experiences.

Dear Father:

I commenced a letter to you yesterday at New Iberia about 10 miles below here and not writing but little before I had to leave it — I will try again. When I wrote you last we were in Franklin. We remained there till last Thursday night — when all of us except Co. I and D got orders to march to New Iberia up about 30 miles. We arrived there after a very pleasant march Saturday AM. The place is about the same size as Franklin but of more consequence to the Rebs as they had a sort of an arsenal where they made shot and shell for their artillery. Also the salt mines are about 3 miles from here and taking every thing into consideration the place was of great benefit to them. Our Col, S.G. Jerrard is commander of the post here at present and a capt. from the 52 Mass [is] provost marshal. Beside our 8 companies there are 4 of the 52nd Mass. there. By the way 50 men were sent from our reg't about a week ago to go to the "front" (with an ammunition train that was to join the Army) as guard. 17 of them were from our Co. We have not heard from them since the 2nd day after they left but expect them down every time a lot of prisoners or a wagon train comes in from the army. The last we heard from the army it was about 100

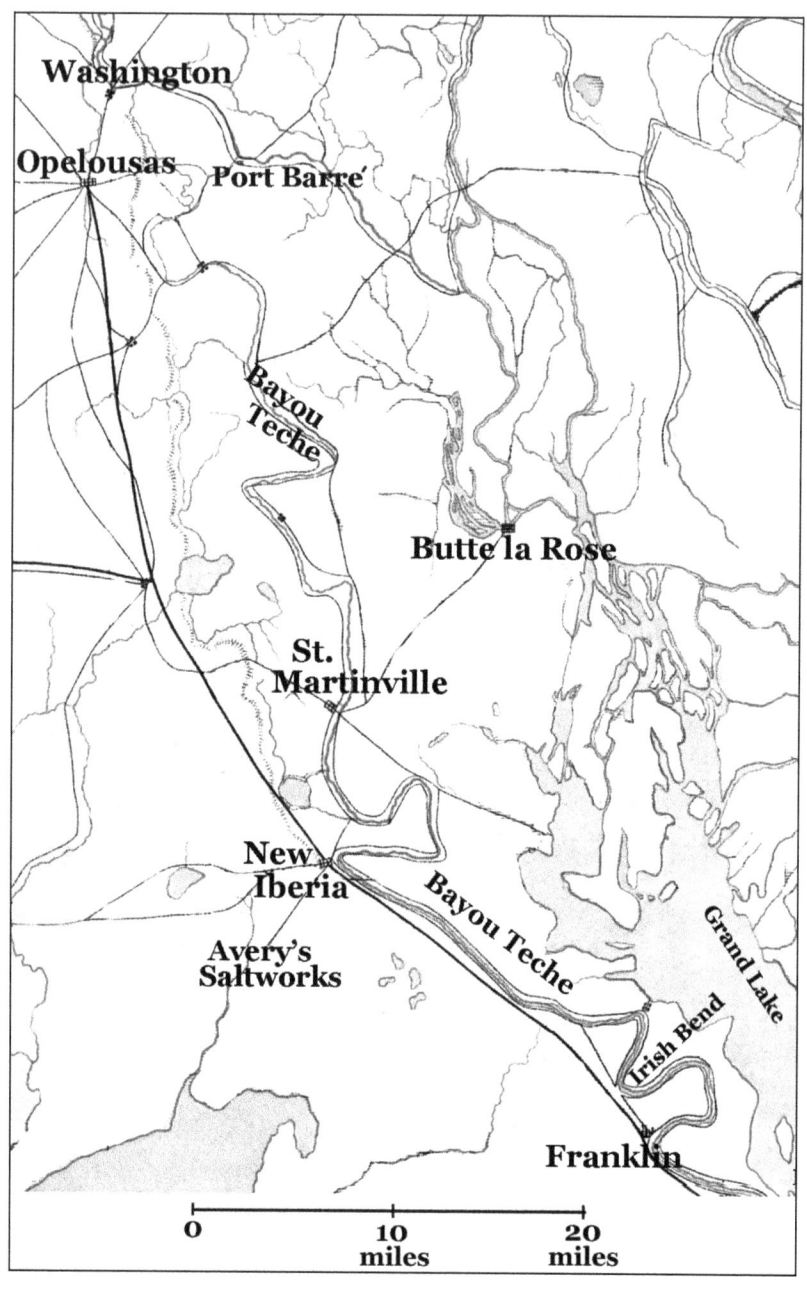

Map adapted from plate CLVI, *The Official Military Atlas of the Civil War*.

13. New Iberia and St. Martinville

miles above here and still on the advance after the rebs and taking hundreds of prisoners and sweeping the country clean of rebels and confiscating property such as cattle, sheep, horses, mules and sugar, molasses, cotton, etc. Last Thursday we met in droves during the day about 15,000 head of all kinds of stock and that is just the beginning. These prairies are covered with them and are more plenty as they approach Texas. Generally the stock is in rather poor condition this season of the year but our folks will get a great many good mules, horses, and any quantity of beef, mutton, etc. for the soldiers in this dept. I tell you they (the rebs) will get enough of the "Bobbin Boy" or Gen. Banks this time! He and such men as Weitzel and Grover etc. have not laid still the past winter for nothing! Banks is just but firm. For instance when he took the salt-mines at New Iberia there was about 700 bbls. on hand which the rebs offered to pay $40.00 per bbl. in specie if he would let them have it! But he said No! and turned it all in to the river! Destroyed the machinery, plugged up the mines and left them, but then you will hear by the papers as much as I can write and get it sooner into the bargain.[1]

While at New Iberia, Francis Ireland's Company E, led by its captain, Henry Wood, was given the responsibility of dealing with a slave insurrection at St. Martinville, about 10 miles away, directed against some of the French landowners. The area was settled by Acadian French, Catholics who had been forced out of Maritime Canada in the mid–1700s when the British gained control of all of Canada and who then became the Cajun French of Louisiana.[2]

Well now you will see that our reg't is (a part of it) at New Iberia and I am here! Well, yesterday 30 men were detailed to come up here with Capt. Wood and Lieut. Brown of Co. A for this purpose, A few reckless stragglers [from the Union Army] have been putting the devil into the niggers' heads and got up an insurrection. They attempted to attack the place Sat. night but did not make out. They have killed several white people and the citizens (French) have shot several in the out skirts of the town where there was about 500 niggers armed with broad axes, knives and a very few guns attempting to get in to the place. They captured and hung over 20 besides. About every citizen is armed and had not slept any for 3 nights till we came here last night. This is an Old French town there being hardly anybody but French here, and they have not any more to do with the rebs than you, being perfectly neutral. Every house that floats the French flag is passed unmolested. The citizens keep a good look-out for the darkies and I don't think they will make any further demonstrations as long as they know we are here. The people here treat us tip top, they brought in a plenty of such as they had, corn cake, baked lamb, etc, and have given our boys that were out on picket a good breakfast this morning. (We guarded the court house a nice two story building. I am up in the jury room sitting in an easy arm chair writing this and some of the boys are in the jury box and Judge's chair, and are spread out generally). Now I must relate a little time I had last night—enjoying the polite manners and hospitality of the French planters.

In a lined off area, Francis has here written: "P.S. I tell this to illustrate the French customs, manners, etc. more than to brag about myself." He then continues.

> Just as we got here a nice coach drove up here with some ladies from a place about 3 miles out and left them at a residence here. One of them, a very polite French lady, wished for a guard to go with the coach back to the place and get a sick man. Capt. Wood assented and told me I might go. I got into the coach with two planters (French) both armed making 3 of us armed. The coachman boy drove us to the residence. I was introduced to the sick man and the porter brought chairs and goblets of water for us. The sick man then told me that he was an officer of the Confederate army, one of Gen. Richard Taylor's staff, and he was taken sick near here and left behind on the place. [He] said that "he had done all he could for the cause and wished me to report to my com. officer (Capt. Wood) accordingly. After talking some twenty minutes the porter came again with splendid whiskey and a pitcher of water and passed it around, each man mixing to his fancy (I of course didn't drink much whiskey) and all drinking at their pleasure. The coachman was called and he drove up, the 2 planters and the sick man got into the coach and I (wishing to see what I could) rode outside with the boy. He told me that the coach harnesses and the horses that they had before the war cost $2500.00 (twenty five hundred dollars), a fair price I should judge from the silver that was on the harnesses and coach! That is the way the planters lived here before the war. The officer told Capt. Wood that the Confederacy was ruined, and whipped and the sooner Jeff Davis gave up, the less [they] would have to starve. At New Iberia, flour was $1.50 per lb. and hardly any to be had at that, tea $40.00 per lb. and other Northern necessities in proportion. At Franklin a rebel citizen showed me his shirt made of common cotton cloth that he paid $3.50 per yd. for. It was in Confederate money of course, but that is just as good to them as green backs as long as they hold a place.[3]

Captain Wood, in his report to Colonel Jerrard, stated that when his company arrived at St. Martinville they were "none too soon," as there were reports from a courier that a large group of slaves were heading toward the town. Captain Wood sent his sergeant major with a group of mounted citizens to judge the strength of the approaching slaves. "Shortly the mounted men returned saying that on their approach the negroes fled, but they thought they were coming up in another direction." Captain Wood "sent scouts out in every direction and found on their return that there was not any immediate danger." He therefore "posted pickets on every road leading into the place, and the night passed off very quietly." In reporting on the Confederate officer who surrendered, Captain Wood states, "I found him to be Capt G.L. Fusilier former aid de camp on Genl. Taylor staff." This officer "immediately surrendered himself to me, he said he considered their cause hopeless and was ready to give himself up."[4]

The statement by the gentleman who claimed to be Captain Fusilier seemed a bit suspect on first reading, since a fusilier is a type of soldier and would appear to be an unusual personal name. It seemed likely that some private soldier might have made up a story, with a name and rank that might result in good treatment as a prisoner. However, Captain Gabriel Leclerc Fusilier, a 60 year old wealthy land owner, was indeed a volunteer aide to Major General Richard Taylor. His story to Captain Wood about the hopelessness of the Rebel cause and his willingness to give up, on the other hand, would appear to have been merely a tale to lull his captors. The captain escaped from Union captivity and, still fighting for the Confederacy, later ended the war as a major in the 7th Regiment, Louisiana Volunteer Cavalry. And, of course, Captain Fusilier's service also demonstrates that not all the French settlers of Southern Louisiana had maintained the "perfectly neutral" attitudes Francis had indicated in his letter.[5]

Captain Wood then reports, "I find that stragglers from our army have done an immense amount of mischief in this neighborhood, they in many instances have gone to the planters houses and after pillaging and plundering they have made the negroes quit working, threatening to shoot them if they did not." To correct this situation, Capt. Wood states that he

> visited several plantations myself and have told the negroes that it is for their interests as well as everybody else's that they should continue to work as heretofore, in every case it has had a good effect, they have gone to work, and I have not had any more complaints from the same quarter.
>
> The citizens here are very desirous that this should be made a permanent military post, and I think myself it will be for the interest of the service if it can be so, I have no doubt that very many of the citizens here will renew their oath of allegiance in good faith, if a military post is made of it, and a provost marshal is placed here. ...
>
> Everything seems to be going along smooth here now, I don't fear any outbreak now but if we are withdrawn, I would not say what the consequences would be, I think a small force will be sufficient to remain here, even if it should be found convenient to keep a force here at all.
>
> On Sunday I sent a corporal and three men to Mr. Durand's plantation, yesterday I went there myself, and found everything as it was represented.... Mr. Durand is a Frenchman, but he is a very strong Union man, and has suffered very much from the rebels in consequence, I left the men there to guard his plantation."[6]

Colonel Jerrard wrote that Captain Wood "by his firmness restored comparative order and security to that parish." Captain Wood was, for a time, appointed acting provost marshal for St. Martinville.[7]

This event was noted briefly in reports which made their way into the *Official Records*, which simply state that on "April 27 a report was received from Colonel Jerrard, commanding at New Iberia, of a disturbance at Saint Martinville, caused by a few white men and a party of negroes, but which was promptly quelled."[8]

The concern about possible violence from angry ex-slaves had been expressed in November of 1862 in a communication from General Butler's chief of staff, George Strong, to General Weitzel. Indicating that all disloyal persons must be disarmed in areas which came under Union Army control, he goes on to state: "We must leave force enough [in those areas] to take care of any rising of the negroes. I think you had better see the most intelligent of the negroes in person ... and caution them that there must be no violence to unarmed and quiet persons."[9]

As Francis' letter of April 27 goes on, the time when the regiment will go home is once again on his mind. This also gives us an indication of the promises and inducements made to those who enlisted for 9 months:

> Now I will change my subject. The probability is that gov't will not let us go home so as to be mustered out before the middle of July. This is not just, not right (we shall have served 9 months the 10th of June) and it causes a great deal of growling but we shall have to grin and bear it. If we could get home by June 20th all hands would like it better, as the most have believed that we should leave for home by May 20th, but if I am in as good health as now it won't make a great difference to me but there are farmers that would like to get home by the first of June and expected to when they enlisted.[10]

As we have seen, the soldiers in the 22nd Maine had, since the previous summer, been concerned, frustrated, and at times angry about the lack of information regarding their date of mustering out of U.S. service. After being called to assemble in Bangor on September 10, 1862, the regiment was not mustered until October 18. A further oddity results from the recorded date of muster in for the men, as opposed to the regiment: the date of muster in for the great majority of the men of the regiment is listed as October 10, which would mean that their 9 months' service would end on July 10, 1863.[11]

But it seems clear that many men considered the September 10 date as the start of their 9 months' service. It is also interesting to note that the men of 22nd Maine received pay starting on September 10, which would seem to support the men's thought that their service began on that date. There also seems, previously, to have been a feeling that the regiment would be sent home before their service was over so that they would be mustered out back in Bangor on the 9 month anniversary of their enlistment date. This feeling, or hope, would explain why a discharge date in late May was mentioned at times — hopes of being home by early June for mustering out.

And, with some brighter news about the health of a couple of his friends, Francis ends his April 27 letter:

> I have heard a sort of a round about way from Charlie that he is doing well and I guess he will be likely to be sent up to the reg't soon. Danl. Leighton joined the reg't yesterday at New Iberia. He wished me to mention him. Tell his folks that he is smart as ever nearly. I have rec'd no letters etc. since your of March 30th. Expect some next mail.
>
> I would write more but have not time and will talk the more when I get home if I am so fortunate as that.
>
> From your son,
Francis A. Ireland
>
> I would write mother and Olin but this must be for all. By the way while I have been writing this a gentleman came in and made us (30) each a present of a gig of tobacco as long as my arm from the elbow down, and as wide as my hand! It came very handy to some of the boys as it is scarce for them to get, and money is played out with the most of us. The lot is worth (at sutlers' prices) $40.00. It is some that they keep by them in these times. I took mine for the fun of it — don't know what I shall do with it! Plenty that would be glad to have it.
>
> F.A.I.[12]

In the last paragraph, we see an indication that Francis may well have written separate letters to other members of his family from time to time. We also learn that Charlie Farrar has been away from the regiment sick. A letter that Charlie wrote home on April 28 was written from Bayou Boeuf, where the 22nd Maine had been camped before moving against Irish Bend. In that letter Charlie wrote that he hopes to rejoin the regiment in a few days and that he had heard that the regiment had not been "called into action in the battles."

Also in this letter he reports on the Confederate prisoners he has seen, saying that perhaps "some 25 or 30 hundred of them" had gone by on their way to New Orleans. Charlie comments that "they was a prety ruged looking set of fellows and seemed to be glad to get out of the show so easy they did not have eny uniform & dressed enyhow that came handy." And, as with Francis, Charlie was quite impressed with the wildlife of the area. "I have seen some large aligaters and snakes, one ratle snake 15 years old, they haint eny of your small stuff."[13]

On April 30 John Ireland began another letter to his son. In it, we get a feel, not only for the anxiety that parents felt for their soldier sons, but the frustration of waiting to hear of events which, in that day, might not be learned of by those at home for quite some time.

> Dear Son:
> Yours of the 4th, 5th, and 6th inst. was taken from the office Tuesday morning. The reason this did not get here before was that the steamer run aground below N.O. [New Orleans] and remained 8 days. Papers from N.O. by the same brought news of the battle which I suppose you participated in. The accounts we have got represent Banks' Army victorious. How much anxiety we felt for you; hope you escaped unhurt.
> This morning Uncle Farrar's folks got a letter from Charlie dated 15th inst. informing them that he was sent back with the sick; So he was not in the battle; sorry to hear he is sick and separated from you. Hope he is on duty again by this time. I see many names of the 26 Maine among the wounded, but no mention of the 22nd yet although Charles says in his letter that he heard there were several killed in Co. A and F of your regiment.[14]

The battle referred to is, of course, the Battle of Irish Bend, or Franklin, which Francis had described in his letter of April 17 — a letter which had not yet arrived. And although the newspapers would include a general account of the battle, the families where still, after 2 weeks, unaware of the details and of the names of killed and wounded. The report from Charlie Farrar of men from Company A and F being killed was not accurate. As stated earlier, there is no record of death or serious wounds resulting from Irish Bend for any company of the 22nd Maine. The 26th Maine, in the leading brigade in that battle, fared much less well, with 33 wounded and 19 killed or died of wounds.[15]

The elder Ireland continues his letter that afternoon, and, as with the Farrars, we learn that the families of some soldiers are sharing the news of their loved ones. Although this must have helped the families cope with their fears, the delay in letters, and the desire to hear directly from a son far away must have been constant sources of frustration and worry. "Since writing the above, Uncle Farrar and I called at Mrs. Wood's and heard a letter read which she received this morning. We were glad to learn from it that your regiment escaped the casualties of the battle. I think we shall get a letter from you by the night mail, and I will therefore suspend writing till tomorrow."[16]

The Mrs. Wood referred to is undoubtedly Mary Wood, the wife of

13. New Iberia and St. Martinville

Company E's commander, Captain Henry Wood. It seems from references in Francis Ireland's letters that her husband was liked and respected by the troops. In a newspaper article written many years later, one veteran of Company E remembered that, although Captain Wood had been given a horse to use, the captain almost never rode it — he made it available to the most tired men in the company whenever the regiment was on the march. And the captain would often be seen carrying a musket or two for footsore and tired privates.[17]

John Ireland writes more news of the town and then continues on Sunday morning May 3, "No letter from you last night, but the paper announced the arrival of a steamer from N.O. April 23rd and we will content ourselves with the belief that we shall get one in a day or two. I am going up to Uncle Farrar's today and will let your mother fill the sheet. J.P. Ireland."

As we next read, this is the only letter seen in which Martha Ireland writes to her son, but of course it is possible that Francis' mother and brothers wrote their own letters to him. In that era, however, it is quite likely that the father of the family wrote for all and would be the person to whom correspondence was addressed.

Sunday Morn

Dear Francis, I will write a few lines in this letter, But will not try to tell you what anxiety we felt when we heard of the battle with Banks' army supposing you must have been in the fight. And then, how thankful to learn that Capt. Wood's company were all safe. My prayer is that God will preserve you in the future as he has in past.

Your father has gone up to Uncle Farrowes [Farrar's] today as we have no meeting at the Methodist Church today. Olin is out with Flora giving her a ride in his carriage. It is a beautiful morn and the people are enjoying it I guess for I can see French, Scotch, Irish, and Yankees walking the streets and strolling over the hills. We got Uncle Andrew's and wife's miniatures in a letter the other day. Hope Charley is with you before this time. Give my love to him and much to yourself.

Your mother[18]

In her list of the national backgrounds of those walking the streets of Dexter, Martha Ireland is noting the makeup of their town since many newly arrived immigrants had come to work in the woolen mills. Just how she defines "Yankees" as opposed to the others is a matter of some question. Do we assume that the Yankees are those who settled in Dexter before that more recent immigrants? That would seem the most likely explanation.[19]

14

No Spring Mustering Out

On May 4, Francis began another letter to his father from St. Martinville to bring his family up to date on the regiment's latest activities. He reports doing very well there.

Court Room of St. Martins Parish
St. Martinville, La. May 4, 1863
Dear Father

Having nothing else to do I will write a few lines home. The first of May has come at last—the time that we expected to be about starting for home when we came out here. Well! I guess this month won't see us start anyhow! As I wrote last we are having nice times here. Are on guard every other night only and none days. We are well supplied with eggs, milk, corn bread, as presents from the people here or exchanged rations for them. I and two others had a good dinner for a soldier. We had fried pork and eggs, coffee with milk, honey, and a good custard made by us. It was without spice, the only fault—on the whole we live very well as there are but a few of us and I hope we shall stay here quite a while.[1]

Francis continues the next day, his hopes to stay in St. Martinville gone, but with a bit more news from Charlie.

New Iberia, La. May 5

Here we are back again. Came last night—and it is said we are to march tomorrow for Opelusa [Opelousas] about 70 miles above here and I will write a line or two before we start. When we got here I got a line from Charlie of Apr 28. He says his health is getting pretty good, has had a hard time with the jaundice, has got over it pretty well only he is weak yet—thought he should join us soon. Says he has some diarrhea but has good doctors and good fare.

And once again, the issue of the date of discharge is mentioned; the length of the regiment's obligation is still unclear.

14. No Spring Mustering Out

The boys are beginning to swear at the prospect of our not getting home till July, or August — well it begins to look as though they meant to keep us in the service, I hear that they are to muster us out in New Orleans thinking that the most of us will enlist over again. Be that as it may I shall go home probably if it takes all my wages to pay fare! I don't like the idea of having to march so far to join the army when our time is so near out, as we shall have to come back in a few weeks at least. But they expect a great battle there soon, I believe, as Kirby Smith is advancing in that direction I hear. I spoke in a former letter of some of our boys being with or after the army. They are at Opelusa [Opelousas].

We have had no mail for some time don't know when we shall get one. Cannot think of any more to write now.

So good bye
F. A. Ireland[2]

Rumors of an impending battle with troops commanded by Kirby Smith proved untrue. Confederate General Edmund Kirby Smith had been given command, on March 7, of the approximately 30,000 Confederate soldiers west of the Mississippi. These troops, however, were spread from northern Arkansas to southern Texas. The troops of General Richard Taylor with whom General Banks' forces had been engaged were a part of this command, but General Smith did not bring more of his force to confront the Union army during the summer of 1863.[3]

As described earlier, after evacuating Fort Bisland and successfully avoiding a major battle or capture by Union forces in the area around Franklin, General Taylor and his dwindling army had moved toward the northwest. General Banks apparently recognized that General Taylor was having trouble keeping his army intact, for in the history of the 19th Army Corps, it is recorded, "Taylor's army began to melt away and his men, as they passed their homes, to fall out without hindrance. Many were of the simple class called Acadians, with scant sympathy for either side of the great war into which they found themselves drawn, and in all the regiments there were many conscripts."[4]

And so, after leaving a small Union force to garrison Franklin, which we have seen included Companies D and I of the 22nd Maine, General Banks' remaining forces began to pursue the retreating enemy. The estimates of numbers are, as usual, difficult to assess, but whatever the exact count, there can be no doubt that the Confederates under General Taylor were greatly outnumbered. In the history of the 19th Army Corps, it is stated that "Banks took up the pursuit with his united force, now outnumbering Taylor's as three to one." This, almost certainly is an overstatement of the size of the Confederate force in comparison to the Union troops. The Union forces that were making this pursuit had probably started the attacks at Franklin numbering around 15,000, but some regiments and companies, as with parts of the 22nd Maine, were sent to garrison various positions along the way.[5]

During the next few days the Confederate forces moved toward Opelousas, "making a strong resistance at Vermillion Bayou, from which position they were quickly driven." Some elements of Dwight's 1st Brigade as well as two batteries of Union artillery were involved in the action at Vermillion Bayou — an attempt to stop the retreating Confederates from burning a bridge and to prevent Banks' troops from rebuilding it. The Confederates were driven off, and the 22nd Maine was apparently not involved in this action.[6]

General Banks reached Opelousas on April 20 and the Confederate forces retreated toward Alexandria in disorder." On that same day, Union gunboats and 4 companies of infantry captured the Rebel works at Butte a la Rose, "which contained two heavy guns and large quantity of ammunition and was garrisoned by a force of 60 men, all of whom were captured."[7]

On May 5, General Banks reported, "Our headquarters at Opelousas were broken up, and the troops moved for Alexandria, a distance of from 90 to 100 miles, making this march in three days and four hours." General Banks stated, "Moving rapidly to the rear of Fort De Russy, a strong work on Red River, we compelled the immediate evacuation of that post by the enemy, and enabled the fleet of gunboats ... to pass up to Alexandria without firing a gun." The navy reached Alexandria on the morning of May 9; the army reached Alexandria that evening. From there, General Taylor's forces retreated in the direction of Shreveport. "In order to completely disperse the forces of the enemy, a force under Generals Weitzel and Dwight pursued him nearly to Grand Ecore, so thoroughly dispersing him that he was unable to reorganize a respectable force until July."[8]

The effectiveness of this action seems to vary considerably according to the one making the report. General Banks stated that the Confederate troops opposing him amounted to 10,000 to 15,000 men and that "during these operations ... we captured over 2,000 prisoners and twenty-two guns; destroyed three gunboats and eight steamers; captured large quantities of small-arms, ammunition ... and the steamers *Ellen* and *Conie*, which were of great service to us in the campaign." In his later memoir, however, General Taylor stated, "At that time my entire force in western Louisiana was under three thousand."[9]

14. No Spring Mustering Out

We may remember that, as a presumed impartial observer, Charlie Farrar wrote of seeing between 2,500 and 3,000 Confederate prisoners sent back during this time period (see chapter 13). While General Taylor had lost substantial numbers of men to desertion during the retreat from Bisland and Franklin, we have great difficulty in coming up with an exact number for the Confederate forces under his command. Should we suspect that, just as General Banks continually overestimated the number of Confederates he faced, so General Taylor would understate the numbers he commanded?

For about 2 weeks General Banks had expected, having "dispersed" General Taylor's Confederate force, to turn his attention to the capture of Port Hudson. General Grant had offered to send 20,000 reinforcements from Vicksburg to assist in that operation. With Port Hudson taken, a small Union force would be left as a garrison, while the remainder joined General Grant at Vicksburg to take that stronghold. On May 12, however, General Banks received a dispatch from General Grant saying that the expected reinforcements would not be sent.

General Banks then reported that his choices were, "First, to pursue the enemy to Shreveport," which he rejected since the enemy was already "captured or completely routed." His second choice was "to join General Grant at Vicksburg." This was rejected since General Banks stated that he lacked sufficient transportation. His third choice was to "invest Port Hudson with such forces as I had at my command." Accepting this option, orders to set this plan in motion were sent out and various scattered Union forces began to be gathered in.[10]

While the 22nd Maine's Company E had been in St. Martinville, and two companies had been left to garrison Franklin, the remainder of the regiment had moved, on May 6, to Washington, Louisiana, arriving there on May 11. The main body of the regiment remained at Washington, while Company E, and the two companies (D and I) that had been left at Franklin, were ordered to rejoin the regiment.[11]

On May 10, Francis wrote to his father from Washington with an update of the regiment's latest movements.

Dear Father;

I will just drop a line to let you know where we are and what we are doing. This place is about 55 miles from New Iberia, and 5 from Opelousas. We that were at St. Martinville were ordered to our reg't — Monday last — and after arriving at New Iberia that night the reg't (the part at New Iberia) got orders to go to Opelousas. We started Wednesday and arrived there the third day after or Friday. Next morning we came here and the 114th N.Y. (which had been with us on the march) kept on the march to the front: and we got orders to wait here for a baggage train and go with that (as guard) to the Front. It may not be here for two days and may be here in an hour. We probably shall have to go as far as Alexander [Alexandria], about 60 or 70 miles above here, as we hear that Banks has taken the place. It will be a long march but I think it will be about our last one. We have heard heavy cannonading all night and till after sunrise this morning in the direction of Port Hudson or Baton Rouge. The citizens here say this morning that Port Hudson is taken! I almost believe it — for there seems to be no end to the good luck of Gen. Banks.[12]

From May 8, the Union warships and gunboats south of Port Hudson had been shelling the Confederate fortress with cannons and mortars. On the night of May 9–10, the Confederates moved 4 of their guns into a position where, it was hoped, they could effectively fire on the Union vessels. A loud and prolonged exchange of artillery fire that night and early on the morning of the 10th resulted in no substantial damage on either side, and no appreciable change in the situation.[13]

As Francis is writing this letter, the 22nd Maine is preparing, along with other components of the Union forces, to bring a wagon train of supplies from Washington back to Brashear City.

Our Cos. I & D have just arrived from Franklin as I am writing and a part of the 175th N.Y. which is to go with us. The train consists of 150 wagons loaded with commissary stores. Our colonel, S.G. Jerrard, will have command and charge of the train. We shall be 7 or 8 days on the road. I am in first rate health and time is passing off very fast. At present it is pretty hot here about like July in Maine, but a breeze most all the time. Next month it will be sultry. The rest of our boys that left us at Franklin to come up here as guard are 9 miles from here [and] will join us before we leave.[14]

We then learn something of the Irelands' literary tastes. Like many in Maine and the nation, they had read the works of Harriet Beecher Stowe, who wrote her best known tale, *Uncle Tom's Cabin*, while in Brunswick, Maine, with her husband, Calvin Stowe, a professor at Bowdoin College. This work was followed by *Dred: A Tale of the Great Dismal Swamp*.

By the way I suppose you are aware (if you recollect) that we are and have been in (lately) the portion of country in which the scenes of Uncle Tom's Cabin are laid out. I believe it mentions in one place Uncle Tom's being at Opelousas, or some such circumstance. At any rate there are a great many descriptions of country, and habits of negroes, much of a planter's life, etc. laid down in that and Dred that are just as near perfect as pen can make them. I have seen a great many Uncle Toms, Old Tiffs [a character in *Dred*] etc. out here!

Francis, perhaps due to the influence of Stowe, is now back to using the term "Negroes." He then goes on:

> I have not heard from Charlie since my last letter to you. We march from sunrise till about 10 o'clock and then rest in the shade till 3 or 4 in the PM and then go on till we find a good place for the night — generally about 5 or 6. The most we have marched was 18 miles last Wednesday as it was a very cool day and we got over the ground pretty fast. But I must be closing my letter. ... I and Willie Hall [the young artist from Dexter] are laying in the shade of a great oak. We came out here to read some books (that we got from the houses where our officers quarter, a deserted palace with books and paintings worth thousands of dollars, all under foot) but Willie has gone to sleep and I am about as near it as I can be.
>
> Good bye
Frank A. I.[15]

On Sunday morning, May 17, John Ireland wrote again to his son. After a bit about an unusual May snowstorm, the elder Ireland wrote of three of the boys from Dexter. The first, Otis Roberts of the 6th Maine, had arrived home on a furlough. A sergeant in the 6th Maine, Otis went on to receive the Medal of Honor for his bravery at Rappahannock Station, Virginia, in November of 1863.[16] But we then learn of two less fortunate young men. "The probability is that Mr. Merrill will not be able to obtain his son's body. This is a very severe blow for them. I understand that Maria is very much afflicted. Friday Elder Gerry preached Saml. Silver's funeral sermon at the Hasseltine school house, in Silver's neighborhood, therefore Uncle Farrar's folks are not down today."[17]

Alonzo Merrill was a private in Co. H of the 6th Maine. When Francis had wondered whether the Dexter boys in the 6th Maine had come through December's battle at Fredericksburg, nobody knew that the regiment would fight there again that coming spring, as a prelude to the Battle of Chancellorsville. Alonzo Merrill was wounded during this second assault on Fredericksburg, May 3, 1863, and died May 5. Maria was his older sister, Sarah Maria Merrill, who helped raise the younger children after their mother died in 1858. Arranging for the bodies of dead soldiers to be sent home for burial was a problem for many, and most certainly so for those whose sons were sent to the Deep South. The family typically had to pay to have the body prepared and then sent north, and both the expense and the logistics presented difficulties. Many gravestones of Civil War soldiers who died during the war serve as a memorial, but are not marking the young man's actual grave in the South.[18]

Samuel Silver had died on March 10, and Francis had told his family of the death in his letter of March 19. This letter from John Ireland telling of the funeral is dated May 17.

John Ireland goes on to write of school starting and passes on news about the presumed mustering out date of the 22nd, news that may have come as a shock to Francis and his comrades, who still had hope of being home in early or mid–June. In these final paragraphs, the elder Ireland gives his feelings, concerns, and faith more voice than usual.

> You will probably see by a statement in the Courier that your time does not expire till July 18th, by what authority the statement is made I know not. I hope 'tis not so; but if it is, it will make only about a month's difference, and that will soon pass. The most I think of is that it will carry you into the heat of summer. But I hope you will keep good courage, as you have exhibited heretofore.
>
> We shall be very glad to witness your return. But alas! how many that went out with you — that friends hoped to welcome home again, that will never return. Far from home and loved ones, they were laid by the hands of their comrades beneath a Southern sky, on the banks of the Mississippi, the roaring of whose water will chant their requiem unobserved by them.
>
> It is very gratifying to friends here, to know they were cared for in their last hours, and had a decent burial. How glad we should be if this war could close speedily and honorably, without the further sacrifice of life. But He who rules in the armies of heaven, and among the children of men, knows what is for the best for this nation.
>
> Hope to get a letter from you soon,
>
> From your father,
J.P. Ireland[19]

A week later, on May 24, John Ireland writes to let Francis know that the family has just received his letter written almost a month earlier.

> My dear son;
>
> Your letter dated at St. Martinsville April 27 and post marked May 5 came in hand last night, and we were glad to hear from you, for we had looked for one for two weeks, and began to be some anxious.
>
> I have been down to Mr. Leighton's this morning to let them know about Daniel. They have been very uneasy about him for a long time, as they have had no letter from him since he was left at Baton Rouge [Francis mentioned Daniel Leighton's return to the regt. in that letter]. They will write him today.
>
> We are glad to hear of Banks great success in his department.[20]

Francis' father also has heard that General Grant expects to have Vicksburg in his hands before long, that the Mississippi River will soon be opened, and he believes that this will have a serious impact on the "Jeff Davis Confederacy."

14. No Spring Mustering Out

Back in November, Francis had written a letter in which he had despaired of Union victory. A more positive view of recent successes, or rumors of success, which Francis had expressed since then, prompted his father to write, "I think your faith in our success must have been strengthened since you stated in a former letter that we should never succeed unless some foreign nation stepped in and put an end to the war." After writing a bit about recent hot weather and Francis' mother's cough, he goes on,

> I will continue to write and send papers so you may get them up to the time of your leaving for home. Drop me a line when it is announced that your regiment is to start for home. ... If you can obtain anything that you can bring home that will be a curiosity, I wish you would do so.
>
> Flora grows finely; you would not recognize her if you were to meet her away from home. She and Billy [her puppy?] have fine times.
>
> I have no more to write at this time; hope you will be as fortunate in future in regard to health, etc. as heretofore.
>
> J.P. Ireland[21]

On May 20, the 22nd Maine had marched from Washington, Louisiana, to Barris Landing (Port Barre), and had been attached to a provisional brigade under Colonel Joseph Morgan of the 90th New York. On the 21st, this brigade — made up of the 22nd and 26th Maine, the 41st and 52nd Massachusetts, and the 110th, 114th, 90th, and part of the 175th New York — was ordered to march to Brashear City as a guard for a large wagon train of supplies. According to Colonel Jerrard, this wagon train included "four thousand contrabands." This train was a part of the vast quantity of supplies that were taken by the Union Army during General Banks' advance from Franklin. The value of the goods seized by legitimate forage (in other words, not counting theft by pillaging) may have amounted to 10 million dollars. In addition, many thousands of slaves left their former owners and were sent back toward Brashear City as a relatively safe haven.[22]

Colonel Jerrard wrote that this march from Port Barre to Brashear City was "decidedly the hardest march of the whole campaign" and was carried out in very warm weather, and with the fear of attack by rebels thought to be operating in the area. The wagon train apparently stretched for some 6 or 7 miles in length and, at one point, moved over 45 miles in 24 hours. After arriving at Brashear City, the regiment was taken by train to Algiers, Louisiana, just across the Mississippi from New Orleans.[23]

Francis wrote to his father on May 28 from "Algiers La. opposite New Orleans" to tell of these movements, to report the death of another young soldier from Dexter, and to say that Charlie Farrar has rejoined the regiment. He also indicates that the regiment expects to be sent to Port Hudson, which he feels will be their last posting before being mustered out. This letter is written at a time when many men of the 22nd had hoped to be preparing for the trip home.

Dear Father;

I take a moments time to write a few lines to let you know our whereabouts. We left Washington [Louisiana] the 20 [th] and went down to Barris Landing (5 miles) and the next morning we and the 26th Me., 110th, 114th 90th and 4 cos. of the 175th New York reg'ts and 41st & 52 Mass. (the 41st — Mounted) started on our march of eight days and 15 miles a day as ordered (to Brashear City). We marched much faster than that however. We were in charge of the Ammunition Train spoken of before and an everlasting train (4,000) of niggers. When we were on the road our train extended about 6 miles in length! But I must leave this to the latter two days. In the P.M. of Monday 25th just after we passed Franklin the rear of the train was attacked by gerrilas said to be backed up by a force of 6,000 that intended to cut us off at Franklin but were an hour too late and we had quite a time that eve getting ready to skedaddle, as our force could not prevent them from getting a part of the train if they chose, it was so long. The train was sent ahead and we started at 11 P.M. in the rear (we had 2 sections of Nims' Battery with us also) and we marched at quick time till day light when we took some sleep till 7 A.M., when we started again. We arrived at Berwick City a little past noon, having marched 44 miles in a little more than 24 hours with no breakfast or dinner till we got to Berwick (fast marching that). The rear regt's on Monday lost one or two men and 3 or 4 officers that were taken prisoners, one died yesterday that was wounded in the breast. We crossed over to Brashear yesterday and last night came here [Algiers] on the cars getting in at sunrise. We are to go up to Baton Rouge from here and I expect to Port Hudson from there. We have been rushed thro for the last week as we were over 200 miles from here a week ago! I stood it, Bully! marched all the way to Berwick City (130) miles. A great part gave out and had to ride. Over tired and sleepy but expect to go on board every minute. Tuesday we got our back mail. I got 4 letters from you and about 20 papers, and have just got one from uncle Eben and two papers from you! But I must hasten, Charlie joined us at Brashear, is smart again. The boys had rather start for home than Port Hudson! But I hope it will come out all right. Jacob Fogg [another young soldier from Dexter] died at Baton Rouge May 18. If we go up there [Port Hudson] I expect it will be the last move of our campaign but a desperate one I fear. I could fill 6 sheets but have no time.

Good bye from your son,
Francis

In 5½ days, 130 miles we marched.[24]

15

On to Port Hudson

The 22nd Maine was, in fact, sent to Port Hudson on May 29, the evening after the previous letter was written. That Confederate fortress, in conjunction with Vicksburg about 100 miles to the north, was preventing Union shipping from freely using the Mississippi River, while at the same time preserving Rebel supply routes to the Eastern Confederacy through Mexico, Texas, Arkansas, and Louisiana. With the Union capture of Alexandria on the Red River, General Banks positioned gunboats there to cut the main Confederate supply lines to Port Hudson's defenders. Beyond that, it was hoped that Confederate troops which might have supported Port Hudson had been scattered. With the decision to focus his attention on Port Hudson, General Banks began moving various units under his command in that direction. These land forces were to be supported with substantial firepower from naval vessels on the Mississippi, positioned both north and south of Port Hudson.[1]

At Port Hudson, Confederate Major General Franklin Gardner had assumed command in December of 1862 and his first priority had been the reorganization and strengthening of the defenses. General Gardner was ranked 17th of 39 in the 1843 graduating class at West Point, where he was trained as an engineer. (U.S. Grant had graduated 21st in that same class.) After West Point, Gardner had served in the Mexican War and received 2 brevet promotions for gallant conduct. Although a New Yorker, Gardner was a Southern sympathizer and had married Marie Celestine Mouton, the daughter of Alexandre Mouton, a former Louisiana governor and U.S. senator. Alexandre Mouton was also a wealthy planter, slave owner, and president of the Louisiana Secession Convention. In May of 1861, Captain Gardner had abandoned his U.S. Army duties in Utah and joined the Confederate Army as a lieutenant colonel. He was promoted to brigadier general in April 1862, and major general in December of that year.[2]

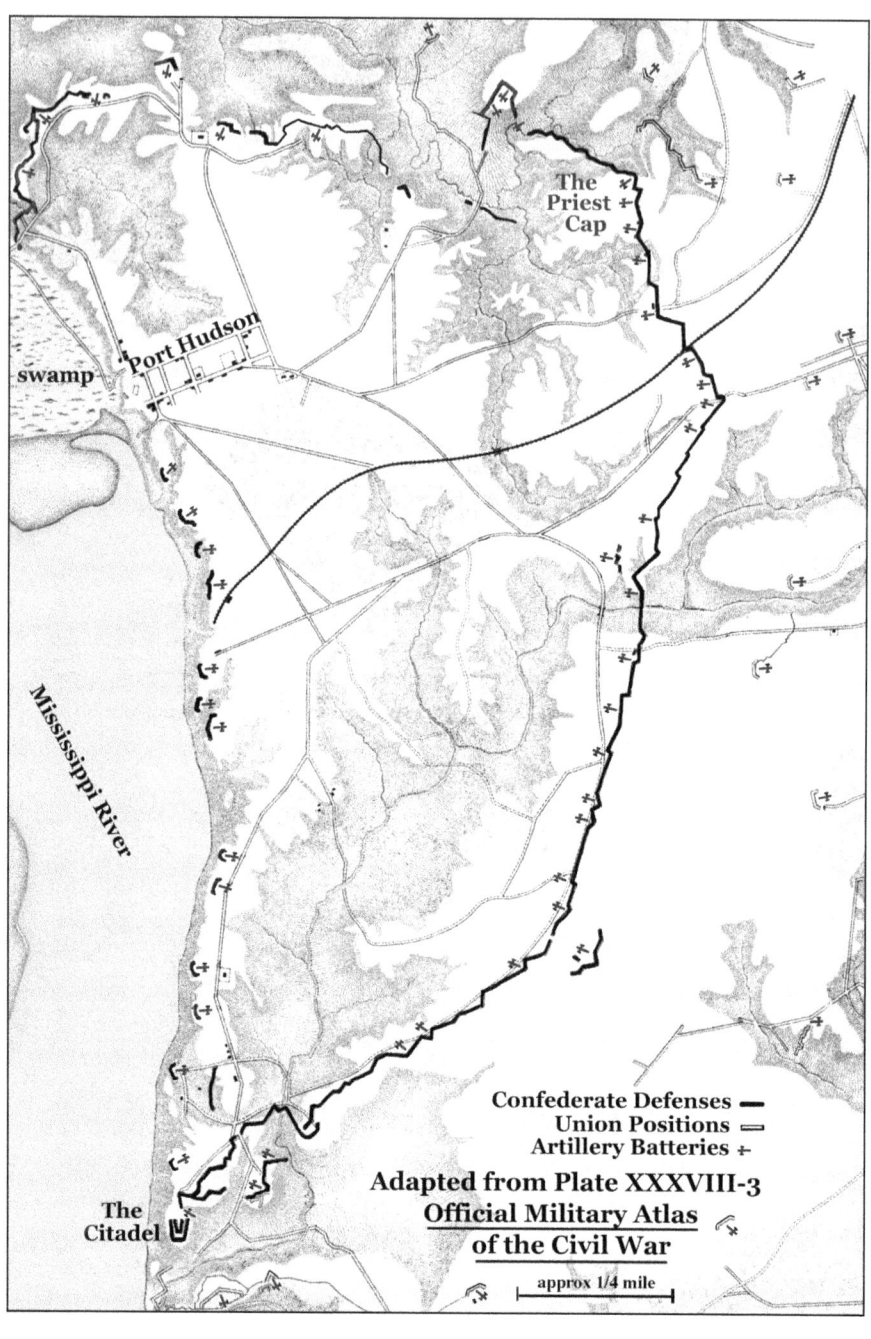

Port Hudson, showing the Confederate defenses and Union positions; adapted from Plate 38–3, *The Official Military Atlas of the Civil War.*

Prior to General Gardner's arrival, the Confederates had recognized Port Hudson's importance as a potential stronghold on the Mississippi. The Confederates, lacking sufficient gunboats, could not hold the Mississippi River, but needed positions on the river which would allow supplies from the Western Confederacy to come up the Red River and across the Mississippi en route to the Eastern Confederacy. In August of 1862, after their defeat at Baton Rouge, the Confederate commanders began the occupation of Port Hudson, which was seen as an ideal location for defending against attacks from both land and river.

As described in an earlier chapter, Port Hudson is located

Major General Franklin Gardner (Library of Congress).

at a sharp bend in the Mississippi that in itself presented a challenge to navigation. Here at the water's edge the Confederate batteries were able to take advantage of high bluffs, rising sharply to as much as 80 feet above the Mississippi. This elevation gave a strong advantage to the Confederate gunners firing down at any Union ships that attempted a passage. On this river side of his defenses, General Gardner repositioned the guns to more effectively concentrate their fire. In making plans to repel an attack by land, the defenders were aided by Port Hudson's terrain of steep sided ravines, ridges, and plateaus. Using these natural barriers to their advantage, they built a series of strongly fortified positions spaced such that any attacker would be subjected to direct and cross fire. General Gardner, with his training as a military engineer, continued this plan and saw to the construction of a line of formidable artillery platforms, breastworks, and trenches which would confront any assault from land.[3]

But while General Gardner was strengthening the physical defenses of his post, he lost a considerable number of his troops. The need for reinforcements at other Confederate positions, such as Vicksburg, was given

The bluffs at Port Hudson showing Confederate batteries (*Review of Reviews*).

priority, and the Port Hudson garrison dwindled considerably from around 16,000 men at the end of March 1863, to fewer than 7,000 by late May.

There was, during May, considerable argument among Confederate commanders about the priorities of Port Hudson versus Vicksburg, or the possible fortification of other towns in Louisiana and Mississippi. A telegram on May 7 from Confederate President Davis to General John C. Pemberton, in command of the Department of Mississippi and East Louisiana, stated that "to hold both Vicksburg and Port Hudson is necessary to a connection with Trans-Mississippi," the Confederate lands and supply route to the west." At that time, General Gardner had already left Port Hudson with a substantial part of the garrison's troops, having been ordered to bring reinforcements to Vicksburg. Having gotten as far as Clinton, he received a message from Pemberton to hold Port Hudson, and with approximately 2,000 of his men, he immediately returned. General Joseph E. Johnston, overall commander of the Confederate's Depart-

One of Port Hudson's river batteries (*Review of Reviews*).

ment of the West, which included Pemberton's Mississippi and Eastern Louisiana, disagreed with Davis' and Pemberton's assessment of Port Hudson's importance. Later in May, therefore, apparently on his own initiative, General Johnston sent orders to General Gardner to abandon Port Hudson. However, by the time the orders arrived and preparations for departure could be made, the Union army's presence made that impossible. And so, with this force of fewer than 7,000 men, the Confederates prepared for the Union assaults.[4]

From May 8, Union gunboats had begun a mortar bombardment of Port Hudson that was intended to soften the defenses in preparation for the arrival of Union troops. On May 18, Union Major General Christopher C. Augur received instructions to leave one regiment of Louisiana Native Guard at Baton Rouge and proceed with the rest of his force to Port Hudson. As his troops neared that Confederate stronghold on May 21, skirmishing with Rebel pickets and cavalry slowed their advance. The superior Union numbers, however, caused the Confederates to withdraw their pickets within the Port Hudson defenses. On May 22, General Banks, with Brigadier General Cuvier Grover and additional Union troops, arrived to join Augur's force. By May 24, the day that General Gardner had planned to abandon Port Hudson, Union troops had the Confederates surrounded with an army of around 13,000 men. And with this almost two to one superiority for Banks' forces, the Union officers and men were confident of victory.[5]

On May 27, before the 22nd Maine's arrival, General Banks ordered the first assault on the Rebel position at Port Hudson. At dawn an artillery barrage was begun along the entire Union front, and was followed at around 6 A.M. by the advance of General Weitzel's division on the right of the Union line. However, the Union attacks were poorly coordinated, perhaps, it is claimed by some, due to the vagueness of General Banks' orders. It seems clear, however, that after meeting with his division commanders the previous evening, General Banks had issued orders for an attack on the morning of the 27th, to be preceded by an artillery cannonade beginning at daybreak. Further, it seems that all division commanders were ordered to begin their attacks by advancing skirmishers during that cannonade.

As the morning wore on, however, and with no other attacks being made, General Weitzel's men, after heavy losses, found they were unable to break the Confederate line. Whatever positions were held by Union troops were only held by remaining behind cover, but further forward movement did not appear possible. After consulting with General Grover, General Weitzel decided to halt the attacks, and wait for other Union forces to advance before making any further attempts.[6]

However, it was not until noon, when General Banks found there were no other Union troops advancing, that he himself rode to one Union commander, General Thomas W. Sherman, and found that general at lunch in his tent with his staff. Hot words passed and Sherman's division soon began its attack on the south (right) of the Confederate line. General Augur, who was waiting for Sherman's men to move forward, then ordered the advance of his division, attacking the center of the Confederate defenses. Thus, more than 6 hours separated the attacks at the north (left) the Confederate defenses and the attacks on the center and right. The lack of simultaneous attacks at many points of Port Hudson's defenses meant that Confederate commanders could shift men to areas where they were needed, and did not need to defend their entire line at any one time. Parts of the Confederate line would have been highly vulnerable otherwise. As the attacks actually materialized, however, they were repulsed by the sparse Confederate garrison, who remained secure in their strong natural and man-made defenses. Almost 2,000 Union soldiers were killed, wounded, or captured. General Sherman was among the severely wounded and had a leg amputated. The total Confederate casualties amounted to less than 250. Another result of the failure of the May 27 attack was that Confederate morale soared, while morale of the Union, which was previously confident of a victory, plummeted. Moreover, this lack of well-defined orders and coordinated attacks was an indication of problems that would hamper future attempts to breach Port Hudson's defenses.[7]

One of the most notable, and yet little known, events of that day occurred when black soldiers of the 1st and 3rd Regiments of the Union Army's Louisiana Native Guards took an active and courageous role in the attack. General Banks had authorized the formation of Native Guard regiments within the Union Army and, at the time of the May 27 attack, 3 of these regiments, the 1st, 3rd, and 4th Louisiana Native Guard, were listed as a part of the Union forces at Port Hudson. At least one of the general officers there, General Godfrey Weitzel, had expressed great displeasure at the creation and presence of these units and was threatening to turn down a command that would include black soldiers. In November of 1862, having written to General Banks to express this displeasure, General Weitzel received a lengthy response from General Banks, written by Assistant Adjutant General George Strong:

> You say that in these [Native Guard] organizations you have no confidence. ... It was arranged between the commanding general [General Banks] and yourself that the colored regiments should be employed in guarding the railroad. You do not complain in your report that they either failed to do their duty in that respect, or that they have acted otherwise than correctly and obediently to the commands of their officers or that they have committed any outrage or pillage upon the inhabitants.
> The general was aware of your opinion that colored men will not fight. You have failed to show, by the conduct of these freemen so far, anything to sustain that opinion. ... You say you "cannot command these negro regiments." Why not?

After addressing Weitzel's stated and implied reasons, General Banks states that he will forward General Weitzel's report and his own reply to higher authority. "In the mean time these colored regiments of freemen, raised by authority of the president, and approved by him as the commander-in-chief of the Army, must be commanded by the officers of the Army of the United States like any other regiment."[8] It is an interesting sidelight on General Weitzel's career that, in December of 1864, he was given command of the newly formed 25th Corps, the only all-black corps in the history of the United States Army.[9]

At the time of the May 27 attack, 2 regiments of Native Guard, the 1st and 3rd, were assigned to General Weitzel for the attacks at Port Hudson. The Native Guard regiments, while having white field officers (colonel, lieutenant colonel, and major), had line officers (captains and lieutenants) who were black. One change that General Banks had attempted to make in the Native Guard regiments was to remove the black line officers and replace them with white officers. In the 2nd Regiment, this was accomplished, but the troops of the 1st, and 3rd Louisiana Native Guard at Port Hudson retained most of their black line officers in command of their companies.[10]

During the attacks of May 27, these two Native Guard regiments under General Weitzel's command had the opportunity to do more than guard the railroad lines, and given their chance, they showed great bravery. Attacking across swampy ground toward a well fortified hilltop position at the northern end of the Confederate defenses, the regiments suffered heavy casualties — the dead including Captain Andre Cailloux, one of the freemen serving as a line officer. The bodies of the dead black soldiers remained on the field where they fell for over 40 days, until the end of the siege of Port Hudson, in spite of the fact that on May 28 General Banks requested and received permission from General Gardner to care for the Union wounded and bury the dead.[11]

There is considerable controversy over the exact number of Native Guard soldiers killed and wounded on May 27. Perhaps, as was done later in the war, it was considered important for morale that reported numbers be kept low. While the *Official Records* (for the period from May 23 to July 8) lists 3 officers and 41 men killed with another 133 of all ranks wounded from the 1st and 3rd Native Guard Regiments, other sources give much higher numbers. One author states that the "lowest believable accounting" is 371 killed and another 150 wounded, while a Confederate soldier who observed and helped repulse the Native Guard attack states that he could see about 250 bodies on the field at the end of the day.[12]

With the failure of the Union army's May 27th attacks, a siege of Port Hudson followed, creating desperate hardship for the Confederate

15. On to Port Hudson

Assault of the Second (Colored) Regiment on the Confederate works at Port Hudson, May 27, 1863 (Frank Leslie's *The Soldier in Our Civil War*, 1893).

defenders as their supplies dwindled. Nevertheless, General Gardner's men used the time to further strengthen their approximately 4½ miles of defenses. A series of trenches, bombproof shelters, and individual "rat holes" or "gopher holes" were dug to protect the defenders, while a maze of blind alleyways, a number of collapsing bridges, a jumble of felled trees, and rows of sharpened stakes were intended to prevent an easy approach by attackers.

For General Banks, the failure of the attacks of May 27 resulted in his decision to bring in more troops from throughout his district, including the 22nd Maine. His force at Port Hudson soon exceeded 30,000 and may have approached 40,000 men by early June, although some number of those present were not available for duty due to sickness.[13]

The 22nd Maine had been transported up the Mississippi on the steamboat *Fulton* to Baton Rouge and had then marched overland, arriving at Port Hudson on June 1. There, the regiment was assigned to the 4th Division under General Cuvier Grover and, with the 1st Louisiana, 90th, 91st, and 131st New York, made up the 1st Brigade of that Division. And immediately upon their arrival, one third of the regiment "acting as skirmishers" found itself in an advanced position in the Union Army's rifle pits in front of the enemy's lines. The remainder were detailed to support artillery batteries — the 1st Indiana Heavy Artillery and the 1st Battery, 1st Maine Light Artillery.[14]

During this time in early June, Confederate cavalry, under the command of Colonels John Logan and Frank Powers, were based around Clinton, to the east of Port Hudson and in the rear of the Union lines. Clinton, connected to Port Hudson by rail, had been a source of supplies to the

Inside Port Hudson's defenses showing "gopher holes" dug as protection from Union bombardment (*Review of Reviews*).

garrison at Port Hudson, and had also provided a route by which supplies which were landed at Port Hudson could be sent eastward to other Confederate states. Although the railroad link from Port Hudson had been cut, the railroad hub at Clinton was still in Rebel hands and was a base for Confederate cavalry. An attempt on June 3 by Union cavalry under Colonel Benjamin Grierson to rid the area of these Confederate horsemen failed and caused another 1,200 or so Union casualties. Then, on June 6, a larger Union force of around 3,000 cavalry, infantry, and artillery under General Halbert Paine was sent to Clinton. The Confederate cavalry, numbering around 1,200 had no desire to face this larger force and abandoned Clinton to its fate. Although failing to force a battle with the Confederate

15. On to Port Hudson

1st Indiana Artillery, Battery K, at Port Hudson (Massachusetts mollus Collection).

cavalry, the Union troops destroyed the railroad station and burned substantial quantities of Confederate supplies. Perhaps as a result of the large cache of Louisiana rum the Union troops found, they also broke into private homes, stole or destroyed private property, and left a considerable part of the town in flames.[15]

Meanwhile, back at Port Hudson, after 10 days of serving on the Union siege line, in the midnight and early morning darkness of June 11, the 22nd Maine took part in an attack against the Confederate defenses. The purpose and scope of this attack was recorded in General Banks' General Order No. 137 of 7:35 P.M. on June 10, which states that at midnight, "With the view of harassing the enemy, of inducing him to bring forward and expose his artillery, acquiring a knowledge of the ground before the enemy's front, ... Generals Augur and Grover will at once make arrangements to advance a line of skirmishers along their respective fronts, who shall cover themselves and open fire upon the enemy." Further, "The batteries, under the direction of General Arnold, chief of artillery, will take advantage of any opportunity offered to dismount the guns of the enemy, or otherwise annoy him." We may question the wisdom of any advance in darkness over very difficult ground and on short notice, but the intention seems clear: a limited forward movement by skirmishers firing from cover upon the Confederate positions to gain knowledge of their artillery positions and strength. Subsequent orders also make it clear that General Banks' intention for June 11 was "a feigned attack by skirmishers."[16]

However, the regiments under the command of General Godfrey Weitzel received orders of a very different nature — orders which led them to actually attack the Confederate lines in a much more determined manner and which resulted in unnecessary deaths. General Weitzel, a West Point graduate and an engineer, seems to have frequently been assigned to responsibilities greater than his normal brigade command. On the night of June 10 he was apparently given responsibility for three brigades, his own 2nd Brigade, 1st Division; Colonel Joseph Morgan's 1st Brigade, 4th Division, which contained the 22nd Maine; and the 2nd Brigade, 4th Division, which was to be held in reserve. General Weitzel's report on June 11 indicates that he had ordered, and expected, the first two of these brigades to advance to, and if possible, take the Confederate works — expectations very much different from General Banks' orders. One explanation for Weitzel's order is that, in his anger at General Banks for ordering this night action, and with his ongoing dislike for the "political" general, General Weitzel had lost his ability to consider the welfare of his men and to make the best of the orders he was given. Or perhaps General Weitzel simply thought his brigades could indeed breach the Confederate defenses if given the opportunity. Whatever the reason, various units under General Weitzel's command received orders that were clearly at odds with General Banks' General Order No. 137 — the orders that General Weitzel had received that night.[17]

In one regiment of the 2nd Brigade, 1st Division, Lieutenant Colonel Frank Peck of the 12th Connecticut received orders from General Weitzel which only in part reflected those given by General Banks. Colonel Peck states that he sent out 4 companies of skirmishers, as ordered, "with the design of compelling the enemy to disclose the positions of his artillery." Going on, however, Colonel Peck adds, "Orders were also given by the brigade commanders to scale and occupy the works, if possible."[18]

Echoing this statement is Captain John William DeForest, also of the 12th Connecticut. He wrote that after receiving dispatches from their brigade commander (General Weitzel), the 12th's Colonel Peck summoned his company commanders to give orders that were "singular, and to us at the time incomprehensible." The majority of the regiment was to be "formed at midnight behind the parapet, ready to advance at a moment's notice." The companies selected to advance as skirmishers were to be sent forward to "carry the enemy's works, and report their success, upon which they were to be supported by the others." Again, the orders given in this report are not consistent with General Banks' original orders.[19]

In the 22nd Maine's 1st Brigade, 4th Division, also subject to General Weitzel's authority, it appears that similar orders were given. But it also appears that, unlike the brigade that included the 12th Connecticut, this brigade sent out not only skirmishers, but entire regiments. The 22nd Maine's Colonel Jerrard reported that he was ordered by his brigade commander, Colonel Morgan, to advance the regiment "on the works in front of the batteries and if possible, carry them." We do not know whether this order came from General Weitzel, or was Colonel Morgan's interpretation of General Weitzel's instructions, or was Morgan's own. Colonel Jerrard had further been directed "that no order be given above a whisper and that there should be no firing unless opposed by a force outside the works." Colonel Jerrard then writes, "My intention was to charge the works with the bayonet if possible, reserving fire for use after."

The regiment moved forward with Companies A and B and Francis Ireland's Company E as the advanced line of skirmishers. The remainder of the regiment followed a few yards behind in line of battle, but given the terrain, felled trees, and other obstructions, this orderly line proved impossible to maintain. The 22nd Maine approached the enemy's works through a ravine while the 90th New York on its right flank and the 131st New York on its left were more exposed to enemy fire. The attackers were hampered during this 600 yard advance not only by darkness and the fire of the defenders, but by felled timbers that littered already difficult terrain. And, the night's action was made all the more miserable by a sudden rain shower, with a surreal touch added by the accompanying thunder and lightning.[20]

During this action one portion of the 22nd Maine's skirmish line became separated in the darkness and, advancing beyond the rest, briefly drove the Confederates from an artillery piece. Without support, however, they soon retreated. Some of the attackers, including men from the 22nd Maine, found refuge from enemy fire in a ravine at the base of the Confederate fortifications. Unfortunately, this particular ravine also contained rotting animal remains thrown there as refuse by the Rebel garrison's butchers. It was here in this disgusting spot that a Rebel counterattack captured 7 Yankees, including Lieutenant George Anson, of the 22nd's Company B.[21]

Felled trees obstructing the Union attacks at Port Hudson (Massachusetts mollus Collection).

References to the Confederate garrison's refuse pit and accompanying slaughter pen has caused some potential confusion regarding the exact location of the attack by 22nd Maine and the rest of Morgan's brigade. In his report of June 11, the 22nd's Colonel Jerrard refers to members of the regiment crossing a "bayou" and becoming engaged with the Rebels near "the Slaughter house." There is, on the east side of the Confederate defenses, a farm owned by a family named Slaughter, and hence known as "Slaughter's farm"—an area where there was heavy fighting during the attacks of May 27. However, from every other description of the action of June 11, it seems clear that the 22nd Maine attacked at the north side of the Confederate defenses near the Rebel slaughter house and not near the Slaughters' farm. The bayou referred to appears to be Sandy Creek, which runs along the base of the northern line of Confederate defenses.[22]

Sergeant Joseph Joy, of the 22nd Maine's Company A, later wrote to his wife and told of the chaos of that night's attack: "Our brigadier [Colonel Morgan] made a mistake in ordering our colonel to advance to the breastworks, when we should have gone only a short distance in order to draw the enemy's fire. Instead of that, we went under the breastworks ...

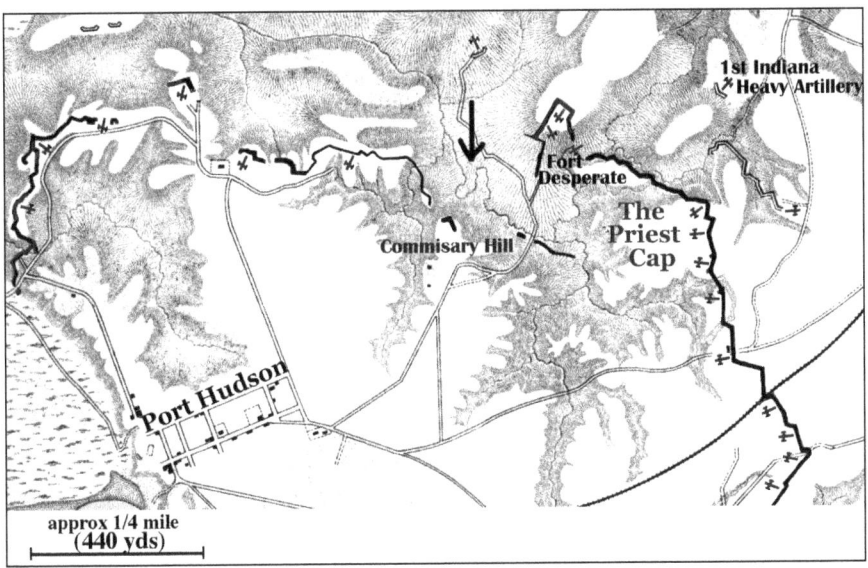

The area of the 22nd Maine's attack in the early morning of June 11, 1863. Adapted from Plate 38-3, *The Official Military Atlas of the Civil War.*

through felled timber, about 300 yards, under heavy fire. Near the breastworks our Captain [Henry Crosby of Hampden, Maine] fell, mortally wounded." Sergeant Joy and other men of the company were unable to get themselves or their dying captain to safety due to their exposed position, so he and 7 others who had been separated from the rest of their company spent the day of June 11 behind a small hill. That night, finally able to withdraw, they used a blanket to carry their captain and struggled back to their own lines. When told by the regiment's surgeon that his wound was mortal, Captain Crosby said, "That is more than I expected. But it is a good cause to die in."23

General Weitzel's report, written on June 11, states:

> The Twenty-second Maine advanced under a heavy fire through the ravine, but owing to the obstructions and heavy fire from the enemy's breastworks, could not maintain their position, and were ordered to fall back, leaving two companies in the ravine, and cannot ascertain their whereabouts as yet. The companies that succeeded in retiring were ordered to support the Ninety-first New York, which was at daylight holding an exposed position within 75 yards of the enemy's breastworks. They have since retired, and are now occupying their old position. ... The Twenty-second Maine reports 6 officers and 53 privates missing."24

As members of the 22nd who had been separated from their comrades made it back to their own lines, the regiment's final casualty count saw 4 killed or mortally wounded during the assault — Captain Crosby and Privates Nathaniel Bailey, Augustus Clewley, and Henry Wilson — and 2 men captured.[25]

Yet, while all of this was going on, another regiment in the 22nd Maine's brigade, and positioned in the same area of the Union line, was inexplicably doing nothing at all, not even standing in reserve. A private

> CO. A. 22. ME. VOLS.
>
> Capt. H. CROSBY, killed at Port Hudson, June 12, 1863.
> Serg. J. E. JOY, killed at Port Hudson, June 23, 1863.
> Corp. J. S. WARD, died at Baton Rouge, La. Mar. 26, 1863.
> Mus'n W. P. WALKER, died at Baton Rouge, Feb. 15, 1863.
> C. B. BAILEY, died at Fortress Monroe, Dec. 15, 1862.
> A. SNOW, died at Fortress Monroe, Dec. 30, 1862.
> E. HUMPHREY, died at Baton Rouge, Jan. 31, 1863.
> A. PORTER, died at Baton Rouge, March 1, 1863.
> S. KNOWLES, died at Baton Rouge, Mar. 12, 1863.
> M. MURCH, died at Baton Rouge, Mar. 11, 1863.
> B. D. TRUEWORTHY, died at Franklin, La. Apr. 27, 1863.
> J. W. KNOWLES, died at Franklin, April 28, 1863.
> J. P. EMERSON, died at Franklin, May 30, 1863.
> Z. COWAN, died at Bellefontaine, O. Aug. 6, 1863.
> Z. GOODELL, Co. D 14 Reg't, died at Hilton Head Sep. 28, 1865.
> W. B. PERKINS, Co. D 30 Reg't, died Sept. 8, 1864.
> — LINCOLN, Co. I 16 Me. died in Andersonville Prison Aug. 6, 1864.
> T. N. RACKLIFF, Co. L 1st Mass. Artillery, died at Fortress Monroe, July 3, 1864.

Monument in Hampden, Maine, honoring Captain Henry Crosby and others of Company A, 22nd Maine (author photograph).

15. On to Port Hudson

in the 1st Louisiana Infantry (Union) recorded in his diary that, on that night of June 10–11, "while the First Louisiana was sleeping, a charge was being made" against the Rebel line "directly in front of our position."[26]

The attack of that night did apparently impress Port Hudson's commander. On the night of June 11, General Gardner sent one of his men, Captain Robert L. Pruyn of the 4th Louisiana (C.S.A.), to ask for help — reinforcements and supplies — from General Joseph E. Johnston. General Gardner had sent men out before to request assistance, but all had been killed or captured. Realizing that it would be nearly impossible to make his way through the Union lines surrounding Port Hudson, Captain Pruyn lashed a number of empty canteens together, and with this aid, swam downriver under cover of darkness. He was spotted by a seaman on one of the Union vessels in the river, but was able to continue, eventually landing on the west bank of the Mississippi some 9 miles below Port Hudson. There, obtaining a boat from Confederate sympathizers, he crossed to the east bank and, after several days' journey, reached General Johnston's headquarters in Jackson, Mississippi. When Captain Pruyn eventually made his way back to Port Hudson, it was only to report that no help was to come. It must have been extremely frustrating but perhaps not surprising to General Gardner that General Johnston, who had wanted Port Hudson abandoned, would not send supplies or men for its defense.[27]

In a later report from April of 1865, General Banks records the June 11 action in very different terms from his original orders of June 10. In this later report he defines the action, not as a limited attack by skirmishers, or as an attempt to gain knowledge of the Confederate artillery, but as an endeavor to move the Union lines forward and "to get within attacking distance of the works." Yet, this revised description of the orders and intentions of the attack still remains at odds with General Weitzel's apparent orders to the brigades under his command that night. To those men who suffered through that assault, arguments about the accuracy of the various versions of their orders, or the intentions of those giving the orders, would be irrelevant. They only knew the grim consequences of the orders they received.[28]

16

Assault on Port Hudson

On June 14 a general assault was planned against the Port Hudson fortifications. The attack was preceded, on June 13, by a bombardment of the Confederate positions from the powerful Union land batteries supported by Union gunboats on the Mississippi. After an hour, a ceasefire was ordered by General Banks and a formal request for surrender was sent to Port Hudson's commander. General Gardner replied, "My duty requires me to defend this position, and therefore I decline to surrender." The bombardment then resumed and continued the rest of that day.[1]

General Banks' overall plan involved attacks toward the northeastern corner of the Confederate lines at the area known as the Priest Cap and simultaneously at the Citadel, a fortification at the extreme south of the Confederate line where that line met the Mississippi. A Priest Cap was a specific type of defensive fortification named for its resemblance to the biretta worn by Catholic priests. The silhouette of a biretta, with its two points, was similar to the shape of a defensive "priest cap" as seen from above — the shape of a capital letter "M." The forward-jutting points of this type of defensive works were designed to force attackers into a crossfire in the spaces between those points.[2]

The attacks at the Priest Cap and Citadel were to be preceded by a diversionary attack on the Confederate lines between these two parts of the Confederate defensive line by 2 brigades of General C.C. Augur's First Division. The Citadel was to be attacked by General Dwight's Second Division. The assaults at the Priest Cap were to be made on both the northern and eastern faces of that Confederate position and were directed by General Grover and General Weitzel, with Grover in overall command of that aspect of the Union attack. The forces attacking the Priest Cap consisted of two divisions: Brigadier General Halbert Paine's 3rd Division, and Grover's 4th Division, now commanded by Colonel Joseph Morgan.

Inside the Priest Cap, showing defensive lines and sharpened stakes (*Review of Reviews*).

They were augmented by General Weitzel's former brigade (2nd Brigade, 1st Division) commanded by Colonel Elisha Smith of the 114th New York. With Colonel Morgan given the responsibility for the 4th Division, Colonel Richard Holcomb of the 1st Louisiana was given command of Colonel Morgan's 1st Brigade, 4th Division, which should have included the 22nd Maine, 1st Louisiana, 90th, 91st, and 131st New York. For the June 14 attack at the Priest Cap, however, the 91st New York was taken from the brigade and placed in the advance line of the attack in order to use hand grenades against the defenders. Hand grenades were, at this time, not in common use by infantry soldiers, but General Banks had requested 500 grenades for this attack from Admiral Farragut. The navy kept a store of hand grenades in readiness on its ships to repel boarders, and it is an indication of this weapon's novelty to infantry troops that Banks also requested a naval officer to instruct his men in the use of the grenades. The most widely used type had fins to guide it to the ground so that, it was hoped, a striking pin at the front of the grenade would hit the surface and set off the explosive charge. These grenades were not particularly reliable or effective when used against infantry, and there are stories of opposing combatants catching grenades and throwing them back at the enemy.[3]

The 22nd Maine's Colonel Jerrard wrote of the preparations for this attack: "Everything being in readiness, Sunday June 14 was appointed for the third and as was believed, the last assault on Port Hudson. Necessary orders were communicated the evening previous and all looked forward to the morning with the highest expectations."

Colonel Jerrard's report is at odds with other reports in some details. He wrote that General Dwight's attack "on the left" was intended as a feint "for the purpose of drawing the enemy from the real point of attack." General Dwight's attack at the Citadel, on the Union's far left, was not, according to other sources, intended as a feint, but the attack by General Auger's 2 brigades, which was to the left (south) of the 22nd Maine at the Priest Cap, but to the right (north) of the Citadel, was the feint. Colonel Jerrard also wrote that the attack in which the 22nd Maine was to participate was carried out by one division — the 4th Division, when in fact the general area around the Priest Cap was attacked, as stated above, by both the 3rd and 4th Divisions. These two divisions were attacking from different directions — from the north and east — however, and so this may explain Colonel Jerrard's statement. In other respects, Colonel Jerrard's report appears clear and accurate, and he continues: "The 1st and 3rd brigades [the 22nd Maine was in the 1st brigade] were held in reserve. At 1 o'clock A.M. the 1st Brigade was in motion, and reached the center where the attack [on the Priest Cap] was to be made at 3½ o'clock and at once took position in rear of the assaulting column."[4]

As we will see later, this position "in reserve" and at the rear of the assaulting column did not last long. According to General Banks' 1865 report of the battle:

> On June 14, a second general assault [he is counting the attacks of May 27 as the first general assault] was made at daylight. A column of a division was posted on the left, under General Dwight, with the intention of getting an entrance to the works [the Citadel] by passing a ravine, while the main attack

16. Assault on Port Hudson

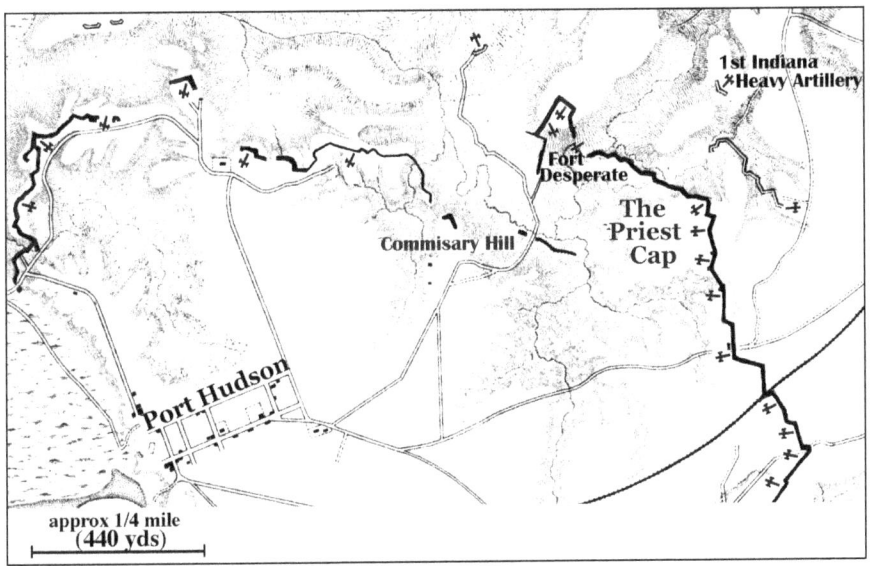

The assault of June 14, 1863; adapted from Plate 38-3, *The Official Military Atlas of the Civil War*. The 22nd Maine attacked as part of Colonel Richard Holcomb's brigade at the north face of the Priest Cap.

on the right [the Priest Cap] was made by the commands of Grover and Weitzel. Neither column was successful in fully gaining its object, but our lines were advanced from a distance of 300 yards to distances of from 50 to 200 yards from the enemy's line of fortifications, where the troops entrenched themselves and commenced the construction of new batteries. ... This day's work was of great importance; but it was now felt that our force was unequal to the task of carrying the works by assault, and the slower, but more certain, operations of the siege were commenced.[5]

In other words, the attacks failed. Among the reasons were the difficult nature of the ground, the strong Confederate defenses, and as on May 27, a lack of coordination in the attacks. At the Priest Cap, where attacks on the northern and eastern face were to be made simultaneously by 2 divisions, the Fourth Division did not attack until an hour after the Third. And at the Union far left, General Dwight, for some reason, waited until 3 hours after the attacks at the Priest Cap to begin his own assault at the Citadel. The diversion by General Augur, although commencing as planned with an artillery barrage at 2:45 A.M., and followed by a feint forward by his skirmishers, apparently did nothing to affect the outcome.[6]

On June 25, Francis Ireland wrote home with his record of these events. For some reason, Francis had not written home for a month, did not write about the events of June 11, and waited about 10 days before writing of "the awful Battle of June 14." Before going into more detail about the specifics of that battle and its aftermath, here is his account :

Dear Father

I wrote to you last at Algiers May 26 and as I have rec'd several letters since then, I will write a bit. ... I am as well as can be altho somewhat worn out with the labors of this siege here. We have been under fire or within rifle shots reach of the enemy works! How much longer we shall stay I cannot tell, but hope that those of us that live will start for home within the next month! I dare not guess when that day will be! I write just to let you know that I am alive but the next minute I may be shot by the stray bullets of the reb sharpshooters from the fort. They are continuously whistling thro the woods here. Of our position, the enemy works, our various skirmishes, and the awful Battle of June 14 I could write had I time and paper. Let it suffice that I have come as near being shot as it generally falls to the lot of men in battle and am not scarred yet. You probably have ere this heard of the loss in our Co. Sergts. Knight and Allen. The later was a near friend of mine. He was instantly killed by a ball thro the head as we were charging the enemy works. He was side of me when he fell and we were speaking together 3 minutes before! Sergt. Knight I saw a short time before he was wounded. The slaughter was awful that day and I must say from causes that were needless ones, for instance drunken officers. But our Reg't is clear of any such charge as that. There were reg'ts whose commanders could hardly stand they were so intoxicated & will such things never end. Hundreds of lives in charge of men that don't know one thing from another hardly, but such things have been and will be till the war ends, I suppose! But enough of this. Another subject that has interested our reg't since the battle. Our brigade lost its acting commander at the first charge. It then fell upon our Col. Jerrard to command. He led us to a ravine near the fort where we remained till he got orders from Gen. Grover to charge and take the works at all hazards, they must be taken! One brigade had gone in with a few men in the morning a few getting inside the works but were all killed or taken prisoners! The rest were laying near the works and every time one lifted his head he was shot sure! Our Col. examined the position and commenced to file his brigade into position to charge, but they were shot so fast that he called them into their old position contrary to the wishes of their drunken colonel, but agreeable to the good judgment of all sober officers, and he told one of the Gens. aides de camp that he could not put his force in without more support for the first brigade would certainly be cut all to pieces, and the 2nd not much better and then we should be at the mercy of the enemy! and that knowing the inevitable result as he did "he considered it folly to put men in there and would not and he would give up his sword and command before doing it." etc. He had hardly made this decision when orders came not to advance! So you see that had he gone in as ordered first, he would have lost

The "rat trap" at the northern side of the Priest Cap. These defenses included two bamboo bridges which were intended to collapse under attackers and drop them onto sharpened stakes below. Sketch by Erastus Palmer, 22nd Maine (Simon G. Jerrard Papers, Mss. 1180, 1266, 1285, Louisiana and Lower Mississippi Valley Collections, LSU Libraries, Baton Rouge, La).

many men and not gained anything at all! We left the field after dark and came back to our old camp leaving the field in the possession of our forces it being of but little account as long as we did not get inside of the works. Col. was arrested then, tried, and dishonorably discharged from the army for using discouraging and seditious language in the presence of his men and to the general's aide in front of the enemy's works June 14. He was a brave and good Col., a better one never drew a sword, and the reg't all consider him innocent — and that he did his duty — as he does himself. Also the most of the brigade think so and 2 of the reg'ts refused to read the general order (expelling him from the army) last night.

The reg't will return to Maine and prove to those at home that he is innocent and that he did what any sober man would have done in the same place, but outside influence of miserable and envious officers ruled the day. I could write a dozen sheets and then be but just begun but this must suffice. I hope we shall be in Bangor by July 18, but it looks very dubious to me at present. But then we may start tomorrow — time will only tell. We have seen and heard enough of war this past month to need a little rest, and hope for it soon. It would be useless for me to attempt to describe this place, but it is a Hard one I tell you and ought to have been taken long ere this but it is not! Had it been we should have probably been on our [way] home now. Never mind, only 15 days to the 10th of July! and no man took an oath to serve beyond that at any rate. But we keep up good courage and shall as long as we are used fair. But I must be closing. This is a poor letter on old poor paper but you can make it out I guess. I will write again if I can before we leave. I hope Mother will be smart as ever soon, for I intend to run around visiting etc. some after I get home to make up lost time! I should be glad to see you at Bangor if convenient when I get there or after if we have to remain there any time.

No more now. Love to mother and all the rest. I hope to see you all soon.

From your son,
Francis A. Ireland[7]

It was Colonel Morgan, in command of Grover's Division, who made the complaint that led to Colonel Jerrard's dismissal from the service. In his report of the day's attacks, Colonel Morgan states that after Colonel Holcomb was killed attempting to advance his brigade, command of the First Brigade was given to Colonel Jerrard. The brigade was then ordered to charge the enemy's works, but Colonel Jerrard refused to obey. Morgan then sent one of his aides, Lieutenant Mayne of the 1st Louisiana, to repeat the order to charge. At this point, according to Colonel Morgan, Colonel Jerrard replied, "Tell Colonel Morgan that I have tried to get my men in position and cannot get but a few of them where they can charge the enemy's works, and if he can get anybody to take command of the brigade to lead the charge he can, for I shall not."[8]

According to another source, Sgt. Charles Wing of the 22nd Maine, Colonel Jerrard had initially led his men forward as ordered by Colonel Holcomb, waving his sword in the air and shouting "Come on my brave boys, follow me!" When the first phase of the assault began to slow and falter, Col. Jerrard is credited by Captain Henry Wood with encouraging the troops forward, stepping to the front of his regiment and shouting, "Men of the 22nd follow me to the enemy's works." It was during this further advance by the First and Third Brigades that Colonel Holcomb was killed, and confronted with strong enemy fire and difficult terrain, the attack came to a halt as men took whatever cover they could find. Having found shelter with others in a ravine which gave some protection from the enemy's fire, Colonel Jerrard received the order to attack once again. At this point one report (other than those already quoted above) has Colonel Jerrard stating, "If General Banks wants to go in there, let him go in and be damned. I won't slaughter my men that way." At this point, Captain Wood quotes Colonel Jerrard as saying that if any other officer would take the responsibility to order the men to advance he [Jerrard] would support with his life if need be. Attempts were then made to move the Union attack forward by gathering volunteers for a storming party to make one more attack against the Rebel works, but Captain Wood states, "Not a man responded to the call." When this was reported to headquarters, the order for further attacks was countermanded.[9]

An officer whose regiment was in another brigade was also able to report on Colonel Jerrard's actions. Captain DeForest of the 12th Connecticut had been in the 2nd Brigade, 1st Division, and had attacked in advance of the 22nd Maine. After that attack had stalled, Captain DeForest found himself and the remnant of his regiment among those placed under Colonel Jerrard's command. Agreeing that Colonel Jerrard pulled together what force he could, Captain DeForest quotes Jerrard as saying to one of General Grover's aides, "Now go back to General Grover. Tell him that I have formed the column, and that, if he wants it to charge, he may come and lead it. I for my part am not going to take it into that slaughter pen." Captain DeForest then goes on, "This defiance cost him his commission, and of course properly, for while he was correct in judging that an assault would fail, he had no right to utter flat disobedience and send taunting messages to superiors." At the time he made the decision not to charge the Confederate works, Colonel Jerrard is described by Captain DeForest as "worried and indignant in expression, but not scared."[10]

In Colonel Jerrard's own report of the events to Maine's Adjutant General, John Hodsdon, he states that after others had hesitated, he and the 22nd Maine advanced to a ravine near the enemy works, but seeing that no other troops from his brigade were supporting this attack, halted there to await orders. At this point, Colonel Jerrard says that he was informed of Colonel Holcomb's death, told to take command of the brigade, and take the enemy's works immediately. When Colonel Jerrard reported that he did not have his whole brigade assembled, he was ordered to attack with whatever troops he had and from whatever point they were found. After discovering that the 90th New York was not in a position to attack and had been "badly cut up by a cross fire," Colonel Jerrard ordered them to withdraw from their current position and move to join him for the assault, but this order was countermanded by Colonel Morgan. The

1st Louisiana, again according to Colonel Jerrard's report, was also unable to join with the 22nd Maine for the attack. With a part of his own regiment and men from the 131st New York, Colonel Jerrard estimated that he had only 245 men available to make the ordered attack. After relaying this information to Colonel Morgan, Colonel Jerrard states that he was told "to charge the works if I should lose every man." After advancing some distance up the ravine, the men of the 131st New York reportedly refused to continue, and faced with this fact, Colonel Jerrard felt it would be a "fruitless sacrifice" to take only his own regiment forward and reported this to Colonel Morgan. Shortly after that, Colonel Jerrard states that he received an order from General Grover countermanding the order to charge.

Colonel Jerrard then states that he was placed under arrest, was not told the charges, and was denied a court-martial. And although he was told that he would soon be released and returned to his command, he received an order on July 22 dismissing him from the service. His offense is listed as "using discouraging and insubordinate language in the presence of a number of officers and enlisted men while forming the brigade for the charge." Colonel Jerrard declares that the nature of the offense was "wholly false, and had [I] been granted an opportunity I would have proved it so."[11]

In his original letter to Maine's adjutant general, on which the above report was based, Colonel Jerrard had stated that Colonel Morgan's order to attack "was more the result of an overdraught of whiskey than of any just conception of his duties or responsibilities." And Colonel Jerrard also wrote,

> Col. Morgan lay under a log during nearly the whole battle. Had he been sober and capable of executing even the most simple combination, the result, with me at least, would have been different.
>
> I will only add that during a more recent engagement he was carried from the field on a stretcher (as was believed) dead drunk. He was placed in arrest, charged with "drunkenness and cowardice on the battle field" and soon after tried by court-martial and dishonorably dismissed [from] the service. This decision was not however approved by the gen. commanding [General Banks] in consequence of some informality in the proceedings of the court.[12]

These comments about Colonel Morgan's drinking were not included in the final version of Colonel Jerrard's report published in the Maine adjutant general's report. However, several letters from officers in support of Colonel Jerrard are included in that published report. In a later letter to the adjutant general, Colonel Jerrard wrote:

16. Assault on Port Hudson 175

In regard to the omissions made by you in publishing my manuscript report of 1863, allow me to say they were entirely approved by me. I was aware at the time that it would require more space than could probably be afforded to it. That part which related to Col. Morgan's drunkenness on the field during the battle of June 14 and his subsequent arrest and trial I very naturally desired to place before the public as is furnished a key to my unfortunate position during that battle. Its many objectionable features doubtless excluded it. I am under obligation to you for the liberal space granted me in your report. The publication of letters from the regimental commanders of the 1st Brigade gave me great satisfaction."[13]

These letters in support of Colonel Jerrard and his conduct on June 14 were written by officers of the 1st Louisiana, 131st New York, and Colonel Morgan's own 90th New York. Company E's Captain Wood, writing on behalf of the officers of the 22nd Maine, records a resolution passed unanimously by those officers. In part this resolution states that their colonel was "unjustly under arrest" and gives their "unqualified approval of his conduct" during the June 14 assault, and "on all previous occasions." The 22nd Maine's Chaplain, John K. Lincoln, confirmed Francis Ireland's report that two of the regiments in the brigade refused to hear the order for Colonel Jerrard's dismissal read, although all regiments were required to do so. Chaplain Lincoln describes Colonel Jerrard as "he who stood first in rank, and first in all that was true and noble" and adds, "I trust, for the vindication of at least one true man, that a faithful history of that day's proceedings may yet be written. ... I believe that such a history would vindicate one whose reputation and honor is very dear to all the members of the 22d Maine. I refer to Colonel Jerrard."[14]

Although not providing direct evidence regarding Colonel Morgan's condition during the attacks of June 14, Morgan's conduct was, in fact, called into question a month later and a court-martial was ordered, and its outcome was as Colonel Jerrard described in his letter to Maine's adjutant general. At that time, General Grover wrote a report to Assistant Adjutant General Lt. Col. Richard Irwin about a failed attack at Donaldsonville, Louisiana, and stated, "Colonel Morgan behaved badly, and I shall cause an investigation into his conduct." And in a second report, General Grover wrote, "The reverse of yesterday was entirely due to the disobedience of orders, drunkenness, and misbehavior before the enemy of Colonel Morgan, commanding brigade. I wish that he may have a speedy trial by court-martial."[15]

On September 10, a court-martial reported Colonel Morgan guilty of "misbehavior before the enemy" and "drunkenness on duty" in the face of the enemy, and ordered that Colonel Morgan be "cashiered, and utterly disqualified from holding office or employment under the government of the United States." However, Major General Banks overruled the court-martial's guilty verdict and suspended the sentence. On October 26 Colonel Morgan was released and returned to duty.[16]

All of that, however, took place well after the attacks of June 14. With the failure of those attacks, General Banks' forces continued the siege of Port Hudson. And with Colonel Jerrard's dismissal from the service, the 22nd Maine was led by their second in command, Lieutenant Colonel Olonzo Putnam of Dover, Maine. In his own brief report of the events after he was placed in command, Colonel Putnam merely states that he was ordered to form his men in line of battle and later to move the regiment to a ravine where they remained until night. The regiment was then ordered to retire back to their encampment.[17]

As a final thought on Colonel Jerrard's actions on June 14, we may consider a comparison with Maine's best known Civil War general, Joshua Chamberlain. During the attacks on Petersburg at the end of Grant's Overland Campaign in the spring of 1864, Chamberlain was faced with a similar difficult decision. In command of a brigade, Chamberlain was ordered to attack a heavily defended Confederate stronghold at Rives Salient. This was the only time Chamberlain was known to question orders, and he later stated that he expected to be dismissed from the service for doing so. Upon receiving the orders to attack, he sent a message to his superiors saying that he faced heavily entrenched infantry and artillery and he assumed that his commanders were not aware of the situation. One brigade, he realized, would have no chance against the defenses he saw before him and on his flank. He received orders in reply repeating his instructions to attack and assuring him or additional support in the form of other brigades. Still feeling that it was a very bad idea, he proceeded to make the attack as ordered, even though the promised support did not materialize. In the process of the attack he was badly wounded and only barely survived; many men in his brigade were killed or wounded, and the attack failed, as he had predicted. And so, who made the right decision? Or is there a "right" decision at such a time?[18]

Chamberlain went on to be a brigadier and major general of volunteers, governor of Maine and president of Maine's Bowdoin College, was awarded the Medal of Honor, and is regarded as a hero. And rightly so — he did his duty and did it extremely well. He was a brave man, a natural leader, and he enjoyed the support and high regard of the men who served under him. He was also well respected by his superiors — recommended for the regular army by General Gouvenour K. Warren and was good friends with 5th Corps commander, General Charles Griffin. When General Grant looked for an officer to accept the surrender of the Confederate Infantry at Appomattox, he chose Chamberlain, although many officers outranked him. Colonel Jerrard, on the other hand, did not make the attack he was ordered to make and his decision no doubt saved many lives that would have been uselessly lost.[19]

17

The Fall of Port Hudson, Up the Mississippi and Home

On June 15, the following exchange of letters took place between General Banks and Port Hudson's commander, General Frank Gardner. The notes reflect what may seem an odd gentlemanly propriety between men whose overall intentions were the killing of each other's soldiers.

Sir: I have the honor to request your permission to send a small quantity of medical and hospital supplies within your works for the comfort of my wounded in your hands and of such of your own as you may desire to use them for.

Very respectfully, your most obedient servant,
N. P. Banks

General Gardner answered:

Sir: In reply to your note of this date, I have the honor to state that I will send out to meet any party you may wish to send in with such medicines and hospital supplies as you may desire to send for your wounded in my possession.
I take the liberty to inform you that you are probably ignorant of the fact that there are a few of your dead and wounded in the vicinity of my breastworks, and I have attempted to give succor to your wounded, but your sharpshooters have prevented it.

I am, sir, very respectfully, your obedient servant,
Frank Gardner[1]

On June 14, General Banks had failed to rally men for a storming party after the failed assault on Port Hudson's defenses. On June 15, General Banks sent another, and more persuasive, call for volunteers to form a storming party of a thousand men to once again attempt an entry into the Rebel stronghold. General Banks' appeal to patriotic sentiment, coupled with the promise of promotion and medals may be seen as a masterpiece of wordcraft.

17. The Fall of Port Hudson, Up the Mississippi and Home

The commanding general congratulates the troops before Port Hudson upon the steady advance made upon the enemy's works, and is confident of an immediate and triumphant issue of the contest. We are at all points upon the threshold of his fortifications. One more advance and they are ours!

For the last duty that victory imposes, the commanding general summons the bold men of the corps to the organization of a storming column of 1,000 men, to vindicate the flag of the Union and the memory of its defenders who have fallen! Let them come forward!

Officers who lead the column of victory in this last assault may be assured of the just recognition of their service by promotion, and every officer and soldier who shares its perils and its glory shall receive a medal fit to commemorate the first grand success of the campaign of 1863 for the freedom of the Mississippi. His name shall be placed in general orders upon the Roll of Honor.[2]

These words had the desired effect, and although their time of enlistment was almost over, eight men of the 22nd Maine — including Company E's Captain Henry Wood and Company H's Captain Isaac Case — volunteered for this assault. The others were Lieut. George Brown, Company A; Sgt. Samuel Mason, Company F; Private Van Buren Carle, Company B; Private Daniel McPhetres, Company B; Private Timothy Erwin, Company G; and Private Amaziah Webb, Company K. The east face of the Priest Cap was seen as offering the best chance for this attack and in preparation, sappers dug to the edge of the Confederate defenses, and a mine was prepared to destroy a portion of the fortifications. However, none of these measures were needed, for no further attack was made. The planned assault was delayed when the Confederates blew up a portion of the Union tunnel, and a further delay resulted from heavy rain. Then, after the fall of Vicksburg on July 6, the Port Hudson garrison, with no prospect of support or resupply, surrendered on July 8, and the Union forces entered to occupy the fortifications on July 9.[3]

The cost in casualties had been high for the Union, for during their time at Port Hudson their losses approached 5,000 killed, wounded, or missing. The Confederate killed or wounded amounted to less than 700. Some statistics of this battle list approximately 7,000 Confederate casualties by counting those who surrendered as captured, and counting them with those killed, wounded, or died of disease. This is unsupportable, however, since roughly 6,000 of those who surrendered were almost immediately paroled on condition they no longer fight against the Union. The parole was promptly declared invalid by the Confederate government and most all of those Rebel "casualties" from Port Hudson were once again in the Confederate Army. Even Port Hudson's commander, General Gardner, was exchanged in August of 1864 and returned to the Confederate Army. Gardner spent the last months of the Civil War in Mississippi, serving under General Richard Taylor until the surrender of that Confederate department in early May 1865.[4]

Back in Dexter, the fall of Vicksburg and the Army of the Potomac's July 4 victory at Gettysburg were celebrated with a jubilee. That ringing of bells and the firing of cannon was also intended to "plague the Copperheads," according to one participant. In much of Maine, and in the nation as a whole, and in history books since then, Vicksburg and Gettysburg far overshadowed the attacks, siege, and surrender of Port Hudson. We are left to wonder how the battle for Port Hudson would be remembered if that Confederate fortress had surrendered or been captured before the fall of Vicksburg. For the families of the 22nd Maine's soldiers, the surrender of Port Hudson meant that their men would be coming home.[5]

Charlie Farrar's letter of July 14 gives his account of the regiment's activities before and after the capture of Port Hudson.

> We have got Port Hudson at last, after having a hard time lying in the woods & being on guard one third or one half of the time. Our posts were in rifle pits where we acted as sharp shooters. Port Hudson is a pretty strong place I will not try to pen the particulars of the fight. ... We are now guarding rebel prisons but they are taking them away very fast, paroling them and sending them off. We shall start for home in a few days as soon as we can get our baggage together. We expect to go home up the river if so we shall see some of the great west. Frank [Ireland] is well. There is so much to tell you that it is no use to try to write eny thing it will all be new to you when I get home.[6]

Francis Ireland's last wartime letter to his parents was written on July 23 from inside Port Hudson's lines. Even using their muster date of October 10 as the start of their service, the regiment had been in U.S. service for longer than their 9 month term (July 10 would have been 9 months from October 10.). But now their journey home could take advantage of the Union-controlled Mississippi River.

> Dear Father;
>
> If all things were as they should be, I could talk with you instead of writing this morning. But here we are, and are likely to be for several days at least, delayed on account of the reg't business not being closed up. There is but one 9 month reg't ready to leave (52 Mass.) and that is waiting for a steamer. I am contented to stay because that is the only way I can do, altho I would like to be at home during berrying season and in the time of green beans, peas, etc., but one thing that we have got to comfort us, we probably shall go up river when we do go.

I am glad we were kept here to see the surrender of this place and to share in the glory after so hard work and hard fighting, but now that is over I want to get North where it is a little cooler and more healthy. As for me, my health is tip top as ever and the hotter it gets the healthier I feel, altho it makes one sweat some. The tendency is to be sickly generally, however at this time.

The boys are very uneasy about going home as we are serving on the 11th month! and we were to serve but 9! As for me I have filled all the obligations I ever came under by oath or otherwise to the U.S. and have been lucky enough to live and enjoy good health thru hard fights and all. Have seen a great deal of the world and expect to see some more before I get home. Have learned something, I hope, for I have not kept my eyes and ears shut all this time. Now, I with all the rest wish to get home and have a rest free from the sound of the bugle and drum. We are resting from the noise of over 40 days of cannonading now, and it is quite a relief I tell you. Our reg't is doing garrison duty in the fort here, but our Co. is down here doing provost guard duty.

By the way, tell Harvey I have got a piece of rock salt from the celebrated mines, near New Iberia and shall bring it home for him. It is just like most any rock salt, but the curiosity is that such an immense quantity should be so clear and pure, solid as any ledge at home.

Charley is pretty well, he wrote a few days ago, I must be closing.

So good bye till I see you,
Frank

It will be useless to write when we leave as a letter would be several days later than we should. We shall pass by where Otis is [Francis' cousin, Otis Day was in Helena, Arkansas]. I wish he knew it — he might see us pass if nothing more.

FAI[7]

It appears that men in other 9 month regiments were even more impatient with delays in returning them to civilian life. In General Banks' 1865 report, he states, "During these operations [after June 14] the nine-months men, whose terms had expired or were about to expire, were dissatisfied with their situation, and unwilling to enter upon duty involving danger. Great embarrassment and trouble was caused by the conduct of some of these troops, one regiment, the 4th Massachusetts, being in open mutiny."[8]

During the weeks after Port Hudson's July 8 surrender, the Union forces were still clearly in enemy territory and still subject to enemy fire. Sergeant Joseph Joy, the young man in Company A who had written to his wife describing the attack of June 11, was the last of the regiment to die from enemy action. He was shot on July 20 while on picket duty at Port Hudson and died on the 23rd. Also among the last to die before the 22nd Maine headed for home was Captain Isaac W. Case — the young man who had volunteered for the "Forlorn Hope" storming party and whose father, Dr. Isaac Case, had written to Maine's governor expressing concern about the regiment's length of service and the health of its men.⁹

Of Captain Case, Colonel Jerrard wrote:

> Captain Isaac W. Case of Company H died of congestive chills after a few hours' illness. He died at the encampment of the storming party, having volunteered to lead a company of "stormers" and if necessary to seal the devotion to his country's cause with his life in a final attempt to take Port Hudson. No soldier more brave or patriot more true has yielded his life in this unfortunate struggle. He died as he had lived, a devoted Christian. His body was embalmed and sent to his friends in Kenduskeag, where it was buried with appropriate military honors.¹⁰

For the rest, Charlie Farrar's sentiment is no doubt typical. "I am out of it with a whole hide and will soon be with you in old Maine."¹¹

The 22nd Maine started for home on July 24, traveling up the Mississippi to Cairo, Illinois. The men of the regiment must have felt some satisfaction in being able to travel that waterway at last. From Cairo they had a lengthy trip by rail to Portland, Maine, arriving on August 5. Sailing from Portland by the steamer *Daniel Webster*, the regiment arrived in Bangor on the 6th of August. They were escorted to their original campground at Camp Pope by a company of cavalry, 2 companies of the State Guard, the Bangor Cornet Band, and the Corinth Cornet Band. There "a bountiful collation was served to the almost famished boys of the 22nd, who had not had a morsel to eat, save what their haversacks furnished, since leaving Boston at noon the day before." They were mustered out of U.S. service on August 14, just over 10 months from their muster-in date, and 11 months from their assembly in Bangor.¹²

Their service, and the battles at Irish Bend and Port Hudson, are not typically seen as major events of the Civil War. Irish Bend is scarcely mentioned in general histories and Port Hudson is often merely a side issue to Vicksburg. Today a national park does commemorate the struggle at Port Hudson where, to continue with General Chamberlain's speech quoted at the start of this work, we can hope that "reverent men and women from afar, and generations that know us not and that we know not of, heart-drawn to see where and by whom great things were suffered and done for them, shall come to this deathless field, to ponder and dream."¹³

At this point, one rather gets the image of actors leaving the stage, the story of the 22nd Maine Volunteers ended. But even for the 9 men killed or died of wounds, and the 160 who died of disease or accident,

17. The Fall of Port Hudson, Up the Mississippi and Home

their lives may have ended, but their stories remained in the memories of family and friends. And for the men who had survived, their stories went on.[14]

For some, their service continued as they re-enlisted in other regiments. Ten or so men were discharged from the regiment before the 22nd left Louisiana in order that they could re-enlist then and there.

As a group in future years, the regiment held reunions and the tales of their time in uniform were told and retold. As individuals, many simply picked up their lives from where they had been when they enlisted, while others had to endure the aftereffects of disease or wounds from their time in the service.

John Lincoln, the 22nd Maine's chaplain, fell from his horse just a week before the regiment headed home. Suffering serious brain damage, he found that he was unable to read words of more than 3 or 4 letters and could not continue as a minister. However, he did lead a Sunday School class, started a weekly religious service at the Penobscot County Jail in Bangor, and apparently was able to continue for a time in his original occupation as dentist. He died May 20, 1887.[15]

Simon Jerrard, the 22nd's commander, was cleared of any misconduct, at least as far as the Maine adjutant general's office was concerned, and was restored to his rank as colonel. He also remained in the good graces of the residents of his home town, continuing after the war to serve for many terms as one of Levant's Selectmen. In 1877 he was elected sheriff of Penobscot County and served for one year during which disputes over the enforcement of prohibition laws made that job quite difficult. He then became well known as a breeder of Jersey cattle and remained in his rural home town as a farmer. He died there in February of 1909 at age 80.[16]

Henry Wood, Company E's Captain, was mustered out with the rest of the regiment, and later re-enlisted, in March of 1865, in the Battalion 12th Maine. The original 12th Maine had served along with the 22nd at Irish Bend and Port Hudson. When the regiment's term of service expired in December of 1864, many of its soldiers were reorganized into the new battalion and served until mustered out in April of 1866. Captain Wood served with that regiment as commander of Company H and, at the end of the war, spent several months on reconstruction duty in Georgia. When he returned to Dexter he became postmaster. He died in Dexter in 1889.[17]

Charlie Farrar also came home to Dexter and he married Mary Leighton in 1869. Charlie was active in the local chapter of the Grand Army of the Republic (GAR), and served as one of the local officers. He

Frank Ireland (standing, left) with brothers Eben and Olin and sister Flora. John P. Ireland is seated (Dexter Historical Society).

died in September 1913 and is buried at Mt. Pleasant Cemetery in Dexter.[18]

Francis Ireland's mother, Martha, died in 1870, and his father, John, apparently went to live with Frank's sister Flora and her husband, Simon Shorey, in New Hampshire. John Ireland died in 1904.[19]

Frank Ireland came home to Dexter and returned to work in the woolen mill. He married Annie Morgan in 1866 and their daughter, Grace, was born the next year. He remained active in the Methodist Church and was a member of the GAR. Annie died in 1883, and in 1885 Frank married Ellen Russell and moved to Pittsfield, Massachusetts. There he worked in Pomeroy's woolen mill, becoming a foreman in 1892. He was later appointed messenger for Berkshire County, Massachusetts, to the general court at the State House in Boston, a position he held for 23 years. After suffering a stroke, he died in 1928 at age 85. He is buried in Dexter, just a few yards from his friend Charlie Farrar.[20]

Appendix A
Raising the Regiments

At the start of the Civil War, and to some extent throughout the war, the process of raising regiments to serve in the Union Army was, at times, difficult, frustrating, chaotic, amusing, and tinged with cronyism and political favoritism. The United States was obviously faced with a crisis, and found itself ill prepared to cope with that crisis. Within the various states, the responsibility to raise troops to meet the military needs of the country fell on men who, to varying degrees, showed their competence, resourcefulness, and preparedness, or the lack of those same qualities. In spite of a wide range of problems, the states did raise the needed men, and the way in which that was done provides an interesting story.

The Maine adjutant general's report for 1861 begins as follows:

> The bombardment of Fort Sumter at Charleston, on the twelfth of April last, by those who should have been its defenders, found Maine as little prepared to furnish troops for maintaining the integrity of the Union as it is possible to conceive. With an enrolled but unarmed militia of some sixty thousand men, no more than twelve hundred, and these merely paper organizations, were in a condition to respond to calls for ordinary duty within the State ... while their uniforms, equipments and camp equipage were of a character totally unfitted for service in the field.

It goes on to state that Maine's legislature

> determined upon furnishing the government, at the earliest possible moment, with ten regiments, fully armed and equipped to serve under a two year's enlistment. In order to facilitate recruiting, and to requite, in some measure, the sacrifices of the soldier, a bounty of two months' pay was appropriated to each non-commissioned officer, musician and private, residents of this State, who should thus enlist and be mustered into the service of the United States.[1]

And while this act of the legislature called for men to serve for two years, "unless sooner discharged," the First Maine infantry, with many in Maine and the nation anticipating an early settlement of the conflict, was mustered into U.S. service for just 3 months of military duty on May 3, 1861. Throughout the war regiments tended to be raised in specific regions of the state, with companies raised from specific towns and cities, or small groups of neighboring towns. This is reflected in the designations of the companies of the 1st Maine, which were named for cities and towns in southern Maine.

Company A: Portland Light Infantry
Company B: Portland Mechanic Blues
Company C: Portland Light Guards
Company D: Portland Rifle Corps
Company E: Portland Rifle Guards
Company F: Lewiston Light Infantry
Company G: Norway [Maine] Light Infantry
Company H: Auburn Artillery
Company I: Portland Rifle Guards
Company K: Lewiston Zouaves[2]

When the Second Maine was then mustered into U.S. service for three years, this change from Maine's 2 year term of enlistment was caused by orders from the U.S. War Department requiring states to have their volunteers mustered into U.S. service for three years. This extended length of service caused that regiment's men to have a number of serious conflicts with the state and federal government, including two mutinies. Their term of service was eventually changed to conform to the two years stated in the Maine Legislature's act, but that two years only applied to the men who were mustered on the date of the regiment's official entry into U.S. service—May 28, 1861. Men who were mustered a day or a week or a month later found themselves under a three year obligation. This, according to many of these men, was not made clear at the time of their muster, and brought on the mutiny of 1863, when the men mustered after May 28 found they were not to be mustered out along with the rest of their regiment when its two years term expired. These men, now refusing to continue to fight for the Union, were transferred as a body to the 20th Maine, the only other Maine regiment in the Fifth Corps. Eventually, all but a handful agreed to serve out their additional year with the 20th Maine.[3] For the remaining 8 Maine regiments of that original 10, the term of U.S. service was clearly stated as three years.

There was a certain level of naive romance in the formation of these early regiments. As stated above, most expected a rapid conclusion to the rebellion of the Confederate States, and some appeared to feel that a show of force might settle the issue without the need for battle. But if battle were required, a quick and decisive Union victory, with a substantial amount of glory to the victors, would certainly be all that was required.

The second Maine, as an example, was made up of companies with colorful names such as the Bangor Tigers (Company G) and the Gymnasium Company (Company H). This latter was made up largely of men who had met and been recruited and organized at a Bangor gymnasium, while the former is reported by one writer to derive from the name of a Bangor firefighting company, while others maintain it was taken from the name given to the men who drove logs down Maine's Penobscot River to Bangor — in either case a statement of purest bravado.

The names of the other companies in the Second Maine again reflect the very regional nature of the companies within a regiment, with names taken from the towns of south central Maine, where the regiment was raised:

Company A: Bangor Light Infantry
Company B: Castine Light Infantry
Company C: Brewer Artillery
Company D: Milo Artillery
Company E: Bangor Company
Company F: Bangor Company
Company K: Old Town Company

Company I was made up of members of Bangor's large community of Irish immigrants and was known as the Grattan Guard. This name is assumed to derive from Henry Grattan, a member of the Irish House of Commons and a proponent of home rule for Northern Ireland.[4]

In a similar fashion, the 1st, 3rd, 4th, 5th, and 6th Maine had their companies named for the towns where they were raised. With the 7th Maine, this practice was discontinued, and companies, although still retaining a local character from the area where they were recruited, were simply known by a letter designation.[5]

Calls for additional troops by the U.S. government added 5 more regiments from Maine to the state's total, and by the end of 1861 Maine had mustered 15 infantry regiments into U.S. service. In addition to these infantry regiments, by the end of 1861 Maine had also raised a company of sharpshooters, one cavalry regiment, and 5 batteries of light artillery.[6]

During the time that these first regiments were being raised, some of the practical aspects of getting the men to a rendezvous for mustering had yet to be worked out. This letter to Maine Adjutant General John Hodsdon, from a gentleman in Northern Maine's Aroostook County, demonstrates some of the very pragmatic details that were not yet resolved.

Houlton Nov. 18, 1861

Sir: There is at this time nearly 500 men for the 15th Regiment about ready to start for Augusta. If we take the men by stage and subsist them at taverns it will cost in addition to stage fare 87½ cts per day. The time we shall be on the road if traveled by stage to Bangor will be as follows, to wit

From Fort Kent to Bangor 5 days
" Ashland to do 4 days
" Presque isle to do 3 days
" Houlton to do 2 days

If we transfer the men by special teams and substitute them as directed by you it will take about double the time that will be required to go by stage and the men must of necessity stop at taverns over night as we have no conveniences for camping out.

Considering the distance we have to travel and the inconvenience in subsisting the men by cooked rations for so long a time and at this season of the year, cannot we be permitted to subsist the men at the taverns on the route as has been done by all the troops that have gone from this section?

Our men are ready & willing to go into camp and take soldiers' fare when the government can provide for them so as to make them comfortable. And they do not object to commencing at the start if there is not help for the inconvenience they must undergo by so doing.

If the army regulations will not permit us to pay 25 cts. per meal for subsisting recruits can't we get at it in some way to contract for transportation and subsistence at the usual stage fare and 87½ cents additional for every 24 hours?

If the United States will pay as above please say so on the wires and write full particulars.

Very Respectfully, Your Ob't Serv't, E. C. Blake[7]

And so, even at the end of the first year of the Civil War, there were still matters of importance to be determined for the raising of Maine's regiments.

In July of 1862, with all thoughts of a quick Union victory a thing of the past, the State of Maine was required to do its part in a call for 300,000 troops to serve for 3 years. Before this call, the 16th Maine was already authorized, and in response to this call, the 17th, 18th, 19th, and 20th Maine were raised. As a part of this process, quotas had been established for Maine's towns based on population, to provide a specific number of recruits to fight for the Union.[8]

As a part of this effort to recruit more troops, Maine offered a bounty of $45 for men who would enlist in new regiments, or $55 for those who would enlist in regiments already in the field. There were good reasons for a higher bounty for those enlisting in existing regiments. First, most men wished to serve with their friends and neighbors — men whom they knew and, it was hoped, could trust in a difficult situation. Second, the chance for rank higher than a private would be greater in a new regiment than in a veteran one where the more or less automatic promotion of corporals to fill sergeant positions and sergeants to lieutenant rank was already established.[9]

The desire by recruits to join new regiments as a group is seen in this August 4, 1862, letter to Governor Washburn:

> You know best, but it seems to me that another reg't had better be organized, for this reason vis. because so many soldiers now stand enlisted with an understanding and promise of going into the new reg'ts. I fear it will make trouble if they are forced into the old reg'ts. I know very well that it is of the first importance that the old reg'ts be filled, but what shall we do? How can we keep faith with these men otherwise than by doing as we promised them; and will not the effect be bad regarding future enlistments?
> Our men are reluctant exceedingly to enter the old. How they might feel provided they were all together in one place and had discussed the matter I cannot say, But now they are much opposed and you know how inexperienced undisciplined new volunteers are disposed to be.
> We must go on recruiting every where. It has cost much time and money to get up this fever. Let us not permit it to subside. We shall soon enough be called upon for more soldiers! More <u>regiments</u> I think. I would not be surprised if the State of Maine whold not be called upon for 25,000 more men. Let us be in some readiness.
>
> Yours Truly, Josiah Crosby[10]

With the state bounty of $45 for recruits for new regiments, a "premium" of $2, and $25 advance bounty, and $13, one month's pay, in advance, a man could expect to receive "$85 in hand, when mustered into service" and a promise of another $75 bounty "due them at the end of their term of enlistment." For men who enlisted in existing regiments, the state bounty of $55, along with other inducements, would give them $97 at the time of their muster into U.S. service.[11]

This "liberal course" was adopted "for the purpose of relieving our cities, towns, and plantation, wholly or in part, from the obligation which they had assumed in offering large bounties for volunteers." It was also hoped that wealthy communities would be discouraged from offering large sums of money to lure men from less affluent towns to enlist in those wealthy communities. This was seen as unfairly relieving some of the burden from the wealthy town's men to meet the town's quota and creating a greater burden for the less wealthy towns to meet their quota from a reduced number of available men. It did not, as we shall see later, accomplish this last goal.[12]

Finding even this July call for troops insufficient to meet the needs of the Union Army, on August 4, President Lincoln called for another 300,000 men — these men to be raised by draft from those enrolled in state militias, and for this call, the period of service was reduced to 9 months. Under this call, Maine's quota would be 9,609 men, and Maine was granted the "privilege of furnishing volunteers instead of drafted men for the whole or any portion of the number." This order also "required the enrollment of all able-bodied male citizens between the ages of eighteen and forty-five years" for the militia. There was also a list of persons within that age group who would be exempt from the draft. The list starts with the vice president of the United States, Maine citizen Hannibal Hamlin, and goes on to specify occupations and religious affiliations that would be exempted. Also, surgeons would be appointed to examine men to see if they were physically fit to serve, and men claiming a disability would have to present a certificate from one of these surgeons. In addition to this list of exemptions, a drafted man of sufficient means had the option of hiring a substitute to serve in his place.[13]

And so, although it is generally thought that the first Union draft of the Civil War was the result of the Enrollment Act of 1863, we can see that a draft — technically a state draft rather than federal — was put in place in 1862.[14]

In mid–August of 1862, as a part of this process of raising 9 month regiments, and after stating that volunteers would be accepted in place of drafted men to meet quotas, the State of Maine ordered that "no State or United States bounty will be paid to such volunteers, and it is hoped that cities and towns furnishing their quotas by voluntary enlistment, will not disregard the wishes of the general government, that nine months volunteers should be raised without bounties. No volunteers will be received in lieu of drafted men from any city or town that shall pay a bounty of more than twenty dollars to each volunteer."[15]

So, with no bounty for the 9 month recruits, it appears that this order was intended to make clear that no money would be paid to those who volunteered for the 9 month regiments. It may well be that the establishing of the draft and quotas in combination with the offer of a 9 month term of service instead of 3 years was seen as sufficient inducement to gather needed numbers. The statement that volunteers would be accepted into the 9 month regiments as a privilege seems to indicate this feeling — a hope that men would in fact come forward for the 9 month regiments without waiting for a draft.

It was further specified that any men who were eligible for the draft for 9 month regiments, but who chose instead to enlist in one of the existing 3 year regiments, would receive the usual $97 when mustered, and would count for their town of residence toward the quota required under the draft. It was an interesting choice for young men to make.[16]

This order that no bounty be given to men enlisting for 9 months was apparently causing an unforeseen problem, since in October of 1862 it was noted that "recruiting officers and others are enlisting men in this state for other states, and offering large bounties therefore in violation of law." In other words, Maine men were being lured to enlist in other states' regiments — an action which would deplete the numbers available for Maine towns to meet their quotas.[17]

This draft was met with mixed reactions, especially before the provision for volunteers to fill quotas was announced. Some seemed to believe that it was a fair way to assure that the task of military service was shared by all male citizens, willing or not, while others felt very differently, as seen below. On August 10, 1862, this lengthy and impassioned letter was written in response to the draft for the 9 month regiments by a man from Dexter to Maine's governor, Israel Washburn. It embodies the patriotic fervor that must have been felt by many.

> Dear Sir, Permit me to address you at this perilous time for our country upon a matter that concerns us all most deeply and upon which depends in a great measure the success of the national army in ther present contest; not by way of dictating a policy to be pursued in raising the new levies of 9 mos. men, but to implore those in authority to do it by volunteer enlistment; instead of by draft, which so far as I know is exceedingly unpopular with the people;

It certainly appears to me, that the whole of Maine's quota might be raised in ten days if the proper inducements were offered, and suitable appeal were made by your excellency, to the patriotic feeling of the people by a proclamation, calling them to the rescue of all they hold dear on earth, the existence of free government. I do believe, men would rush to arms, to fill up our quota as our fathers did of yore; from every town, and city, and hamlet, until ther was no [want] for more.

The people generally, are not alive to the momentous issues of the hour, the imminent danger that threatens us. When this Union shall break up, and the heritage of national glory, that [?] and the old flag is gone, oh what man in all our domain will wish to live longer for one spring that the humiliation may never be mine, that my eyes may close in death ere it comes.

I appeal to you sir as the chief magistrate of the state that you stand forth before the people, and in clarion notes speak, burning words, to them that shall touch their inmost souls, and, cause them to rush to arms, as they would to save their dwellings from the flames;

For what is wealth, or homes, or friends, ... [or] worldly possessions and, no country, no ancient fame, no patriot fathers' graves, exept it be covered with shame, and disgrace; God forbid that it ever be. Strip me of everything, and leave me my country, one and entire, with the dear old flag waving, oer me and, I can be content.

Let no unwilling hands be brot to the work, force no man, into our armies for, if will be a living disgrace to our country, to do it, if free institutions cannot be sustained without conscriptions, then call our experiment a failure, for conscription never can;

It is the resort of despotism, and has always been our boast that we were safe without it; whatever Maine may do, or not do, dim not the glory thus, rather awaken a storm of outbursting enthusiasm that shall sweep oer the whole land, filling the ranks of our volunteer army, untill its rushing tide sweeps from ocean to ocean, from the lakes to the gulf, crushing treason and rebellion, restoring our country to its former greatness.

Cease to appeal to their selfish natures and urge motives that are worthy of freemen.

Let the voice of the past, speaking, from Concord, Lexington, Bunker Hill, Camden, Saratoga, & Yorktown, with the ancient battle cry of our fathers sing[ing] out all oer the lands; and, our citizen soldiers shall take their lives in their hands, an offering to their country, and shoulder to shoulder, and voices [lifted?] on high, "Cry, Father, of Earth, and Heaven, we call thy name, around us, the smoke of battle rolls, Father, sustain our untried soldier souls, or life or death whichever be the goal, that, closes around this [struggling?] hour thou knowest of [Eve?] from my spirit stole one deep [?] prayer, twas that no cloud might lower on my countries fame. Oh hear, thou God of Eternal Power, this is the spirit that should be aroused, and all that of dollers and cents, thrust aside, while willing hands, with brave hearts, come to the rescue; Let Maine set an example, and twould spread like a Mainia, and so might peace soon return to bless us;"

Excuse this long epistle, and, if error has crept into it, attribute it to my great anxiety lest some step is about to be taken that will render this war, odeous to freemen; please give the matter that consideration it deservesand be sure that no irretrievable error crept into our state policy that will prolong our struggle or destroy our fondest hopes of our countries founders.

Yrs Truly, Geo Cutler[18]

Another letter addresses the question of a draft in a very different tone. In a letter written at about the time the draft for the 9 month regiments was announced, but quite apparently before the news that the quotas could be filled by volunteers, Josiah Crosby penned on August 12, 1862, "I judge from the orders that there will be no such thing as volunteering, that it must be a draft. I think we could easily fill our quota by volunteering but still I see no great objection to a draft. Will there be any volunteering arrangement?"[19]

And then there is this sentiment, expressed in several copies of the same petition, and all sent to Governor Washburn:

> We the undersigned citizens of Piscataquis, most humbly but earnestly represent that in our opinion a draft of soldiers to supply the quota of the State of Maine for the National Army would have a very deleterious effect. We believe that soldiers so raised would not generally do effective service....
>
> We therefore would further represent that in our opinion [the legislature] should take action to offer such bounties as will induce sufficient enlistment....
>
> There is something revolting to the minds of the people in the idea of compulsory service but all will readily consent that property may be taxed, no matter how high, as needful for its own protection.[20]

With this draft, or threat of a draft, came a variety of problems, many of which were apparently unforeseen, and even seemingly simple choices could be effected by various considerations. For example, with the possibility for exemption from the draft based on a physical ailment or disability, the choice of who would be the examining surgeons became a matter of concern. In this letter to Adjutant General Hodsdon, we see an example of the factors that could contribute to the choice.

Dover, Aug. 18, 1862
Gen. Hodsdon

> Sir. What arrangement has been made. if any, for the examination of invalid soldiers subject to the draft? If regimental surgeons are to be appointed permit me to suggest the name of John W. Cook, M.D., of Dover as well qualified for the place, having a central location in the County, with no modern Dem-

ocratic proclivities to lead him to exempt men able and liable to do military duty....

Josiah Jordan, Regs. of Deeds[21]

And from later that year, we read the following from C.W. Lowell in Foxcroft, Maine, who had the commission to hold that town's draft. After writing that two neighboring towns have had a draft, he states, "I understand that in both of these towns drafted able-bodied men cheated the examining surgeon by falsehoods and previous preparation and thus obtained certificates. Could not another examination be had?"[22]

The crediting of men to the quota of their town of residence rather than the town where they enlisted often caused conflicts, as shown in letters such as the following, written to Adjutant General John Hodsdon. That the third letter was written more than a year after the first two also demonstrates that the problem was not quickly resolved. And, as with a small fraction of the letters addressing this same issue, they also give an indication of the sort of arguments that the Adjutant General's office was being asked to resolve.

Hampden Sept. 15, 1862
Genl. John L. Hodsdon

Sir: Yours of the 5th inst. informing the selectmen of Hampden that Canaan claimed Chas H. Fitzgerald who enlisted in Hampden for the 20th Reg't as a citizen of that town is rec'd — Charles H. Fitzgerald was a citizen of Hampden at the time of his enlistment — and had been residing there for some months before, and claimed Hampden as his home, and rec'd our bounty — he went into the 18th Reg't.

Truly Yours, Edmund Dudley, in behalf of Selectmen Hampden[23]

Dexter Sept. 16, 1862
Gen. Hodsdon
Dear Sir:

Jacob H. Whittier, claimed by Ripley as one of their 9 month quota, is a native of this town & has always lived here till the 29th of June last when he married & moved to a farm in Ripley, still owned by his father.

He & his wife have been at his father's in Dexter nearly half the time since they were married. Monday Sept. 8 he moved himself and his wife & most of his goods to his father's, was enrolled here & warned to appear for draft. When he left his father's farm in Ripley he told him to make no dependence upon his going onto it again on his return from the war.

The above facts we have from Jacob's parents, who say positively that he did not leave Ripley to avoid the draft. Monday morning when he moved to Dexter we had enlisted less than half of our quota though it was more than full before night.

From the above facts we are fully satisfied his change of residence was real & not to avoid a draft.

 Very Respectfully, J. H. Gould, J. S. Sawyer, Selectmen of Dexter[24]

The regulation, stated in General Order 32, that men volunteering and counting on a town's quota in place of drafted men would receive no bounty over $20 was apparently being ignored in some places. This, too, was leading to problems regarding town's quotas.

Foxcroft, Dec. 3, 1862
Dear Sir,

 In accordance with instructions of Nov. 29th I have seen the town authorities of Parkman and they say that they will pay to the towns that stole their men the maximum bounty allowed by the governor to be paid volunteers in lieu of drafted men in General Order No. 32. They think it rather hard when they attempted to live up to that General Order, and their drafted men sell themselves to other towns for large bounties, for the governor to then require them in order to have the credit of these men to pay instead of $20 the maximum of General Order 32, a bounty of $100. It seems that the government in giving credit to towns for men should look above the question of town bounties, set their face against the whole thing and entirely disregard it, and credit those towns with the men, and those only that have really resided there.[25]

The writer then goes on to plead on behalf of Parkman, saying that they had done their duty. He gives the numbers of men who have gone into U.S. Service, asking that they not be required to send another dozen, and tells that 3 of their men have come home, discharged, "with bullets in their bodies." And all of this in spite of the fact that "God knows it is a secesh hole."

In 1863, with the national draft now in place, Maine towns were once again faced with quotas to fill. And with town bounties again being offered openly, the concern about crediting the town of residence, rather than the town where men enlisted, resurfaced. It seems that a "bidding war" was again a consideration, as various towns lured recruits with ever increasing bounties. The different amounts of bounty which were being offered by different towns is reflected in the following letters, again sent to Adjutant General John Hodsdon.

Nov. 20th, 1863
General Hodsdon, Dear Sir,

 There are five of our Palmyra Boys who have recently enlisted, viz. Cyrus Millet — William Chase — George Hubbard — Albert Applebee & Onslow W. Damons — They were enlisted by recruiting Officer Whiting of Newport — and came to Augusta last Tuesday — They are all residents of Palmyra — & all minors & if they are accepted & mustered into the United States service we shall expect them to be credited to our quota for the present call.

Respectfully Yours, Etc. Sam'l Clements Cha. of Selectmen of Palmyra[26]

Dexter, Nov. 21, 1863
Bro. Hodsdon,...

We have a town meeting today — can't say what we shall do.

There must be a draft in very many towns I think Impossible that the poor towns can pay $200 per man.

Your Truly, Josiah Crosby[27]

Dexter Nov. 23, 1863
John S. Hodsdon, Esq.

Dr. Sir, we have voted to pay $200 to each volunteer & are going to do ourbest to raise our quota....

Nathan Wyman   Stephen Leighton   E. S. Juniper[?]
Selectmen of Dexter[28]

Dexter, Nov. 28 1863
Bro. Hodsdon,

The evil of allowing towns to pay bounties instead of having the state offering a liberal bounty equal thus in the whole state is beginning to show itself if as some suppose the towns are not protected by the acting of Me. state or national authorities.

For instance three young persons from this town just before our town meeting go to Augusta, enlist the week of meeting, and take 200 bounty from Portland tis said.

This town votes $200 bounty. ... Now one of the returned [soldiers] takes one or more men with him & they enlist taking the Sangerville bounty of $250 & Bath a wealthy town better able to pay 500 than the 200 offers 350. So tis said. Now how this got to go in this way that our young men can take the bounty of other towns & we get no credit it. We have lost credit before in this way and it threw a double burden on us. ... Will you explain about this & relieve anxious inquiries if possible....

Yours Truly, Samuel McClellan

Tax payers like myself are also slightly interested in the above especially those who like myself are taxed heavily for unproductive property and whose business instead of being made lucrative is ruined by the war. Our town voted to raise 8000 [dollars] by immediate tax to pay bounties. My part is about $85, I conclude.[29]

Dexter, Dec. 8, 1863
Bro. Hodsdon,...

Our young men are still enlisting in better paying towns and I think you will have to decide that each town must have credit for their own men — No other rule will work here. S. McClellan[30]

And then there is this letter to Governor Washburn, which calls into question the issue of patriotism and the "fairness" issue, and suggests that the draft was not as thoroughly observed or regulated as some would wish and this was causing friction among communities.

Dexter, Dec. 22, 1862
Hon. I. Washburn

Dear Sir: We would respectfully suggest that, while this town in common with a great many others, has furnished her quota of soldiers for the defense of the country against traitors in arms, and having done so at great expense and effort on the part of her patriotic citizens, some towns through the efforts of unpatriotic citizens and from other causes have failed to answer the calls of the government for soldiers and rendered the draft of no effect. We think that it is unjust towards towns like Dexter that Parkman an adjoining town, should be let off without an enforcement of the draft and we would recommend if their quota has not been filled that the law should be strictly enforced in that town. If good reasons exist for not exacting a strict observance of the draft and the law in relation thereto we cheerfully submit to your actions. We say nothing above in a spirit of dictation but wish to know if our citizens have been justly dealt with.

Very respectfully, Your ob't Servants,
Nathaniel Dustin   Hiram Carr[31]

The fairness of the administration of the draft was also addressed in a lengthy letter signed by 36 citizens of Houlton, Maine, in northern Maine's Aroostook County. Their grievance centered on the fact that the French speaking communities of the northernmost part of the county were not being required to provide men for the draft in proportion to their part of the county's population.

Houlton, August 25, 1862
To Hon. Israel Washburn, Governor of Maine

The undersigned citizens of Houlton have noticed with surprise and regret that under the recent requisition of the gov't, a draft has been made upon the Town of Houlton and upon the southern and middle of Aroostook County for a considerable number of men.

That these portions of the county have not been deficient in earnest participation that they are ready and willing, if necessary, to send the last man and expend the last dollar in the prosecution of the war in which they believe the existence of their country is at stake is sufficiently shown by the number of their soldiers already in the field, and by their votes at the polls....

We desire to call the attention of your excellency to the fact, that the northern portion of the county, commonly called the French Plantations, constitute more than one fourth part of its entire population, the population of the county according to the last census being 22,449 and that of the Plantation 5,630.

According to the last report of the adj. gen'l of this state the northern section had furnished only 46 volunteers, while the southern and middle portion of the county, with a population of 16,819 had furnished about 700 and yet the northern section is almost entirely relieved from a draft, while the southern and middle section are required to furnish 200 more men. But since the date of that report we have furnished over 300 additional volunteers and also 126 men for the regular army, making in all over 1100 men. ... These portions of the county [the southern and middle sections] have therefore done their whole duty and more than their duty already....

It may perhaps be said, that a draft is not practicable in the northern section of this county because its inhabitants speak a different language from ours, and have not to any considerable extent been enrolled in the militia.

Our reply is that if they are not eligible as soldiers then they should not be counted as a port of our population from which a draft is to be made. ... We would respectfully urge that the plainest principles of justice and equity require that this section of the county [the French Plantations] should be made to furnish its share of men, or if for any reason that is deemed impracticable, that their quota should not be charged upon the rest of the county, already severely taxed....

If these are facts, and your excellency has the record before you by which to test them, surely if there is a town in Maine which ought to be excused from the draft it is the town of Houlton. We claim to be the banner town of Maine. We assure your excellency that we shrink from no duty but we earnestly ask that we may be credited for what we have already done and we are unable to see upon what principle of justice and equity a further call can be made upon a town already taxed severely.

We are assured that your excellency upon examining this matter will readily see that no further call should be made upon us.

Very Resp. your ob't sev't
[signatures of 36 men][32]

Other concerns of fairness, the loyalty of citizens, as well as the amount of money offered as a bounty by the wealthier communities is reflected in the following letter. Other letters below, however, make one wonder whether the writer was simply making excuses. In addition, this letter mentions a thought found in other correspondence — that the draft, or threat of a draft, was largely seen as an inducement for men to enlist. (In this first letter and other letters from the same writer, his spelling has been left as written.)

Dexter, Dec. 18, 1863
Gen. Hodsdon,

Dear Sir: I received the small lot of inlistments papers have used them all up out of my own town. Finding it impossible to inlist men in Dexter for a bounty of 200$ we have caled [called] for another town meeting to rais more money and now the men begin to inlist. Have got 3 today on the promise of 300$ town bounty others together with the idear that the draft is near is making quite a [storm?]. We have a large number of copperheads and foreigners hear which makes it a hard chance for us, but I think we shall fill our quota or nearly so as the thoughts of the draft is a greater help than the bounty. Still without either it would be impossible to do a thing hear.

Please send me enlistment papers enough for 40 men and oblige your ob't servent, E. B. Fifield, Dexter, Me.[33]

There were, of course, considerations other than the amounts or bounty offered, or the presumed patriotism of various towns and individuals that impacted the willingness of men to volunteer. The personality of the recruiting officer, including the Mr. Fifield of the previous letter, could be a factor in the success of enlisting volunteers.

In a letter from S. McClellan, previously quoted in part, there is this sentence: "Fifield [the] recruiting officer is obnoxious — especially to all belonging formerly to the company in the service of which he was a lieutenant."[34]

Edward Fifield of Dexter had been a lieutenant in Company D, 20th Maine. He (along with the captain of that company) had resigned his commission in November of 1862. At that time, the 20th Maine had seen some of the war, being at Antietam, but was not engaged in that battle. They had, however, come under Rebel fire as they followed the Confederate withdrawal from Antietam to Shepherdstown Ford.

A month after the letter above regarding Fifield's personality, we read,

Dexter, Dec. 25, 1863
Gen. John L. Hodsdon, Adj. Gen., Maine
Dear Sir:

I herewith introduce to you Rev. Wm. W. Lovejoy of Dexter who has enlisted in the First Maine Cavalry. Mr. E. B. Fifield of Dexter, recruiting officer has concluded to turn the business of recruiting over to Mr. Lovejoy and has delivered all his papers to him. I have no doubt that Mr. Lovejoy will be a more successful recruiting officer than Mr. Fifield. He knows of a number who are ready to enlist with him. He is reliable in every respect. I think you will do well to issue proper recruiting papers to him, and hope you will send them forthwith....

Resp'ly, Your Ob't Serv't, Josiah Crosby

We the undersigned selectmen of the town of Dexter do hereby confirm the above statements and recommend that recruiting papers be immediately sent to Mr. Lovejoy.

Nathan Wyman   Stephen Leighton   Selectmen of Dexter[35]

Whatever the town politics or personality concerns, Fifield, in February of 1864, was writing as follows:

> Adj. Gen. Hodsdon
> Dear Sir:
> I recruited one man bugaler for 2d M Cav. by the name of Edward Drake. I am not certain but Edward is his middle name and I learned from the directions sent me that arrangements were made to pay for recruiting for that organization the same as for old reg. If so will you pleas send it to me (15$) and this shall be your receit for the same.
> Yours Truly, E. B. Fifield
> I am gitting some recruits this weak for Bakers Cavalry. Shall I present them at Augusta or at Capt. Lary Bangor?[36]

With all of these other considerations, the prospective company officers under whom men would serve was also a concern, as we see in the following letter written to Adjutant General Hodsdon.

> Dexter, July 21, 1862
> It is utterly impossible for us to enlist our quota of volunteers if they are obliged to go into a company under Mr. Williams. But we have no doubt we shall be able to raise the requisite number in a few days if they can have Mr. Haskell as commanding officer. We are informed by citizens of Garland & Exeter that the same feeling prevails in those towns.
> Yours Truly, Russell S. Merrill and [name illegible][37]

Isaac Haskell of Dexter had been captain of Company D, 20th Maine. He had resigned his commission at the same time as Lieutenant Fifield. In the minds of these writers, at least, Captain Haskell seems to be held in higher regard than his former lieutenant, Edward Fifield. Company D of the 20th Maine seemed to have an inordinate number of problems with its commissioned and noncommissioned officers. Two of the company's sergeants were reduced to the ranks, as were 4 of its corporals. In addition, after the resignation of Captain Haskell and Lieutenant Fifield, 7 men from that company deserted from late 1862 through late 1863.[38]

In this appendix, I hope to have given a reasonably clear explanation for a reasonably confusing situation. Briefly stated, the way in which Union regiments were raised, as typified by Maine and its 22nd infantry regiment, was very foreign to our current ways of thinking. One could become a lieutenant or captain by raising numbers of men to serve. One could become a colonel or other regimental officer through personal, political, or professional contacts with military experience of little consequence.

For a look beyond this state and local context, we may examine the backgrounds and qualifications of those chosen for much higher rank. Commanders of the Army of the Potomac such as Joseph Hooker, George McClellan, Ambrose Burnside and even George Meade (despite his success at Gettysburg) were heavily criticized for a lack of ability to lead armies to victory. Although graduates of West Point, these men had not achieved high rank prior to the Civil War. This was not unusual, of course, due to the smaller army with fewer opportunities for promotion. But some who would go on to very high rank had not maintained a military career at all.

Hooker, an 1837 graduate of West Point, had no commission higher than lieutenant colonel during the Mexican American War, and held a colonel's commission in the California Militia when the Civil War broke out. Burnside, West Point class of 1847, had been a lieutenant in the war with Mexico and had served for a time on the western frontier after that war. He resigned his officer's commission in 1853 and, in addition to becoming an arms manufacturer, worked for the Illinois Central Railroad under George B. McClellan. McClellan, another Mexican war veteran, had graduated from West Point in 1846. He entered the army with the rank of lieutenant and was given a brevet commission as captain for his actions at the battle of Chapultepec. His peacetime activities included returning to West Point to help train cadets, the translation of a French manual of bayonet tactics, and the writing of a manual for cavalry tactics. When he resigned his commission in 1857, he became an engineer and vice president of the Illinois Central Railroad. George Meade, perhaps the most "professional" soldier of that group, was an 1835 graduate of West Point who also fought in the Mexican War. Before the Civil War he held the rank of captain of engineers, and spent much of his time working on lighthouse and breakwater construction. For all 4 of these men, the Civil War brought them quickly to the rank of general — indeed to the rank of major general — a rank for which they had no experience.[39]

Other generals, also much criticized, such as Benjamin Butler, Nathaniel Banks, and Dan Sickles, were purely "political" generals — owing their ranks to political connections and perhaps to the support they might bring to the Union cause from their constituents.

As an indication of the value some placed on the military training and experience of those given high command, "Grant's choices of Meade and Sherman for promotion [in the spring of 1864] were meeting resistance, for there were politicians who urged consideration of the mind-boggling duo of Butler and Sickles for the appointments, defending these candidates with theories of the necessity of diminishing 'West Point influence.'"[40] This may serve to demonstrate that it was not just at the state level, or at the level of regimental colonels or company commanders, that we see a very different set of standards and expectations from today.

Appendix B
Causes of Death in the Different Theaters of the War

Statistics are, of course, tricky. It is often stated that many more men died in the Civil War from disease than from combat-related causes. While that is true, it can also be seen that the ratio of deaths from disease vs. battle varied considerably from one geographic locale to another.

It is fairly easy to compare figures for Maine's 9 month regiments, since they tended to spend their entire term of service in one area. Here we can see the number of deaths due to disease for regiments that were sent to the Gulf of Mexico and for those kept nearer Washington.

Department of the Gulf:

22nd Maine: 160 from disease (9 killed)
21st (Gulf— Port Hudson): 145 from disease (27 killed)
24th (Gulf— Port Hudson): 190 from disease (1 killed)
26th (Gulf— Irish Bend, Port Hudson): 131 from disease (23 killed)
28th (Gulf— Port Hudson, Donaldsonville): 143 from disease (11 killed)

Defense of Washington:

23rd (Defense of Washington): 56 from disease
25th (Defense of Washington): 20 from disease
27th (Defense of Washington): 22 from disease

For Maine's 3 year regiments, the comparisons are a bit more difficult, since some moved from one theater of the war to another while others, which had lost heavily in battle, had their ranks renewed with fresh recruits. But, here is a comparison of two regiments that spent their time in one area.

    15th Maine (Gulf & Texas): 343 from disease (5 killed)
    20th Maine (Virginia, Pennsylvania, etc.): 146 from disease (147 killed)

Other 3 year Maine regiments:

    12th (Gulf '62 and '63 and later Va.) 239 from disease (52 killed)
    13th (Gulf and Texas) 181 from disease (14 killed)
    14th (Gulf '62 and '63 and later Va.) 332 from disease (86 killed)
    17th (Virginia) 163 from disease (207 killed)
    19th (Virginia) 184 from disease (192 killed)

Appendix C
Roster of the Twenty-Second Regiment

The following is compiled from the 1862 and 1863 Maine adjutant general's reports, which cover the period of the 22nd Maine's service. Age and marital status are given as they were as of the time of enlistment.

Name	Residence	Date of Rank	Remarks
Col. Simon G. Gerrard	Levant	Sept. 23 '62	'63: discharged from service June 14 by order of Gen. Banks
Lt. Col. Olonzo G. Putnam	Dover	"	
Maj. John O. Brackett	Palmyra	"	
Adj. Frank G. Flagg	Hampden	Oct. 7	
Q.M. Lyman C. Bailey	Calais	"	
Surg. Josiah Jordan	Dover	"	
Asst. Surg. Jason Huckins	Corinth	[not given]	
2Asst. Surg. John W. Cook	Dover	[not given]	'63: never commiss'd and must'd out of service Dec. 3, '62
Chap. John W. Lincoln	Bangor	Oct. 5	'63: Injured by fall; left sick at Port Hudson July 24
Sgt. Maj. Roscoe G. Rollins	Bangor	Sept. 27	
Q.M. Sgt. Edward M. Young	Kenduskeag	Oct. 4	'63: sick at New Orleans
C. Sgt. William Lowney	Bangor	Sept. 10	'63: reduced to ranks trans. to Co. H
C. Sgt. Samuel J. Gallagher	Calais	March 1, '63	'63: trans. from Co. F
Hosp. Std. Eugene B. Sanborn	Machiasport	Sept. 30	
Drum Maj. Oliver D. Richardson	Mapleton Pl.	Oct. 4	'63: returned to Co. G
Fife Maj. George W. Grant	Bangor	"	'63: returned to Co. H

Appendix C

Company A

Name	Residence	Age/Marital Status	Muster Date	Remarks
Commiss'd Officers				
Henry Crosby	Hampden	39 / S	Oct. 10	'63: died from wounds June 12
Thomas J. Knowles	Hampden	45 / M	"	'62: Absent sick; resignation tendered '63: resigned Nov. 30, '62
James P. Ireland	Corinna	34 / M	"	'62: Honorably discharged Nov. 12
Sergeants				
George E. Brown	Hampden	21 / S	"	'63: Promoted 1st lieutenant
Hiram T. Batchelder	Hampden	23 / S	"	'63: Promoted 2nd lieutenant; resigned Dec. 20, '62
Samuel M. Homsted	Hampden	24 / M	"	
Daniel T. Mayo	Carmel	39 / M	"	'63: promoted 1st sergeant
Gipson C. Patten	Corinna	24 / M	"	'63: promoted 2nd lieutenant
Corporals				
Joseph E. Joy	Hampden	35 / M	"	'63: promoted sergeant; died of wounds June 23
John E. Tribou	Hampden	30 / M	"	'63: promoted sergeant
Austin Pomroy	Hampden	37 / M	"	'63: promoted sergeant
John M. Sullivan	Hampden	24 / S	"	'62: sick in hospital at Alexandria '63: disch. for disability Jan. 13
Alfred W. Bussell	Argyle	37 / M	"	'62: left at home sick; 63: returned to ranks as private
John S. Ward	Hampden	43 / M	"	'63: died March 26
George W. Knowles	Hampden	28 / S	"	'63: returned to ranks as private
James Patten, Jr.	Hermon	20 / S	"	
Musicians				
Melville Walker	Hampden	21 / S	"	
William W. Walker	Hampden	20 / S	"	'63: died February 15
Wagoner				
Isaiah C. Deane	Hampden	32 / M	"	

Name	Residence	Age/Marital Status	Muster Date	Remarks
Privates				
Arey, Melvin F.	Hampden	18 / S	Oct. 10	'63: promoted corporal
Atkins, Justin R.	Corinna	18 / S	"	'62: sick in hospital
Bailey, Charles R.	Hampden	19 / S	Oct. 20	'62: sick in quarters; later died
Blaisdell, Charles E.	Corinna	18 / S	Oct. 10	
Blaisdell, George C.	Corinna	26 / M	"	'63: died February 21
Blaisdell, William F.	Corinna	23 / S	"	
Bradford, Bartlett	Carmel	18 / S	"	
Bradford, William W.	Carmel	20 / S	Oct. 20	
Bussell, Jason L.	Carmel	18 / S	Oct. 10	
Bussell, Robert	Carmel	45 / S	"	'62: sick in hospital at Fort Monroe
Clement, George A.	Orneville	18 / M	"	
Clifford, Gersham W.	Hermon	19 / S	"	
Cole, Henry M.	Hampden	21 / S	"	
Copeland, Wm. O.P.	Corinna	18 / S	"	'62: sick in hospital; '63: died Feb. 3
Copp, Edward	Corinna	18 / S	"	
('63 report has his name as Edward Cobb)				
Cowan, Zenas	Hampden	44 / M	"	'63: died August 6
Dyer, Albert C.	Etna	20 / S	"	
Emerson, Daniel W.	Charleton	35 / M	"	'62: sick in hospital
Emerson, Jonathan P.	Hampden	41 / M	"	'63: died May 19
Emery, John, Jr.	Hampden	19 / S	"	
Fletcher, Charles W.	Hermon	19 / S	"	'62: sick in hospital at Washington; '63: disch. for disability Feb. 7
Foster, Alonzo Y.	Newburg	20 / S	"	'63: promoted corporal
Freeze, William W.	Argyle	21 / S	"	'62: left at home sick
Gerow, Abram G.	Newburg	22 / S	"	'63: promoted corporal
Goss, John F.	Hampden	30 / M	Oct. 20	
Grant, Lorenzo	Argyle	26 / S	Oct. 10	
Hewes, Cyrus E.	Hermon	21 / S	"	
Hitchcock, Samuel	Hampden	26 / M	"	
Hole, Owen R.	Corinna	18 / S	"	
Hubbard, Wilbur F.	Corinna	23 / S	"	
Humphrey, Cyrus, Jr.	Hampden	18 / S	"	
Humphrey, Edward	Hampden	23 / S	"	'63: died January 30
Humphrey, John B.	Hampden	21 / S	"	'62: present; not mustered
Jewell, Frank H.	Hermon	18 / S	"	
Knowles, Ephraim S.	Hampden	34 / S	"	'63: died March 12
Knowles, John W.	Hampden	20 / S	"	'63: died April 29
Lake, Daniel	Hampden	33 / M	"	

Appendix C

Name	Residence	Age/Marital Status	Muster Date	Remarks
Leighton, Lewis F.	Corinna	21 / S	Oct. 10	'63: died June 21
Leighton, Charles H.	Corinna	12 / S	"	'63: died August 12
Loring, George F.	Hampden	18 / S	"	
Lufkin, Thomas B.	Hampden	35 / S	"	
Mann, Alexander	Argyle	30 / M	"	
Mann, Isaac	Argyle	23 / M	"	
Marsh, Mark T.	Argyle	28 / M	"	'63: died March 10
Mayo, Prentis M.	Carmel	20 / S	"	
McAuliffe, Malachi	Hampden	40 / M	"	
Miller, Alonzo E.	Hampden	19 / S	"	
Miller, George A.	Hampden	18 / S	"	
Miller, George W.	Hampden	18 / S	"	
Morse, Isaac	Corinna	44 / S	"	'63: died May 8
Morton, John D.	Carmel	20 / S	"	'63: died April 14
Murch, Martin	Hampden	22 / S	Oct. 20	'63: died March 14
Newcomb, Augustus	Newburg	18 / S	Oct. 10	
Palmer, Leonard	Corinna	19 / S	"	'63: died June 28
Partridge, Ichabod F.	Carmel	30 / M	"	
Porter, Alphozo	Hampden	24 / S	"	'63: died March 4
Rogers, Harrison W.	Hampden	26 / S	"	
Sawyer, Edward K.	Hampden	23 / S	Oct. 20	
Shaw, Charles L.	Orneville	18 / S	Oct. 10	
Simpson, Jedediah	Hampden	22 / S	"	
Small, Daniel B.	Carmel	18 / S	"	
Smith, Daniel, Jr.	Hampden	44 / M	"	'63: promoted corporal
Smith, Sumner, Jr.	Hampden	26 / M	"	'63: promoted sergeant
Snow, Augustus	Hampden	22 / S	"	'63: died Dec. 30, '62
Speed, James, Jr.	Bradford	29 / M	"	
Stewart, Forest E.	Corinna	30 / M	"	
Stone, Hiram	Bangor	32 / M	"	
Swett, Charles B.	Hampden	21 / S	"	
Thayer, Alonzo	Hampden	18 / S	"	'62: sick in hospital; disch. for disability March 27, '63
Tracy, Cleaves C.	Hermon	18 / S	"	'62: sick in hospital at Baltimore
Trueworthy, Benj. B.	Hampden	19 / S	"	'62: sick in hospital; died April 27, '63
Veazie, Alfred	Corinna	31 / M	"	
Ward, Charles	Hampden	25 / M	"	
White, David F.	Corinna	19 / S	"	'63: disch. for disability March 27
White, Lewis W.	Corinna	31 / M	"	
Young, Abram	Corinna	43 / M	"	'63: died March 8
Young, Luther	Corinna	34 / M	"	

Name	Residence	Age/Marital Status	Muster Date	Remarks
Company B				
Commis'd Officers				
James W. Wllliams	Bangor	31 / M	Oct. 10	'63: resigned Dec. 16, '62
John T. Gilman	Bangor	27 / M	"	'63: promoted captain
George H. Anson	Bangor	27 / M	"	'62: promoted 1st lieutenant December 16, '62; disch for promotion August 11, '63
Sergeants				
Samuel W. Knowles	Bangor	28 / S	"	'63: promoted 2nd lieutenant
George T. Rowe	Holden	22 / S	"	'63: promoted 1st sergeant
Bradford C. Clark	Holden	31 / M	"	'63: died March 5
Benjamin H. Darling	Hudson	31 / S	"	'63: died February 15
George R. Mann	Hudson	28 / M	"	'63: returned to ranks
Corporals				
Joseph P. Tyler	Bangor	33 / M	"	'63: promoted sergeant
Seth E. Drinkwater (listed as private in '62 report)				'63: promoted sergeant
Joseph E. Hanscom	Dedham	33 / M	"	'62: red. to ranks; sick at Ft. Mon.
Abiather W. Carll (listed as Abiather W .Carle in '63 report)	Hudson	35 / M	"	
Rufus E. Whitmore	Hudson	21 / S	"	'63: returned to ranks
Jacob Tasker	Bradford	37 / M	"	
William E.S. Rice	Bangor	26 / M	"	'63: promoted sergeant
James E. White	Holden	24 / S	"	
Joshua S. Kenney	Holden	37 / M	"	
Musicians				
George W. Grant	Holden	38 / M	"	
Horace C. Griffin	Holden	19 / S	"	'63: returned to ranks
Wagoner				
Arthur E. Blakeley	Bangor	23 / S	"	
Privates				
Ames, William H.	Bradford	21 / S	"	
Bagley, Henry C.	Bangor	18 / S	"	
Bailey, Nathaniel W.	Glenburn	21 / S	"	'63: killed in action June 11
Bailey, Orin N.	Bradford	18 / S	"	
Bailey, Ransom	Glenburn	18 / S	"	

Name	Residence	Age/Marital Status	Muster Date	Remarks
Beale, Charles E.	Bangor	27 / M	Oct. 10	
Bean, George W.	Hudson	19 / S	"	'63: died February 24
Bean, Joseph N.	Hudson	24 / M	"	
Blood, Augustus	Dedham	26 / M	"	
Brown, Charles E.	Bangor	20 / S	"	
Bryant, Charles H.	Lagrange	18 / S	"	'63: died May
Carll, Van Buren	Hudson	18 / S	"	
(listed as Carle, Van Buren, in '63 report)				
Cates, Daniel	Bangor	33 / M	"	
Chamberlain, Charles P.	Hudson	18 / S	"	
Chamberl'n, Lorenzo D.	Hudson	18 / S	"	
Chase, Oscar T.	Hudson	18 / S	Oct. 18, '62	
Clewley, Augustus D.	Brewer	18 / S	Oct. 10	'63: killed in action, June 11
Collins, Daniel S.	Bangor	24 / M	"	
Dickey, Herbert V.	Veazie	18 / S	"	'63: discharged July 23
Drinkwater, Seth E.	Bangor	22 / S	"	'62: promoted to 2nd corporal
Goodwin, Daniel	Hudson	21 / S	Oct. 18, '62	
Griffin, Roscoe M.	Holden	21 / S	Oct. 10, '62	
Hanscom, Joseph E.				'63: disch. for disability April 27
(listed as corporal in '62 report)				
Hanson, Edward W.	Bangor	42 / M	"	'62: sick at Newport News; '63: died May 10
Holt, John S.	Bradford	21 / S	"	'63: died February 13
Houston, William, Jr.	Holden	39 / M	"	'62: sick at Newport News; disch. for disability Dec. 2, '62
Howard, Silas	Holden	36 / M	"	
Howe, George W.	Hudson	27 / M	"	
Inman, Charles	Veazie	35 / M	"	
Johnson, Edwin S.	Bangor	18 / S	"	
Kent, William	Veazie	20 / S	"	
Kimball, Benjamin	Bangor	31 / S	"	
Kinney, Joshua H.	Holden	22 / M	"	
Kinney, Martin	Stetson	23 / S	"	
(Martin "McKenney" in '62 report)				
Lowney, William	Bangor	40 / M	Oct. 10, '62	'62: app't coms'y sergeant
(listed as private in '63 report)				
Lyshon, Albert T.	Hudson	19 / S	"	
Mann, Joel	Hudson	44 / M	"	
Mann, John F.	Dednam	23 / S	"	'63: disch. for disability May 20
McKenney, Martin	Stetson	23 / S	"	
(listed as Martin "Kinney" in '63)				
McLaughlin, Thomas J.	Dedham	23 / S	"	'63: died February 26

Roster of the Twenty-Second Regiment

Name	Residence	Age/Marital Status	Muster Date	Remarks
McPhetres, Daniel	Veazie	18 / S	Oct. 10, '62	
Miles, Franklin N.	Hudson	19 / S	"	
Moore, Franklin B.	Holden	21 / S	"	'63: died Jan. 24
Montgomery, John	Bangor	22 / S	"	'62: sick at Fortress Monroe
Morris, George W.	Veazie	18 / S	Oct. 18	'63: died of wounds July 3
Navy, James E.	Holden	44 / M	Oct. 10	'62: sick in Washington
Nichols, Albert A.	Holden	21 / S	"	
Orcutt, Andrew J.	Holden	34 / S	"	
Orcutt, Elijah B.	Holden	26 / M	"	
Page, Christopher A.	Bangor	39 / M	"	'63: promoted sergeant
Phillips, Timothy E.	Veazie	19 / S	"	
Potter, Andrew J.	Hudson	21 / S	"	
Pritchard, George A.	Brewer	20 / S	"	'63: promoted corporal
Reid, Charles H.	Bangor	18 / S	"	
Richardson, Amos H.	Bangor	39 / M	"	
Rollins, Roscoe G.	Bangor	27 / S	"	'62: appointed sergeant major
Rose, Thomas H.	Abbot	20 / S	"	'63: promoted corporal
Rowe, William A.	Holden	19 / S	"	'63: discharged July 23
Sanborn, Andrew	Brewer	18 / S	"	'63: discharged July 23
Sawyer, George	Bangor	21 / S	"	
Scribner, Edmond C.	Bangor	18 / S	"	'63: disch. for disability May 27
Severance, William A.	Lincoln	19 / S	"	'63: discharged July 23
Smith, Elijah	Charleston	24 / S	"	'63: promoted corporal
Spratt, James S.	Bangor	24 / M	"	'62: appointed wagon master
Steams, Orin	Hudson	25 / M	"	
Strange, William	Bangor	27 / M	"	'63: disch. for disab. Dec. 11, '62
Webster, Frederick E.	Bangor	18 / S	"	'63: died March 13
White, Edwin E.	Holden	20 / S	"	
White, Horatio G.	Holden	28 / S	"	'62: sick at Newport News
Wilson, Charles W.	Bangor	21 / M	"	
Wilson, Gustavus V.	Hudson	22 / S	"	
Wilson, Henry O.	Bangor	19 / S	"	'63: killed in action, June 11
Work, Henry	Bangor	41 / M	"	
Work, Moses	Bangor	34 / M	"	
Wotton, Marcellus	Bangor	21 / S	"	
Young, Alvah M.	Bangor	30 / M	"	
Young, Harrison C.	Bangor	25 / M	"	'63: drowned July 26

Name	Residence	Age/Marital Status	Muster Date	Remarks
Company C				
Commis'd Officers				
George A. Bolton	Orrington	29 / M	Oct. 10, '62	
Jasper Hutchins	Brewer	27 / S	"	'63: discharged July 29
Joseph A. Baker	Orrington	25 / S	"	'63: discharged June 28
Sergeants				
Alvah P. Bennett	Brewer	29 / M	"	'63: discharged July 24
Alonzo F. Smith	Orrington	32 / M	"	'62: sick at Newport News; '63: disch. for disability in January
Jacob Bemis	Lagrange	30 / M	"	'63: returned to ranks
Cyrus W. Penney	Eddington	23 / S	"	'63: discharged July 24
Rufus O. Page	Brownville	30 / S	"	'63: promoted 1st sergeant
Corporals				
Nathaniel Ripley	Waite Pl.	28 / S	"	'63: promoted sergeant
Joseph A. Stearns	Brewer	19 / S	"	
Hiram R. Stevens	Eddington	27 / S	"	
Daniel T. Thomas	Bradley	20 / S	"	'63: died February 10
Peter C. Smith	Orrington	29 / S	"	
Samuel E. Burr	Brewer	22 / S	"	
Elon R. Comins	Eddington	23 / S	"	
George Glidden	Brewer	20 / M	"	
Musicians				
Enoch R. Nye	Orrington	22 / S	"	
John N. Ames	Orrington	29 / M	"	
Wagoner				
Emery B. Lufkin	Orrington	21 / S	"	'62: at home, sick
Privates				
Ames, Sumner T.	Amherst	18 / S	"	
Badershall, Fred'ick W.	Orrington	23 / S	"	
Bakeman, George R.	Brewer	22 / S	"	'63: left sick at Baton Rouge, March 26
Baker, Elijah A.	Orrington	33 / M	"	
Baker, Isaiah A.	Orrington	37 / M	"	
Beckford, Charles A.	Orrington	19 / S	"	
Bowden, Charles	Orrington	36 / M	"	
Bowden, Charles H.	Orrington	21 / S	"	'63: died May 6
Bowden, Jeremiah T.	Orrington	31 / M	"	
Bowden, John E.	Orrington	25 / M	"	
Bumpus, Calvin	Orrington	27 / M	"	
Chapin, Eugene A.	Orrington	18 / S	"	'63: died February 26
Clewley, Henry W.	Eddington	21 / S	"	

Roster of the Twenty-Second Regiment

Name	Residence	Age/Marital Status	Muster Date	Remarks
Conant, Amasa L.	Orrington	18 / S	Oct. 10, '62	
Cowan, George	Glenburn	22 / S	"	
Crane, Charles L.	Orrington	32 / M	"	'63: died December 23, '62
Danforth, William N.	Lagrange	19 / S	"	
Davis, Horace B.	Eddington	22 / S	"	
Dow, James E.	Waite Pl.	21 / M	"	
Dow, John	Waite Pl.	24 / S	"	
Dunning, Francis E.	Williamsb'g	32 / M	"	
Dunsmoor, Henry F.	Talmadge Pl.	24 / S	"	
Eastman, Freeman H.	Brewer	18 / S	"	'63: discharged July 24
Fisher, Jason C.	Waite Pl.	22 / S	"	'63: died February 18
Freeman, James W.	Orrington	40 / M	"	'63: died May 2
Gilbert, George B.	Brewer	21 / S	"	
Glidden, Charles	Brewer	22 / M	"	
Glidden, Daniel S.	Jefferson	19 / S	"	'63: died April 27
Harriman, Amos W.	Brewer	18 / S	"	
Harriman, James, Jr.	Orrington	44 / S	"	
Holyoke, Richard H.	Brewer	20 / S	"	
Howe, Melzar B.	Eddington	21 / S	"	
Innis, John C.	Eddington	44 / M	"	'63: disch. for disability Feb. 14
Libbey, William A.	Brewer	18 / S	"	
Little, Daniel P.	Orrington	24 / M	"	'62: at home, sick; died April 9, '63
Maddox, John S.	Eddington	25 / S	"	
Marble, Isaac J.	Brownville	23 / S	"	
McGranaghan, James	Waite Pl.	29 / M	"	
Mills, Edward E.	Eddington	20 / S	"	
Nickerson, Amos M.	Orrington	30 / M	"	'63: discharged July 24
Nickerson, William P.	Orrington	19 / S	"	'63: died April 20
Orcutt, Marcus M.	Amherst	19 / S	"	'63: died May 29
Parker, Foster	Brewer	18 / S	"	
Parker, Lorenzo	Brewer	23 / S	"	
Pierce, Henry A.	Brewer	28 / M	"	
Pinhorn, Humphrey	Orrington	21 / S	"	
Pond, Preston I.	Orrington	18 / S	"	
Reed, Davis C.	Waite Pl.	21 / S	"	
Robinson, Samuel J.	Orrington	28 / M	"	
Rollins, Charles W.	Milo	18 / S	"	'63: promoted corporal
Sherburn, Oliver L.	Milo	18 / S	"	
Silsby, William H.	Amherst	22 / S	"	
Smith, Albert P.	Orrington	23 / S	"	
Smith, John H.	Orrington	39 / M	"	'63: promoted corporal
Smith, Howes R.	Orrington	36 / M	"	

Name	Residence	Age/Marital Status	Muster Date	Remarks
Smith, Richard	Talmadge Pl.	21 / S	Oct. 10, '62	'62: sick; disch. for disability Dec. 4, '62
Stevens, Levi L.	Eddington	21 / S	"	
Sumner, Nathan P.	Amherst	28 / M	"	
Taylor, Leander	Aurora	37 / S	"	'63: left sick at Bellefontaine, Ohio, August 2
Torrens, John W.	Orrington	23 / S	"	
Wardwell, Irving A.	Orrington	31 / M	"	'63: promoted chaplain March 10
Wentworth, Calvin	Orrington	20 / S	"	'63: left sick at Union, Ohio, August 2
Weymouth, Andrew J.	Milo	27 / M	"	
Weymouth, Frank C.	Medford	18 / S	"	'63: died July 4
Williams, Andrew	Talmadge Pl.	44 / M	"	'63: died March 5
Winslow, Albert R.	Brewer	19 / S	"	

Company D

Commiss'd Officers

Charles H. Union	Addison	30 / M	Oct. 10	
Ephraim P. Dorman	Harrington	43 / M	"	
Nathaniel White	Columbia	23 / M	"	

Sergeants

Lincoln Rhoades	Columbia	28 / S	"	'63: died June 6
George W. Hall	Addison	25 / S	"	'63: promoted 1st sergeant
Jerome W. Peasley	Jonesport	22 / S	"	
David F. Wass	Columbia	27 / M	"	'62: died Chesapeake General Hospital, Nov. 16
James F. Mathews	Cherryfield	29 / M	"	

Corporals

Edward K. Emerson (listed as sergeant in '63)	Addison	24 / M	"	'62: promoted to sergeant
Henry T. Parritt	Harrington	21 / S	"	'63: died March 2
Edward W. Brackett	Harrington	21 / S	"	'63: died at New Orleans
Isaac N. Allen	Columbia	20 / M	"	
Harrison Look	Addison	23 / S	"	
Jeremiah B. Norton	Jonesport	25 / M	"	
William H. Soule	Jonesport	19 / S	"	
Lysander C. Smith	Jonesport	23 / M	"	
Frederick L. Nash (listed as private in '62; promoted to corporal)				

Name	Residence	Age/Marital Status	Muster Date	Remarks
Musicians				
Uriah N. Merritt	Harrington	42 / M	Oct. 10	
Eli A. Leighton	Addison	19 / S	"	'63: returned to ranks as private
Wagoner				
Francis Foss	Jonesport	42 / M	"	
Privates				
Allen, Alphonzo M.	Harrington	23 / S	"	
Allen, Samuel B.	Harrington	28 / S	"	'63: died at New Orleans
Allen, Temple C.	Harrington	25 / S	"	
Allen, William H.	Columbia	26 / M	"	'63: wounded in action, June 14
Alley, Nathaniel S.	Jonesport	20 / M	"	'62: deserted Oct. 16
Brazell, John	Columbia	37 / M	"	
Caler, William	Jonesport	34 / M	"	'63: disch. for disability Jan. 31
Callighan, Luther L.	Centerville	25 / S	"	
Carroll, William A.	Harrington	18 / S	"	'63: died
Carter, Lewis	Harrington	42 / M	"	
Church, Charles W.	Jonesport	36 / M	"	
Colson, William A.	Cherryfield	18 / S	"	'63: wounded in action, June 14
Cox, James	Harrington	44 / M	"	
Dinsmore, Gilbert M.	Harrington	18 / S	"	
Dobbin, Daniel	Jonesport	25 / S	"	
Door, Joseph P.	Jonesport	21 / S	"	
Door, William I.	Columbia	42 / M	"	
Emerson, John T.	Addison	21 / S	"	'63: died at Baton Rouge
Farnsworth, Charles H.	Jonesport	19 / S	"	'63: died at Baton Rouge
Farnsworth, George W.	Jonesport	44 / M	"	
Foss, John C.	Jonesport	19 / S	"	
French, Venleson E.	Columbia	21 / S	"	'63: left sick at New Orleans July 24
Grace, Leonard D.	Harrington	27 / M	"	
Grant, George M.D.	Columbia	18 / S	"	'63: died Nov. 29, '62
Grant, John B.	Columbia	26 / M	"	
Grant, Horace S.	Medford	18 / S	"	
Hartford, Jethron P.	Columbia	23 / M	"	
Huntley George W.	Harrington	19 / S	"	
Hussey, Henry A.	Blanchard	24 / M	"	
Joy, Melvin G.	Ellsworth	40 / M	"	
Kelley, Uriah M.	Addison	22 / S	"	

Appendix C

Name	Residence	Age/Marital Status	Muster Date	Remarks
Leighton, Alfred E.	Columbia	18 / S	Oct. 10	
Leighton, Barney B.	Addison	44 / M	"	
Leighton, Howard C.	Cherryfield	24 / S	"	'63: died April 28
Leighton, Jotham S.	Columbia	21 / S	"	
Leighton, Warren G.	Columbia	23 / S	"	'63: died January 22
Leighton, Wentworth A.	Columbia	21 / S	"	'63: died Dec. 27, '62
Lowe, Henry	Columbia	24 / M	"	
Makenzie, Joseph D.	Columbia	44 / M	"	'63: left sick at New Orleans March 12
McDowell, George I.	Columbia	25 / M	"	
Merchant, Robert, Jr.	Jonesport	24 / M	"	'62: deserted Oct. 16
Merritt, Isaiah N.	Addison	40 / M	"	
Nash, David J.	Harrington	26 / M	"	
Nash, Frederic L.	Harrington	20 / S	"	'62: promoted to corporal
Nash, Judson R.	Harrington	18 / S	"	
Pribble, Sidney L.	Columbia	18 / S	"	'63: died May 17
Sanborn, Eugene B.	Machiasport	27 / S	"	'63: promoted hospital steward
Sinclair, Charles	Columbia	26 / S	"	
Smith, Frederic M.	Jonesport	21 / S	"	
Smith, James W.	Jonesport	22 / S	"	'63: disch. for disability March 28
Stevens, Chester H.	Harrington	22 / M	"	
Tabbut, Robert A.	Addison	42 / M	"	'63: disch. for disability March 28
Tabbut, Rufus 2d	Columbia	18 / S	"	'63: died March 27
Tabbut, Jotham M.	Centerville	23 / M	"	
Tucker, Amos H.	Columbia	23 / M	"	'63: died March 13
Webb, John	Columbia	24 / M	"	'63: disch. for disability March 28
Wilber, David R.	Eastbrook	21 / S	"	'63: died June 14
Williams, George S.	Lagrange	37 / M	"	
Wilson, Walter W.	Harrington	27 / S	"	'63: died Nov. 27, '62
Wood, David R.	Centerville	24 / S	"	
Wood, Isaac	Centerville	34 / M	"	'63: left sick at Centerville, Maine, Oct. 21, '62
Worster, Algernon A.	Columbia	23 / M	"	
Worster, Asa T.	Columbia	32 / M	"	
Worster, James	Columbia	37 / M	"	'63: died February 20
Worster, Moses	Columbia	44 / M	"	'63: disch. for disability Feb. 28
Worster, William G.	Columbia	35 / M	"	'63: died at Boston, Mass.

Name	Residence	Age/Marital Status	Muster Date	Remarks
Company E				
Commiss'd Officers				
Henry L. Wood	Dexter	30 / M	Oct. 10	
W. Prince Hersey	Lincoln	26 / M	"	'63: died Feb. 22
Thomas J. Pekes	Charleston	28 / M	"	'63: promoted 1st lieutenant
Sergeants				
Joseph S. Bowler	Lee	21 / S	"	'63: promoted 2nd lieutenant
Charles H. Knight	Dexter	25 / S	"	'63: died of wounds June 15
Charles G. Wing	Dexter	27 / S	"	'63: promoted 1st sergeant
William M. Cornforth	Springfield	23 / M	"	
John E. Allen	Lincoln	22 / S	"	'63: killed in action June 14
Corporals				
John C. Lamb	Carroll	30 / S	"	'63: disch. for disability Feb. 10
DeWitt C. Warren	Macwahoc Pl.	23 / M	"	'63: promoted sgt; died May 26
Jonathan Drew	Charleston	27 / S	"	
Franklin H. Dyer	Charleston	27 / M	"	'63: promoted sergeant
Nelson Rollins	Charleston	29 / M	"	
George M. Toward	Dexter	23 / S	"	'63: promoted sergeant
Danville S. Chadbourn	Macwahoc Pl.	19 / S	"	'63: promoted sergeant
Charles L. Lothrop	Prentiss	20 / S	"	'63: died April 11
Musicians				
James Crawford	Dexter	43 / M	"	
Joseph J. Elder	Corinna	19 / S	"	'63: left sick at Bellefontaine, Ohio, August 2
Wagoner				
Jefferson P. Richardson	Dexter	19 / S	"	
Privates				
Akiey, Caleb B.	Patten	29 / M	"	'63: disch. for disability at N.O.
Barker, Charles E.	Crystal Pl.	19 / S	"	
Bodwell, Martin V.	Lincoln	22 / S	"	'63: promoted corporal
Brawn, Sumner	Dexter	18 / S	"	
Campbell, J. Sanborn	Dexter	18 / S	"	
Carle, Constantine E.	Hudson	26 / M	"	
Carpenter, Asa S.	Charleston	44 / M	"	'63: died March 7

Appendix C

Name	Residence	Age/Marital Status	Muster Date	Remarks
Chamberlain, Walter R.	Hudson	21 / S	Oct. 10	
Clifford, Daniel	Lee	44 / M	Oct. 18	
Conant, Charles W.	Patten	23 / S	Oct. 10	
Cooper, Bowman	Bradford	26 / M	"	
Crabtree, Mark T.	Topsfield	32 / M	"	
Curtis, George H.	Carroll	26 / M	"	'62: deserted Oct. 16
Darling, Joseph	Hudson	42 / M	"	
Davis, Bartlett	Hudson	36 / M	"	'63: died May 6
Doane, Ivory F.	Lincoln	44 / M	"	
Ewings, Seth W.	Prentiss	25 / S	"	
Farrar, Charles W.	Dexter	21 / S	"	
Fitzgerald, Henry C.	Dexter	18 / S	"	'63: died January 2
Fogg, Jacob B.	Dexter	20 / S	"	'63: died May 18
Haines, Roscoe	Dexter	20 / S	"	
Hall, William M.	Dexter	21 / S	"	
Hall, Benjamin F.	Prentiss	31 / M	"	
Hall, Samuel	Charleston	33 / M	"	
Hamilton, John M.	Bancroft	33 / M	"	'63: promoted corporal
Hart, Alfred	Dexter	26 / M	"	'62: discharged Nov. 23
Hathorn, George H.	Lincoln	21 / S	"	
Hill, Charles E.	Topsfield	18 / S	"	
Hunt, James L.	Charleston	24 / S	"	
Hutchinson, Jonas	Dexter	35 / M	"	'63: promoted corporal
Ireland, Isaiah K.	Dexter	28 / M	"	'63: died January 16
Ireland, Francis A.	Dexter	19 / S	"	
Jipson, George F.	Prentiss	19 / S	"	'63: trans. to 2nd Rhode Island Cav., March 18
Johnson, William M.	Dexter	43 / M	Oct. 20	'63: promoted corporal
Jordan, William H.	Charleston	18 / S	Oct. 10	
Judkins, Andrew J.	Orneville	34 / M	"	'62: appointed color corporal; disch. for disability April 9, '63
Kimball, Charles F.	Macwahoc Pl.	21 / S	"	'63: died May 16
Lamb, Salmon	Carroll	32 / S	"	'62: sent home '63: disch. for disab. Oct. 17, '62
Leighton, James H.	Dexter	28 / M	"	'63: disch. for disab. Feb. 15, '63
Leighton, Daniel P.	Dexter	22 / S	"	
Lemont, Angus	Pictou, NS	25 / S	"	'63: died February 22
Leslie, Melvin F.	Patten	18 / S	"	
McLaughlin, William	Dexter	23 / S	"	'63: died May 13
McPherson, Isaac	Bancroft	31 / M	"	

Roster of the Twenty-Second Regiment

Name	Residence	Age/Marital Status	Muster Date	Remarks
Merrill, Ithamer B.	Dexter	32 / M	Oct. 10	
Moores, Menander O.	Charleston	23 / S	"	
Morrill, Solomon	Dexter	19 / S	"	
Mountain, Charles N.	Dexter	20 / S	"	
Remick, Daniel H.	Dexter	41 / M	"	
Ricker, Moses	Lee	33 / M	"	'63: died May 19
Roberts, George, Jr.	Milo	30 / M	"	'62: in hospital at Camp John Pope; left sick at Bangor, Oct. 21, '62; never heard from
Sanders, William G.	Crystal Pl.	18 / M	"	'63: promoted corporal
Scales, Augustus	Dexter	18 / S	Oct. 20	'63: died December 26, '62
Silver, Samuel F.	Dexter	19 / S	Oct. 10	'63 died March 10, '63
Smith, Joseph H.	Dexter	27 / S	"	'62: sick in hospital; died December 10, '62
Southard, Zachariah S.	Bradford	32 / M	"	'63: promoted corporal
Spaulding, Liberty B.	Springfield	20 / M	"	
Spaulding, Charles	Springfield	21 / S	"	
Spaulding, John W.	Springfield	18 / S	"	
Stickney, Charles H.	Prentiss	18 / S	"	
Stinchfield, Benj. A.	Brownville	18 / S	"	
Strout, Isaiah	Charleston	18 / S	"	
Swanton, Silas B.	Dexter	23 / M	"	
Swanton, Samuel A.	Dexter	30 / M	"	'62: in hospital in Philadelphia
Thurlow, Henry J.	Lee	24 / M	"	
Tucker, Philemon	Lee	18 / S	"	
Ward, Aurelius F.	Bradford	44 / M	"	
Weymouth, Edward W.	Webster	36 / M	"	
Whittemore, Jacob H.	Dexter	22 / M	"	'63: died February 27
Whittemore, Charles E.	Dexter	18 / S	"	'63: died March 6

Company F

Commiss'd Officers

Name	Residence	Age/Marital Status	Muster Date
William B. Taylor	Calais	36 / M	Oct. 10
Benjamin F. Waite, Jr.	Calais	27 / S	"
Gibbs F. Libby	Robbinston	38 /S	"

Sergeants

Name	Residence	Age/Marital Status	Muster Date
Joseph C. Rockwood	Calais	27 / S	"
John A. Nebethel	Calais	44 / M	"
Peter C. Lamb	Calais	22 / S	"

Name	Residence	Age/Marital Status	Muster Date	Remarks
Daniel M. Gardner	Calais	28 / M	Oct. 10	'62: sick at camp; disch. for disability, April 2, '63
Samuel S. Mason	Calais	32 / M	"	

Corporals

Name	Residence	Age/Marital Status	Muster Date	Remarks
John Gayor	Calais	44 / M	"	
Prentiss M. Vose	Robbinston	21 / S	"	
Weston Haycock	Calais	21 / S	"	
Samuel W. Haycock	Calais	24 / S	"	
Henry S. Young	Calais	30 / M	"	
Henry H. King	Calais	21 / S	"	
Samuel Ross	Robbinston	27 / M	"	
Martin Cone	Calais	27 / S	"	'62: changed rank to wagoner
(63: listed as wagoner; returned to ranks)				

Musicians

Name	Residence	Age/Marital Status	Muster Date	Remarks
Hezekiah L. Lane	Calais	33 / M	"	'63: disch. for disability Feb. 14
Edgar Townsend	Calais	23 / S	"	'62: sick at Camp Seward; disch. for disab. Dec. 19, '62

Wagoner

Name	Residence	Age/Marital Status	Muster Date	Remarks
John B. Burnham	Calais	28 / M	"	'62: appointed ordnance sergeant; '63: listed as private

Privates

Name	Residence	Age/Marital Status	Muster Date	Remarks
Andersen, John	Calais	19 / S	"	
Bailey, Stillman H.	Crawford	19 / S	"	'63: died January 12
Baker, Frederick W.	Calais	19 / S	"	'63: discharged July 23
Beckwith, Robert	Calais	25 / S	"	'63: promoted corporal
Berry, Samuel	Calais	24 / S	"	'63: appointed wagoner
Blackwood, Benjamin	Robbinston	35 / M	"	
Boardman, George H.	Calais	19 / S	"	
Brewer, John N.M.	Robbinston	28 / S	"	'63: died April 3
Brown, William H.	Alexander	32 / M	"	
Burbank, Henry J.	Cooper	25 / S	"	
Carson, Samuel	Robbinston	31 / M	"	'62: sick at Camp Seward; disch. for disability April 2, '63
Crafts, William H.	Alexander	21 / S	"	'63: died April 27
Diffin, George	Robbinston	18 / S	"	'62: sick in hospital
Duncan, David	Calais	26 / S	"	
Dutch, Robert	Calais	31 / M	"	'62: musician
Eye, Henry A.	Calais	18 / S	"	

Roster of the Twenty-Second Regiment

Name	Residence	Age/Marital Status	Muster Date	Remarks
Flewellyn, Edward	Calais	44 / M	Oct. 10	
Foster, Charles A.	Calais	18 / S	"	
Fowler, John	Calais	42 / M	"	
Frost, George	Calais	21 / S	"	
Gallagher, Samuel J.	Calais	19 / S	"	'62: on extra duty in Q.M.'s dept.; 63: promoted commissary sgt.
Gates, Horatio	Robbinston	19 / S	"	
Gates, Humphrey	Robbinston	18 / S	"	'63: disch. for disability March 27
Getchell, William A.	Topsfield	28 / M	"	
Greenlaw, Augustus	Calais	19 / S	"	
Hayman, Andrew S.	Calais	19 / S	"	
Hayward, Charles E.	Cooper	18 / S	"	'63: died July 2
Henderson, Benjamin	Cooper	30 / S	"	
Henderson, Levi	Cooper	21 / S	"	
Hickey, Patrick	Calais	18 / S	"	
Hitchings, Hiram	Cooper	20 / S	"	'63: died April 21
Howe, Ephraim W.	Calais	40 / M	"	
Johnson, Frederick S.	Robbinston	27 / S	"	
Jones, George K.	Calais	18 / S	"	
Kelly, George	Calais	24 / M	"	
Lane, Elias S.	Calais	26 / M	"	
Lane, Francis P.	Cooper	18 / S	"	'62: sick at Camp Seward
Lane, Willard C.	Calais	33 / M	"	
Leahan, Edward	Calais	18 / S	"	
Leighton, Samuel	Robbinston	22 / S	"	
Libby, Dallas H.	Calais	18 / S	"	'63: died March 8
Louden, Robert	Calais	20 / S	"	
Lowe, Watson	Crawford	22 / S	"	
Lyons, Greenwood	Alexander	19 / S	"	'62: died in hospital in Philadelphia
Mullen, Daniel	Calais	20 / S	"	'62: sick at Camp Seward; disch. for disability Jan. 15, '63
Munson, John	Alexander	25 / S	"	'63: died April 29
Nash, Augustus	Calais	18 / S	"	
Nodding, Isaac J.	Crawford	22 / S	"	
Perkins, Daniel	Crawford	21 / S	"	
Poor, William H.	Robbinston	34 / M	"	
Rand, Elijah	Baring	44 / M	"	'63: died March 2
Redding, Henry A.	Calais	18 / S	"	
Rowe, Charles E.	Calais	22 / S	"	
Sawyer, Joseph W.	Calais	28 / M	"	
Sawyer, Stillman O.	Calais	19 / S	"	

Name	Residence	Age/Marital Status	Muster Date	Remarks
Scott, George	Calais	24 / M	Oct. 10	'62: transfer to band 3d brigade; transfer to band, 25th Maine Volunteers, Nov. '62
Seamans, Samuel	Alexander	40 / M	"	
Smith, John E.	Calais	24 / M	"	
Spearing, Jefferson	Alexander	24 / S	"	
Stanhope, George	Robbinston	18 / S	"	'63: died February 4
Tarbell, Jesse G.	Meddybemps	37 / M	"	'62: nurse at Camp Seward
Tracey, Thomas	Calais	18 / S	"	
Tucker, John	Robbinston	40 / M	"	
Vose, Benjamin L.	Robbinston	18 / S	"	
White, John N.	Topsfield	26 / S	"	
Young, Daniel	Calais	25 / M	"	

Company G

Commiss'd Officers

Name	Residence	Age/Marital Status	Muster Date	Remarks
Aziel W. Putnam	Houlton	26 / S	Oct. 10	
Robert H. Outhouse	Hodgdon	28 / M	"	
Henry H. Putnam	Houlton	20 / S	"	

Sergeants

Name	Residence	Age/Marital Status	Muster Date	Remarks
Albert Eddy	Linneus	38 / M	"	
Eli H. Bunker	Houlton	21 / S	"	'63: disch. for disability July 24
Joshua C. Pollard	Hodgdon	26 / M	"	
Alexander Thompson	Mattawamkeag	26 / S	"	
Thomas E. Wiggin	Hodgdon	38 / M	"	

Corporals

Name	Residence	Age/Marital Status	Muster Date	Remarks
William H. Hammond	Houlton	30 / M	"	
Hiram H. Chase	Weston	24 / M	"	'63: died March 18
William Gellerson	Weston	23 / S	"	
Greenv'le M. Hopkinson	Ft. Fairfield	28 / M	"	'63: died March 20
Oliver A. Cole	N. Limerick	34 / M	"	'62: sick at Washington; disch. for disability Jan. 29, '63
William O. Foster	N. Limerick	30 / M	"	'62: sick at Camp John Pope; returned to ranks in '63
Stephen R. Smith	Weston	24 / S	"	
John Stewart	Belfast	26 / M	"	'63: disch. for disability Feb. 2

Name	Residence	Age/Marital Status	Muster Date	Remarks
Musicians				
Oliver D. Richardson	Ashland	44 / M	Oct. 10	
Adelbert A. Stackpole	Monticello	21 / S	"	'63: returned to ranks; left sick at Brashear City, La., May 26
Wagoner				
James M. Gordon	Monticello	30 / S	"	'63: died March 17
Privates				
Adams, Isaac L.	N. Limerick	25 / M	"	
Austin, Robert	Littleton	21 / S	"	
Bean, Lyman B.	Monticello	18 / S	"	'63: died April 8
Bean, Oscar L.	Houlton	29 / S	"	'63: promoted corporal
Benn, Samuel	Hodgdon	27 / S	"	'63: died May 6
Berry, Eben L.	Bridgewater	30 / M	"	
Blanchard, Solomon	Houlton	19 / S	"	'63: died March 14
Bishop, James	Hodgdon	28 / M	"	'63: promoted corporal
Bradbury, Ohristop'r C.	Bridgewater	41 / M	"	'63: promoted corporal
Boynton, Arthur W.	Monticello	19 / S	"	
Brown, John W.	Linneus	32 / M	"	
Butterfield, George W	Danforth	20 / S	"	'63: promoted corporal
Butterfield, John H.	Danforth	30 / M	"	
Campbell, Chandler H.	Houlton	26 / S	"	'63: died May 1
Campbell, John	Kingsbury	26 / S	"	
Campbell, William H.	Houlton	22 / S	"	
Chase, Marcellus	Belfast	19 / S	"	'63: died March 9
Chesley, Franklin	Mattawamkeag	42 / S	"	'63: died May 3
Conant, Joseph A.	Ft. Fairfield	32 / M	"	
Dodge, Herbert R.	Shirley	23 / M	"	
Donoho, Thomas	Houlton	26 / S	"	
Downs, Joshua	Wellington	20 / S	"	'63: died February 9
Dunnin, Bernard	Littleton	27 / S	"	'63: died April 10
Ellis, Atkins	Wellington	41 / M	"	
Ellis, Otis	Wellington	18 / S	"	
Ervin, Timothy N. (spelled "Erwin" in '63)	Littleton	23 / M	"	
Fox, Daniel	Houlton	18 / S	"	
Gerow, Israel M. (spelled "Grow" in '63)	Hodgdon	20 / S	"	
Gilman, Leonard	Bridgewater	21 / S	"	
Gilkey, Edward	Houlton	18 / S	"	
Harding, Brydone S.	Danforth	22 / S	"	
Howe, Harrison	Belfast	21 / S	"	'62: died at Baltimore Oct. 30
Hoyt, Joshua	Ft. Fairfield	24 / S	"	'63: died March 10
Hoyt Orin	Ft. Fairfield	26 / S	"	

Name	Residence	Age/Marital Status	Muster Date	Remarks
Huff, Charles	Wellington	18 / S	Oct. 10	
Kane, Michael	Houlton	19 / S	"	
Lassell, Benjamin F.	Houlton	39 / M	"	
Mason, Alexander	Linneus	44 / M	"	'63: left sick at Union City, Indiana, August 2
Merrill, John C.	Houlton	18 / S	"	
Monson, Marion	Houlton	19 / S	"	
Moses, Eli N.	Wellington	20 / S	"	'63: died May 1
Nevill, Michael H.	Littleton	18 / S	"	
Newman, David	Houlton	18 / S	"	
Oliver, Henry N.	Houlton	18 / S	"	
Perkins, John G.	Linneus	25 / S	"	
Pollard, Thomas B.	Hodgdon	22 / S	"	'62: discharged Oct. 3
Pomroy, John	Bancroft	40 / M	"	'62: absent without leave; deserted at Bangor, Oct. 4, '62
Pullen, Stephen	Houlton	21 / S	"	
Pyle, Amos	Ft. Fairfield	22 / M	"	
Rigbey, John R.	Smyrna	33 / M	"	
Rowell, George W.	Hodgdon	24 / S	"	
Scudder, Silas H.	Monticello	29 / M	"	
Seaborn, Robert	Littleton	25 / S	"	'63: disch. for disability July 24
Smith, Warren	Weston	22 / S	"	
Sibley, Albert	Ft. Fairfield	18 / S	"	
Suiter, John W.	Houlton	31 / M	"	
Taylor, Francis F.	Houlton	36 / S	"	'63: left sick at Brashear City, La., May 26
Taylor, Theodore B.	Hodgdon	22 / S	"	
Thibodeau, David	Hodgdon	24 / M	"	
Towle, La Forest V.	Ft. Fairfield	23 / S	"	
Townsend, Charles H.	Ft. Fairfield	42 / M	"	
Tweedy, George A.	Littleton	20 / S	"	
Washburn, Albert	Wellington	31 / M	"	'62: deserted Oct. 2: not mustered
Whitney, William	Weston	22 / S	"	'63: died May 1
Woodard, Israel R.D.	Bowerbank	20 / S	"	'63: transferred to Co. I

Company H

Commiss'd Officers

Isaac W. Case	Kenduskeag	39 / M	Oct. 10	'63: died July 2
Joseph Richardson	Corinth	37 / M	"	
Anson C. Jerrard	Plymouth	27 / M	"	

Roster of the Twenty-Second Regiment

Name	Residence	Age/Marital Status	Muster Date	Remarks
Sergeants				
Joseph L. True	Garland	21 / S	Oct. 10	
Isaac R. Worth	Corinth	21 / S	"	
Asa W. Thompson	Exeter	30 / M	"	
Nicholas G. Reed	Garland	35 / M	"	
William M. Chapman	Corinth	22 / S	"	
Corporals				
Henry W. Jordan	Stetson	20 / S	"	'63: died August 13
Erastus L. Palmer (listed as private in '63)	Garland	28 / M	"	'62: appointed right guide of regt.
Abner G. Clark (listed as private in '63)	Levant	27 / M	"	'62: appointed left guide of regt.
Danville L. Wyman	Levant	30 / M	"	
Chester M. Herrick	Corinth	22 / S	"	
John M. Morrison	Corinth	25 / S	"	
George O. Varney	Greenville	37 / M	"	'63: disch. for disability March 11
Henry C. Spooner	Kenduskeag	32 / M	"	
Edward J. Smart (listed as private in '62)				
Calvin Titcomb (listed as private in '62 report)				'63: died March 28
Musicians				
George W. Buzzell	Plymouth	18 / S	"	
Wagoner				
George F. Davis	Levant	25 / S	"	
Privates				
Allen, Ivis M.	Plymouth	26 / S	"	
Allen, John O.	Stetson	19 / S	"	
Ames, Henry J.	Kenduskeag	37 / M	"	
Badger, John		38 / M	"	'63: left sick at New Orleans July 24
Baker, Dow C.	Kingsbury	23 / S	"	'63: wounded in action June 14
Batchelder, Alonzo F.	Garland	19 / S	"	
Blanchard, David J.	Kenduskeag	43 / M	"	
Booker, Joseph W.	Levant	32 / M	"	
Booker, Orin	Levant	30 / M	"	
Bran, Abner M.	Greenville	24 / S	"	'63: transfer to Gen Banks' bodyguard July 22
Bran, William L.	Levant	20 / S	"	'63: transfer to Gen Banks' bodyguard July 22

Appendix C

Name	Residence	Age/Marital Status	Muster Date	Remarks
Brown, Albert	Kenduskeag	36 / M	Oct. 10	'63: disch. for disability March 27
Brown, Allen H.	Levant	23 / S	"	
Brown, William	Garland	31 / M	"	
Buzzell, Stephen S.	Hermon	22 / S	"	'63: died March 27
Clark, Abner G. (listed as corporal in '62)	Levant	27 / M	"	
Chandler, John B.	Corinth	25 / S	"	
Daniels, John E.	Lee	18 / S	"	'62: furloughed Oct. 26 for 5 days, not returned; deserted at Bangor Oct. 20, '62
Davis, John A.	Garland	18 / S	"	
Ellis, Alden B.	Garland	40 / M	"	'63: taken prisoner in June, '63
Farmer, Randall	Garland	19 / S	"	'63: died March 31
Gardiner, Levi	Corinth	22 / S	"	'62: sick in hospital; died Dec. '62
Gile, William F.	Corinth	23 / S	"	'63: promoted corporal
Gerald, Rufus D.	Levant	27 / M	"	'63: died March 19
Glidden, John J.	Sebec	20 / S	"	
Gouid, Gorham H.	Levant	25 / S	"	'63: died March 3
Gould, Ransom C.	Corinth	22 / M	"	
Ham, Sumner T.	Corinth	24 / S	"	
Hammons, Albra G.	Corinth	20 / S	"	
Haskell, Alphonzo	Levant	20 / S	"	'63: promoted corporal
Haskell, Bennett A.	Garland	18 / S	"	
Haskell, Jason F.	Garland	18 / S	"	
Herrick, George W.	Corinth	20 / S	"	
Holbrook, Edgar E.	Plymouth	21 / S	"	
Holbrook, Franklin	Plymouth	21 / S	"	
Holbrook, Peter	Plymouth	30 / M	"	'63: died May 2
Houston, Cyrus H.	Levant	43 / M	"	
Houston, George W.	Corinth	21 / S	"	
Hoyt, Alfred	Kenduskeag	40 / M	"	'63: prisoner June 27; paroled
Langley, George W.	Stetson	18 / S	"	'62: sick in hospital; died Jan. 4, '63
Langley, William A.	Stetson	20 / S	"	
Loud, Rufus D.	Plymouth	21 / S	"	
Loud, John C.	Plymouth	20 / S	"	
Lovejoy, Levi A.	Garland	25 / M	"	
McKusick, Ambrose C.	Levant	22 / S	"	'63: died April 1
Mitchell, Wilfred A.	Kenduskeag	26 / M	"	'63: died February 25
Morey, Arthur H.	Kenduskeag	20 / S	not mustered	sick at Kenduskeag
Palmer, Erastus L. (listed as corporal in '62)				

Roster of the Twenty-Second Regiment

Name	Residence	Age/Marital Status	Muster Date	Remarks
Ramsdell, Austin	Garland	21 / S	Oct. 10	
Robinson, Frank M.	Corinth	18 / S	"	'63: disch. for disability March 27
Russell, Milford	Bridgton	21 / S	"	
Sargent, Edgar	Corinth	24 / S	"	'63: died March 14
Sawyer, Phineas H.	Elliotsville	35 / M	"	
Shores, Clifford W.	Corinth	28 / S	"	
Skillin, Charles E.	Garland	26 / S	"	
Skillin, David	Garland	18 / S	"	
Smart, Edward J.	Plymouth	21 / S	"	'62: promoted to 7th corporal
Small, Calvin	Plymouth	35 / S	"	
Smith, Ellis	Kenduskeag	18 / S	"	
Staples, Charles H.	Levant	20 / S	"	'63: died May 5
Staples, William D.	Levant	18 / S	"	'63: died May 14
Stevens, Benjamin M.	Corinth	33 / M	"	
Thompson, Mark	Exeter	21 / S	"	'62: sick in hospital; died Feb. 5, '63
Tiplady, James A.	Garland	18 / S	"	
Titcomb, Calvin	Kingsbury	19 / S	"	'62: promoted to 8th corporal
Towle, Edward B.	Kenduskeag	40 / M	"	
Turner, Pirzirvid B.	Levant	20 / S	"	
Whittier, Henry A.	Corinth	19 / S	"	
Wiggin, Robert F.	Stetson	22 / S	"	'63: died December 12, '62
Wing, Ansel O.	Levant	36 / M	"	
Wing, Joseph M.	Levant	18 / S	"	'63: died May 12
York, Walter E.	Stetson	20 / S	"	'63: died February 21

Company I

Commiss'd Officers

Name	Residence	Age/Marital Status	Muster Date	Remarks
Archibald C. Lambert	Dover	29 / M	Oct. 10	
Montville C. Bailey	Sangerville	33 / M	"	'63: resigned January 14
Owen B. Williams	Sangerville	26 / M	"	'63: promoted 1st lieutenant

Sergeants

Name	Residence	Age/Marital Status	Muster Date	Remarks
Hiram E. Hatch	Guilford	34 / M	"	'63: promoted 2nd lieutenant
Edwin Lambert	Dover	31 / M	"	'63: promoted 1st sergeant
William E. Turner	Dover	37 / M	"	'63: promoted 1st sergeant; died May 13
Owen W. Bridges	Sangerville	26 / M	"	
Nelson B. Haskell	Guilford	23 / M	"	'63: died May 21

Appendix C

Name	Residence	Age/Marital Status	Muster Date	Remarks
Corporals				
William Hussey, Jr.	Dover	38 / M	Oct. 10	'63: died May 20
Adoniram J. Herring	Guilford	32 / M	"	'63: promoted sergeant
William W. Blethen	Atkinson	28 / M	"	'63: disch. for disability Feb. 16
Al Spaulding	Dover	29 / S	"	'63: promoted sergeant
Gilman C. Fisher	Foxcroft	21 / S	"	'63: promoted sergeant
Enoch M. Tucker	Guilford	34 / M	"	'63: returned to ranks; died March 16
Sumner L. Hurd	Dover	20 / S	"	
Luther F. Rice	Guilford	20 / S	"	
Musicians				
Elam Palmer	Sangerville	20 / S	"	'63: died January 24
Joseph M. Ames	Dover	21 / S	"	
Wagoner				
Frank W. Gray	Sangerville	30 / M	"	
Privates				
Ball, Love H.	Foxcroft	18 / S	"	'63: died March 15
Booker, Alvin L.	Dover	24 / M	"	'63: died March 1
Bragdon, Ora	Dover	18 / S	"	'63: died February 10
Brett, George W.	Sangerville	18 / S	"	'63: died March 31
Bridges, Jacob A.	Sangerville	19 / S	"	
Bridges, Joshua, Jr.	Sangerville	34 / M	"	'63: sick at New Orleans since March 14
Brockway, Orison A.	Sangerville	21 / S	"	'63: left sick at Union, Indiana, August 2
Brown, Albert	Dover	45 / M	"	'62: disch. for disability Nov. 5
Brown, Frank A.	Dover	21 / S	"	
Cass, Samuel H.	Sebec	28 / S	"	
Carter, Jonathan	Foxcroft	42 / M	"	
Chandler, Isaac G.	Atkinson	45 / M	"	
Chase, Christopher C.	Dover	29 / M	"	
Chase, Napoleon B.	Sebec	18 / S	"	
Clough, Samuel N.	Sangerville	37 / S	"	
Craig, James	Dover	25 / S	"	'63: died March 8
Crocker, Jackson G.	Sangerville	28 / M	"	
Cross, Asa V.	Sangerville	18 / S	"	
Damon, Augustus W.	Sangerville	19 / S	"	
Douglass, Harmon L.	Dover	18 / S	"	
Earl, Ebenezer	Foxcroft	18 / S	"	
Elliott, Thomas P.	Dover	18 / S	"	
Ellis, Mellen F.	Guilford	19 / S	"	
Farnham, Luther F.	Sangerville	20 / S	"	

Roster of the Twenty-Second Regiment

Name	Residence	Age/Marital Status	Muster Date	Remarks
Farnham, William J.	Sangerville	18 / S	Oct. 10	
Fish, Webster A.	Dover	19 / S	"	'63: died May 22
Garey, Samuel B.	Foxcroft	28 / M	"	
Gatchel, Abial	Sebec	19 / S	"	
Gilman, David	Sangerville	33 / M	"	
Glass, Henry H.	Guilford	23 / S	"	'63: died March 9
Goodwin, Charles E.	Dover	18 / S	"	
Gould, John H.	Foxcroft	19 / S	"	'63: died February 12
Hawes, Henry L.	Sangerville	41 / M	"	
Harriman, Justus G.	Guilford	25 / S	"	
Herring, Ruel	Guilford	18 / S	"	
Holmes, Arthur	Sangerville	18 / S	"	'63: died July 3
Hurd, Horace M.	Dover	18 / S	"	'63: sick at Ft. Monroe since December 1, '62
Hussey, Benjamin F.	Dover	30 / M	"	
Hussey, George L.	Dover	19 / S	"	
Jenks, Edwin S.	Atkinson	20 / S	"	
Lambert, George F.	Dover	24 / M	"	
Larrabee, William F.	Dover	20 / S	"	'63: wounded in action June 7
Leathers, Thomas J.	Dover	20 / S	"	
Lewis, Frank R.	Sangerville	18 / S	Oct. 18	
Lovell, Stephen W.	Abbot	33 / M	Oct. 10	'63: disch. for disability March 27
McGrath, Charles H.	Guilford	24 / M	"	
Merrill, Andrew B.	Dover	20 / S	"	'63: promoted corporal
Mitchell, George W.	Dover	22 / M	"	'63: left sick at Bellefontaine, Ohio, August 2
Morgan, Asa H.	Guilford	18 / S	"	
Nichols, Allen B.	Bangor	22 / M	"	
Ordway, George J.	Sangerville	21 / S	"	
Philbrick, Alonzo	Bangor	18 / S	"	
Philbrick, Greenlief	Sangerville	28 / M	"	
Pratt, Benjamin F.	Foxcroft	23 / S	"	
Pratt, Edwin N.	Foxcroft	18 / S	"	
Rice, Flavel C.	Guilford	21 / S	"	'63: died March 11
Richardson, Charles	Dover	31 / M	"	
Robbins, George A.	Guilford	19 / S	"	
Robinson, Anson J.	Dover	18 / S	"	
Robinson, David H.	Dover	20 / S	"	'63: discharged in 1862
Rogers, Cyrus A.	Dover	19 / S	"	'63: died January 27
Rose, John F.S.	Guilford	23 / S	"	'63: disch. for disability Feb. 16
Smith, Eleazer B.	Sangerville	37 / S	"	

Name	Residence	Age/Marital Status	Muster Date	Remarks
Spaulding, Joseph B.	Dover	23 / S	Oct. 10	
Spencer, Walter	Dover	18 / S	"	
Stearns, Charles W.	Guilford	44 / M	"	'63: sick at New Orleans since April 8
Stearns, Charles	Guilford	18 / S	"	'63: sick at New Orleans
Staples, Charles H.	Atkinson	18 / S	"	
Stevens, Benjamin E.	Guilford	44 / M	"	
Stowe, Nathan C.	Dover	19 / S	"	
Swanton, Seth J.	Dexter	19 / S	"	
Trundy, Marshall H.	Dover	19 / S	"	'63: promoted corporal
Tucker, Francis A.	Guilford	37 / M	"	
Turner, Charles H.	Dover	28 / M	"	'63: promoted corporal
Weymouth, Lewis	Guilford	25 / M	"	
Wharff, Albert F.	Guilford	18 / S	"	'63: died January 15
Whittier, James P.	Dover	44 / M	"	
Whittemore, Andrew J.	Sangerville	20 / S	"	
Woodard, Israel R.D.	Bowerbank	20 / S	"	'63: transfer from Company C

Company K

Commiss'd Officers

Name	Residence	Age/Marital Status	Muster Date	Remarks
Turner W. Whitehouse	Newport	24 / S	Oct. 10	
Amos B. Matthews	Hartland	25 / S	"	
Edwin W. Trueworthy	Newport	22 / S	"	

Sergeants

Name	Residence	Age/Marital Status	Muster Date	Remarks
Arnold Stedman	Hartland	23 / S	"	
Edwin A. Parker	St. Albans	24 / M	"	
Sprague W. Marsh	Palmyra	27 / S	"	
George W. Martin	St. Albans	19 / S	"	'62: sick at Fortress Monroe
Albert F. Learned	Newport	19 / S	"	

Corporals

Name	Residence	Age/Marital Status	Muster Date	Remarks
Andrew Skinner	Exeter	32 / M	"	
Henry T. Nutter	Exeter	18 / S	"	
Chester Trueworthy	Newport	24 / M	"	
Hiram G. Steward	St. Albans	30 / M	"	'63: wounded in action, June 14
Stephen A. Steward	Newport	19 / M	"	
James H. French	Palmyra	24 / M	"	'63: discharged for disability
Fernando Miles	Newport	21 / S	"	'63: returned to ranks
Orin A. Parkman	Palmyra	25 / S	"	'63: left to take care of sick at Union, Ohio, August 2

Name	Residence	Age/Marital Status	Muster Date	Remarks
Musicians				
Jacob H. Steward	Newport	24 / M	Oct. 10	
Oliver I. Folsom	Etna	20 / S	"	
Wagoner				
George W. Pennell	St. Albans	35 / M	"	
Privates				
Abbott, Leonard	Etna	40 / S	"	'63: disch. for disability Feb. 15
Allen, Harrison B.	Palmyra	18 / S	"	
Applebee, Henry	Palmyra	18 / S	"	
Applebee, Benjamin F.	Palmyra	20 / S	"	
Atwell, Oliver S.	Dixmont	21 / S	"	
Bates, Constantine	St. Albans	30 / M	"	'63: died March 7
Bigelow, Melvin	St. Albans	18 / S	"	
Call, Ephraim	Palmyra	30 / S	"	'63: died July 13
Carter, Benjamin F.	Etna	18 / S	"	
Caverly, Charles H.	Newport	20 / S	"	
Caverly, Amos	Newport	18 / S	"	
Cole, John W.	Palmyra	23 / M	"	
Colbath, Nathan P.	Exeter	18 / S	"	'62: deserted Oct. 13
Cook, Charles A.	Hartland	18 / S	"	
Day, John H.	Newport	20 / S	"	
Davis, John A.	Palmyra	33 / M	"	
Emery, Sylvanus	St. Albans	18 / S	"	
Estes, Henry W.	Exeter	21 / S	"	
Farnham, John M.	Palmyra	22 / S	"	
Farnham, Isaac L.	Palmyra	25 / S	"	'63: died June 21
Fernald, Mark	Newport	25 / M	"	
Fernald, Tobias A.	Newport	22 / S	"	'63: died January 8
Folsom, Henry W.	Etna	23 / S	"	
French, Edwin	Palmyra	19 / S	"	
Friend, William	Exeter	19 / S	"	
Hoisington, Henry C.	Hartland	28 / M	"	'63: promoted to corporal
Hutchings, Hanson	Etna	19 / S	"	
Hutchinson, James B.	Palmyra	20 / S	"	
Johnson, Joseph T.	St. Albans	23 / S	"	
Judkins, Herbert S.	Palmyra	18 / S	"	
Lawrence, Demarquis L.	Newport	25 / S	"	
Libbey, Daniel W.	Mattawamkeag	22 / S	"	
Lombard, Mark B.	Exeter	28 / S	"	'62: sick at Fortress Monroe; 63: disch. for disability Feb. 13
MacKay, Isaac N.A.	Newport	19 / S	"	
Marsh, Alphonzo G.	Palmyra	19 / S	"	

Name	Residence	Age/Marital Status	Muster Date	Remarks
McKenney, Alonzo	Palmyra	20 / S	Oct. 10"	'63: died January 2
McLure, Charles	Palmyra	23 / S	"	
McLure, Martin	Palmyra	22 / S	"	
Mellows, Job	St. Albans	33 / M	"	'63: died February 22
Murch, John	Palmyra	19 / S	"	
Nay, Stanley E.	Palmyra	18 / S	"	
Nickerson, James W.	St. Albans	18 / S	"	
Nye, Russell M.	St. Albans	24 / M	"	
Nye, George	St. Albans	23 / M	"	
Orff, Charles A.	Exeter	22 / M	"	
Osborn, Peter B.	Hartland	18 / S	"	
Page, George H.	Hartland	40 / M	"	'62: left at hospital in Bangor; '63: disch. for disability Feb. 1
Parkman, Frank O.	Palmyra	20 / S	"	'63: left sick at Union City, Ohio, August 2
Pease, George A.	Exeter	18 / S	"	
Pease, John L.	Exeter	18 / S	"	
Pollard, Thomas J.	Palmyra	20 / S	"	
Powers, Levi	St. Albans	19 / S	"	
Pushor, Albert	Hartland	21 / S	not mustered	sick in Bangor
Robert, Charles	Newport	18 / S	Oct. 10	'63: died February 26
Robinson, Nathaniel B.	Palmyra	19 / S	"	
Robinson, Lorin D.	Exeter	19 / S	"	
Seavey, John M.	Newport	21 / M	"	'62: sick at Alexandria
Sinkler, William P.	Palmyra	18 / S	"	
Spaulding, John S.	Palmyra	22 / S	"	'63: wounded in action, June 14
Spratt, Stowell S.	Etna	18 / S	"	
Stedman, Isaac	Hartland	33 / S	"	
Stevens, Royal L.	Exeter	19 / S	"	
Stevens James F.	Hartland	19 / S	"	
Steward, Benjamin	St. Albans	22 / S	"	
Stuart, John O.	Newport	23 / S	"	
Treworthy, Henry E.	Newport	21 / S	"	
Waldron, Cyrus	Hartland	36 / M	"	'63: died June 20
Webb, Amaziah W.	St. Albans	18 / S	"	
Webber, Joseph H.	Hartland	44 / M	"	
Webber, Allen	Hartland	22 / M	"	
Wedgwood, James	Newport	18 / S	"	'63: died February 26
Wedgwood, John	Newport	20 / S	"	'63: died February 5
Whitney, Eben	Hartland	20 / S	"	'63: left sick at Brashear City, Louisiana, May 5
Wood, Henry P.	St. Albans	18 / S	"	
Woodbury, Isaiah	Hartland	21 / M	"	

Chapter Notes

Introduction

1. Joshua Lawrence Chamberlain, "Dedication of the Maine Monuments at Gettysburg, Speech, Evening of October 3, 1889." In *Bayonets Forward: My Civil War Reminiscences*. Gettysburg, PA: Stan Clark Military Books, 1994, pp. 202.

Chapter 1

1. "Abolition of the Atlantic Slave Trade in the United States," *Harper's Weekly*, 8 March 1862, retrieved 4 February 2005 from wwwl.american.edu/TED/slave.htm.

2. *New York Times*, 15 May 1861.

3. "Celebrate America's Freedom: The Declaration of Independence," retrieved 6 February 2005, www.glencoe.com/sec/socialstudies/btt/celebratingfreedom/caf_01.shtml.

4. "What Lincoln and Other Yankees Knew: The Evidence That Pre–Civil War U.S. Slavery Was Illegal and Unconstitutional," retrieved 7 March 2006, http://medicolegal.tripod.com/slaveryillegal.htm. "Signers of the Declaration of Independence: Benjamin Franklin," retrieved 7 March 2006, www.ushistory.org/declaration/signers/franklin.htm.

5. Diane Monroe Smith, *Fanny and Joshua: The Enigmatic Lives of Francis Caroline Adams and Joshua Lawrence Chamberlain*, Gettysburg, PA: Thomas, 1999, pp. 108–109.

6. Ibid.

7. Mark Hatfield, "Vice Presidents of the United States: Hannibal Hamlin (1861–1865)," retrieved 12 January 2008, www.senate.gov/artandhistory/history/resources/pdf/hannibal_hamlin.pdf+Hannibal+Hamlin&hl=en&gl=us.

8. "United States Presidential Elections: 1856," retrieved 20 October 2007, www.historycentral.com/elections/1856.html. "The American Presidency Project: Election of 1856," retrieved 20 October 2007, www.presidency.ucsb.edu/showelection.php?year=1856.

9. "United States Presidential Elections: 1860," retrieved 20 October 2007, www.historycentral.com/elections/1860.html. "The American Presidency Project: Election of 1860," retrieved 20 October 2007, www.presidency.ucsb.edu/showelection.php?year=1860.

10. Sylvia Sherman, Maine State Archives, personal communication, 6 August 2007. William Whitman and Charles True, *Maine in the War for the Union: A History of the Part Borne by Maine Troops in the Suppression of the American Rebellion*, Lewiston, ME: N. Dingley, Jr., 1865, p. 21.

11. Junius P. Rodriguez, ed., "German Coast Uprising (1811)," in *The Encyclopedia of Slave Resistance and Rebellion*, Westport, CT, and London: Greenwood Press, 2007, pp. 213–216. Adam Rothman, *Slave Country: American Expansion and the Origins of the Deep South*, Cambridge, MA: Harvard University Press, 2005, pp. 106–116.

12. John D. Winters, *The Civil War in Louisiana*. Baton Rouge: Louisiana State University Press, 1991, pp. 3–13.

13. "Biographical Directory of the United States Congress: Breckinridge, John Cabell," http://bioguide.congress.gov/scripts/biodisplay.pl?index=b000789. Mark Hatfield, "Vice Presidents of the United States: John C. Breckinridge," http://docs.google.com/gview?a=v&q=cache:6DbqVZwHT9cJ:www.senate.gov/artandhistory/history/resources/pdf/john_breckenridge.pdf+john+c+breckinridge&hl=en&gl=us.

14. Winters, *The Civil War in Louisiana*, pp. 6–28.

15. Ibid.

Chapter 2

1. James M. McPherson, *Battle Cry of Freedom: The Civil War Era*. New York: Ballantine Books, 1989, pp. 348, 491.
2. Joseph Joy, letter to Governor Washburn, 11 August 1862, Maine State Archives, Civil War Town Correspondence, Hampden.
3. John Benson, letter to Governor Washburn, 28 July 1862, Maine State Archives, Civil War Regimental Correspondence, 22nd Maine.
4. Horace Shaw and Charles J. House, *The First Maine Heavy Artillery, 1861–1865*. Portland, Maine, 1903. *Annual Report of the Adjutant General of the State of Maine*, Augusta, Maine: Stevens and Sayward, 1861, 1862, 1863, 1864.
5. Josiah Crosby, letter to Governor Washburn, 12 August 1862, Maine State Archives, Civil War Town Correspondence, Dexter.
6. Josiah Crosby, letter to Governor Washburn, 18 August 1862, Maine State Archives, Civil War Town Correspondence, Dexter.
7. Ibid.
8. Hutchings to Hodsdon, 23 October 1861; Hutchings to Washburn, 23 October 1861; Hewes, et al. to Washburn, 24 October 1861, Maine State Archives, Civil War Regimental Correspondence, 1861. Godfrey to Washburn, 29 October 1861; Bartlett to Washburn, 7 November 1861, Maine State Archives, Civil War Regimental Correspondence, 22nd Maine.
9. Cushman, Alfred, et al. ("Members of Aroostook Bar") to Washburn, July 1862; Hall to Washburn, 9 August 1862, Maine State Archives, Civil War Regimental Correspondence, 22nd Maine. "Summary Unit Histories and Related Materials," Maine State Archives, retrieved 18 July 2006, www.maine.gov/sos/arc/archives/military/civilwar/15meinf.htm. "Summary Unit Histories and Related Materials," Maine State Archives, Retrieved 18 July 2006, www.maine.gov/sos/arc/archives/military/civilwar/22meinf.htm.
10. Norcroft to Washburn, 4 September 1862, Maine State Archives, Civil War Regimental Correspondence, 22nd Maine.
11. Jordan to Washburn, 30 August 1862, Maine State Archives, Civil War Town Correspondence, Dover.
12. Crosby to Washburn, 4 September 1862, Maine State Archives, Civil War Regimental Correspondence, 22nd Maine. Paul Emerson, "Hampden, Maine Soldiers and Sailors of the Civil War," non–circulating manuscript, Bangor (Maine) Public Library. *Annual Report of Adjutant General*, 1862, Hampden, Maine, Historical Society.
13. Hanson to Washburn, 9 September 1862. Maine State Archives, Civil War Regimental Correspondence, 22nd Maine.
14. Jerrard to Hodsdon, 4 September 1862. Maine State Archives, Civil War Town Correspondence, Levant.
15. Putnam to Washburn, 1 May 1862, Maine State Archives, Civil War Town Correspondence, Dover.
16. Spaulding to Hodsdon, 27 August 1862; Putnam to Washburn, May 1862, Maine State Archives, Civil War Town Correspondence, Dover.
17. Rice to Hodsdon, 3 September 1862. Maine State Archives, Civil War Town Correspondence, Dover.
18. *Annual Report of the Adjutant General*, 1862.
19. Ibid.
20. Ibid.
21. Diane Monroe Smith, Chamberlain author, personal communication, 5 August 2006.
22. *Annual Report of the Adjutant General*, 1862.

Chapter 3

1. *Eastern Gazette* (supplement), Dexter, Maine, August 4, 1904. *History of Penobscot County, Maine*. Cleveland, OH: Williams, Chase, 1882.
2. Dexter Historical Society, Henry Wood biography; Local History column, *Gem and Gazette*, Dexter, Maine, 22 February 1945. Anson Jerrard, letters, Levant Historical Society. Anson Jerrard, Simon Jerrard's younger brother, became a lieutenant in the 22nd Maine's Company H.
3. *History of Penobscot County, Maine*.
4. Francis Ireland, letter, 27 September 1862, University of Maine, Fogler Library, Special Collections. Josiah Jordan of Dover, Maine, became surgeon with Jason Huckins of Corinth as assistant.
5. Batchelder to Washburn, letter, 14 October 1862, Maine State Archives, Civil War Regimental Correspondence, 22nd Maine.
6. Francis Ireland, letter, 29 September 1862, University of Maine.
7. Francis Ireland, letter, 5 October 1862, University of Maine.
8. *Annual Report of the Adjutant General*, 1862.
9. Dexter Historical Society: Charlie's

mother, Elizabeth Day, was the sister of Francis's mother, Martha Day.
  10. Francis Ireland, letter, 29 September 1862, University of Maine.
  11. John Lincoln biography, Bangor Theological Seminary Library. John Lincoln had originally trained and worked as a dentist.

Chapter 4

  1. *Annual Report of the Adjutant General*, 1862. Chesley to Hodsdon, 24 March 1863, Maine State Archives, Civil War Regimental Correspondence, 22nd Maine.
  2. *Annual Report of the Adjutant General*, 1862.
  3. Francis Ireland, letter, 19 October 1862, University of Maine.
  4. Francis Ireland, letter, 25 October 1862, University of Maine. 5. United States War Department, *The War of the Rebellion: A Compilation of the Official Records of the Union and Confederate Armies*. Washington, DC: Government Printing Office, 1880–1901. Series 1, Vol. 26, Part 1, pp. 5–18, online at Cornell University Library, http://digital.library.cornell.edu/m/moawar/waro.html (hereafter *Official Records*). *Annual Report of the Adjutant General*, 1862. *Who Was Who in the Union* states: "There is little in the career of Francis Fessenden to explain his phenomenal rise in rank, but he was the son of William P. Fessenden, a U.S. senator from Maine, who was also Lincoln's secretary of the treasury." Fessenden was wounded at Shiloh, was assigned to the defenses of Washington for 9 months, was named colonel of the 30th Maine, and fought with that regiment in the Red River Campaign, where he lost his right leg. Returning as a brigadier general, he was assigned to duties guarding supply bases and supply trains in the Shenandoah Valley. At the end of the Civil War, it was Francis Fessenden, much to the surprise of many, who was given the rank of major general, instead of Maine's Joshua Chamberlain. Chamberlain had been recommended for the rank of full major general, and a glowing letter from General James Rice commends Chamberlain's many qualities of leadership. However, because Maine had a limited quota for high ranking officers, the choice was made to give the promotion to Fessenden. See Smith, *Fanny and Joshua*, pp. 295–296.
  6. Isaac Case, letter, 16 November 1862, Isaac W. Case Memorial Library, Kenduskeag, Maine.
  7. John Ireland, letter, 31 October 1862, University of Maine.
  8. *Official Records*, Series 1, Vol. 26, Part 1, pp. 5–18.
  9. *Harper's Weekly*, 6 December 1862. Stewart Sifakis, *Who Was Who in the Union*, New York: Facts on File, 1989. Mark M. Boatner, *The Civil War Dictionary*. New York: Vintage Books, 1991.
  10. Carol Bundy, *The Nature of Sacrifice: A Biography of Charles Russell Lowell, Jr.* New York: Farrar, Straus and Giroux, 2005.
  11. Simon Jerrard to Hodsdon, 18 February 1864, Maine State Archives, Civil War Regimental Correspondence, 22nd Maine.
  12. *Annual Report of the Adjutant General*, 1862 and 1863.
  13. Francis Ireland, letter, November 4 1862, University of Maine.
  14. Knowles to Washburn, 9 November 1862, Maine State Archives, Civil War Regimental Correspondence, 22nd Maine.
  15. *Annual Report of the Adjutant General*, 1862 and 1863. Hampden (Maine) Historical Society. Paul Emerson, "Hampden, Maine Soldiers and Sailors of the Civil War."
  16. Francis Ireland, letter, 5 November 1862, University of Maine.

Chapter 5

  1. Simon Jerrard to Hodsdon, 18 February 1864. Simon Jerrard, "Brief History of the 22nd Maine Reg't," letter to Adjutant General John Hodsdon, February 1864, Louisiana State University Libraries Special Collections.
  2. John Ireland, letter, 31 October 1862, University of Maine.
  3. *Annual Report of the Adjutant General*, 1862. Jerrard, "Brief History." Jerrard to Hodsdon, 18 February 1864.
  4. Isaac Case, letter, 16 November 1862.
  5. Francis Ireland, letter, 14 November 1862, University of Maine. 6. Isaac Case, letter, 16 November 1862.
  7. John Concannon, "Making a Stand," *The Wild Geese Today*, retrieved 19 August 2006, http://thewildgeese.com/pages/corcpt2.html. Sifakis, *Who Was Who in the Union*. After battle experiences, imprisonment, and facing Longstreet's Corps at Suffolk in the spring of 1863, Michael Corcoran died not in battle, but from injuries suffered when he fell from his horse on December 22 of that year.
  8. William C. Davis, *Fighting Men of the Civil War*. New York: Gallery Books, 1989. Civil War enlistment cards, Maine State Archives.
  9. Francis Ireland, letter, 14 November 1862.

10. Isaac Case, letter, 16 November 1862.
11. Sifakis, *Who Was Who in the Union*. Edward L. Pierce, "The Contrabands at Fortress Monroe," *Atlantic Monthly*, November 1861, pp. 626–640. U.S. Army, Fort Monroe Web site, retrieved 20 July 2005, www.monroe.army.mil/Monroe/sites/about/history.aspx.
12. Francis Ireland, letter, 15 November 1862, University of Maine.
13. Isaac Case, letter, 16 November 1862.
14. "Distribution of Arms," chart, LSU Libraries, Special Collections. *Annual Report of the Adjutant General*, 1862. Crosby to Jerrard, 19 November 1862, Maine State Archives, Civil War Regimental Correspondence, 22nd Maine. Jerrard to Ripley, 15 November 1862, Maine State Archives, Civil War Regimental Correspondence, 22nd Maine. The 9 month regiments raised in the summer of 1862 were issued a variety of older weapons, including the converted flintlocks and French and Prussian .71-caliber smoothbores, while previous 3 year regiments had been given priority for the newer Springfield and Enfield rifled muskets.
15. Francis Ireland, letter, 15 November 1862. Benjamin Ireland, "Uncle Ben," is John Ireland's brother; Dexter Historical Society.
16. For a view of the Antietam Campaign as a turning point in the war, see McPherson, *Crossroads of Freedom: Antietam*; for foreign intervention see McPherson, *Battle Cry*, pp. 382–391.
17. McPherson, *Battle Cry*, p. 247.
18. Francis Ireland, letter, 15 November 1862.

Chapter 6

1. Francis Ireland, letter, 24 November 1862, University of Maine.
2. *Annual Report of the Adjutant General*, 1862.
3. Francis Ireland, letter, 24 November 1862, University of Maine.
4. Richard B. Irwin, *History of the Nineteenth Army Corps*, New York: Putnam's Sons, 1892. "Nineteenth Army Corps," retrieved 12 June 2007, www.civilwararchive.com/CORPS/19thcorp.html.
5. Francis Ireland, letter, 24 November 1862, University of Maine.
6. Dexter Historical Society. *Annual Report of the Adjutant General*, 1862.
7. Francis Ireland, letter, 24 November 1862, University of Maine. The frock coat issued to the 22nd Maine and other Union infantry regiments is likely what Francis refers to as a "dress coat," of longer cut than the everyday blue blouse or sack coat, and similar to the coat more often associated with an officer's uniform.
8. Francis Ireland, letter, 27 November 1862, University of Maine.
9. "Distribution of Arms," chart, LSU Libraries. Joe Bilby, "The Lorenz," retrieved 16 August 2004, www.washingtonbluerifles.com/bilbylorenz.htm. Davis, *Fighting Men of the Civil War*.
10. McPherson, *Battle Cry*. William C. Davis, *Battlefields of the Civil War*, New York: Smithmark, 1991.
11. New York made it an annual celebration in 1817 and by the mid–1800s many other states had done the same.
12. Francis Ireland, letter, 27 November 1862, University of Maine.
13. Isaac Case, letter, 16 November 1862.
14. Francis Ireland, letter, 27 November 1862, University of Maine.
15. Francis Ireland, letter, 27 November 1862, University of Maine.
16. Charlie Farrar, letter, November 30 1862, Dexter Historical Society.
17. Charlie Farrar, letter, November 30 1862, Dexter Historical Society.
18. John Ireland, letter, 27 November 1862, University of Maine.
19. Dexter Historical Society.
20. John Ireland, letter, 27 November 1862, University of Maine.
21. Boatner, *The Civil War Dictionary*. McPherson, *Battle Cry*. *Annual Report of the Adjutant General*, 1862. Regimental and Town Correspondence, Maine State Archives.
22. John Ireland, letter, 27 November 1862, University of Maine.

Chapter 7

1. Simon Jerrard to Hodsdon, 18 February 1864. Jerrard, "Brief History," LSU.
2. Francis Ireland, letter, 3 December 1862, University of Maine.
3. Francis Ireland, letter, 3 December 1862, University of Maine.
4. Sifakis, *Who Was Who in the Union*. Donald Webster, "Rodman's Great Guns," retrieved 22 June 2006, www.civilwarartillery.com/inventors/Rodman.htm.
5. Francis Ireland, letter, 3 December 1862, University of Maine. *Annual Report of the Adjutant General*, 1862.
6. John Ireland, letter, 7 December 1862, University of Maine. *Annual Report of the Adjutant General*, 1862.

7. John Ireland, letter, 7 December 1862, University of Maine.
8. Dexter Historical Society.
9. John Ireland, letter, 7 December 1862, University of Maine.
10. McPherson, *Battle Cry*. Davis, *Battlefields of the Civil War*. Boatner, *The Civil War Dictionary*. Given Burnside's previous poor performance at Antietam, his appointment to lead the Army of the Potomac is seen by many as ill-considered. Burnside himself may have shared this view, since he had twice before refused that command and even resisted accepting it in November of 1862. He accepted at the urging of other generals who did not want to see General Joseph Hooker have the position.
11. John Ireland, letter, 7 December 1862, University of Maine.
12. Simon Jerrard to Hodsdon, 18 February 1864. Simon Jerrard, "Brief History." *Annual Report of the Adjutant General*, 1863.
13. James G. Hollandsworth, *The Louisiana Native Guard: The Black Military Experience During the Civil War*, Baton Rouge: Louisiana State University Press, 1995.
14. James G. Hollandsworth, "Union Soldiers on Ship Island During the Civil War," retrieved 3 August 2007, http://mshistory.k12.ms.us/articles/211/union-soldiers-on-ship-island-during-the-civil-war.
15. Winters, *The Civil War in Louisiana*. *Annual Report of the Adjutant General*, 1863. Simon Jerrard to Hodsdon, 18 February 1864. Simon Jerrard, "Brief History."
16. Richard S. West, Jr., *Lincoln's Scapegoat General: A Life of Benjamin F. Butler*, Boston: Houghton Mifflin, 1995. McPherson, *Battle Cry of Freedom*, pp. 419–420. Winters, *The Civil War in Louisiana*, pp. 85–102
17. *Official Records*, Series 1, Vol. 15, Chapter 27, pp. 906–908.
18. West, *Lincoln's Scapegoat General*. Benjamin F. Butler, *Butler's Book*.
19. Francis Ireland, letter, 18 December 1862, University of Maine.
20. Isaac Case, letter, 15 February 1863, Isaac W. Case Memorial Library, Kenduskeag, Maine.
21. "Manassas," *Dictionary of American Naval Fighting Ships*, retrieved 21 July 2008, www.history.navy.mil/danfs/cfa6/manassas.htm. Lincoln P. Paine, "CSS *Manassas*," *Ships of the World: An Historical Encyclopedia*, New York: Houghton Mifflin Harcourt, 1997.
22. Francis Ireland, letter, 18 December 1862.
23. Isaac Case, letter, 15 February 1863.
24. Francis Ireland, letter, 18 December 1862.

Chapter 8

1. Winters, *The Civil War in Louisiana*. Simon Jerrard to Hodsdon, 18 February 1864. *Annual Report of the Adjutant General*, 1863.
2. Francis Ireland, letter, 18 December 1862.
3. Simon Jerrard to Hodsdon, 18 February 1864. Simon Jerrard, "Brief History." *Annual Report of the Adjutant General*, 1863. Captain Case's February letter to his sister, cited above, states that the 22nd was the second regiment ashore, but that difference is of little consequence.
4. Francis Ireland, letter, 18 December 1862.
5. *Annual Report of the Adjutant General*, 1863.
6. Francis Ireland, letter, 18 December 1862.
7. Isaac Case, letter, 15 February 1863.
8. Simon Jerrard to Hodsdon, 18 February 1864. Simon Jerrard, "Brief History."
9. Francis Ireland, letter, 18 December 1862.
10. Simon Jerrard to Hodsdon, 18 February 1864. Simon Jerrard, "Brief History."
11. Francis Ireland, letter, 18 December 1862.
12. Francis Ireland, letter, 25 December 1862, University of Maine.
13. Ibid.
14. Isaac Case, letter, 15 February 1863.
15. Francis Ireland, letter, 25 December 1862.

Chapter 9

1. Francis Ireland, letter, 2 January 1863, University of Maine.
2. *Annual Report of the Adjutant General*, 1862 and 1863. Davis, *Fighting Men of the Civil War*, pp. 186, 188.
3. Isaac Case, letter, 15 February 1863.
4. Simon Jerrard to Hodsdon, 18 February 1864. Simon Jerrard, "Brief History." *Annual Report of the Adjutant General*, 1863.
5. Francis Ireland, letter, 2 January 1863.
6. Carol Feurtado, Dexter Historical Society, e-mail to author, 15 November 2005. Enlistment cards file, Maine State Archives. U.S. Census for Maine, 1860.
7. *Annual Report of the Adjutant General*, 1862 and 1863.
8. Francis Ireland, letter, 2 January 1863.
9. Francis Ireland, letter, 2 January 1863.

10. Sifakis, *Who Was Who in the Union*. *Harper's Weekly*, 11 May 1861.
11. Simon Jerrard to Hodsdon, 18 February 1864. *Annual Report of the Adjutant General*, 1863.
12. *Official Record*, Series 1, Vol. 15, p. 626. Sifakis, *Who Was Who in the Union*.
13. Francis Ireland, letter, 2 January 1863.
14. U.S. Census for Maine, 1860. *Annual Report of the Adjutant General*, 1862 and 1863.
15. Francis Ireland, letter, 2 January 1863.
16. Francis Ireland, letter, 6 January 1863, University of Maine.
17. Ibid.
18. *Bangor Daily Whig & Courier*, 22 June 1863.
19. *African American Registry*, retrieved 5 January 2009, www.aaregistry.com/african_american_history/2420/Nigger_the_word_a_brief_history. Randall Kennedy, *Nigger: The Strange Career of a Troublesome Word*. New York: Pantheon Books, 2002.
20. *Annual Report of the Adjutant General*, 1863.
21. Francis Ireland, letter, 6 January 1863.

Chapter 10

1. Francis Ireland, letter, 25 January 1863, University of Maine.
2. "Croton Oil," retrieved 14 July 2005. http://59.1911encyclopedia.org/C/Cr/CROTON_OIL.htm. "Croton Oil," retrieved 14 July 2005, www.lclabs.com/PRODFILE/A-C/C-3669.php4. "Croton Oil," *Dorland's Illustrated Medical Dictionary*, retrieved 14 July 2005, www.mercksorce.com/pp/us/cns/cns_hl_home.jsp. Maud Grieve, *A Modern Herbal*, online edition, retrieved 14 July 2005, www.botanical.com/botanical/mgmh/c/croton118.html#med.
3. Davis, *Fighting Men of the Civil War*.
4. Francis Ireland, letter, 25 January 1863.
5. Ibid.
6. Francis Ireland, letter, 7 February 1863, University of Maine.
7. Ira M. Rutlow, *Bleeding Blue and Gray: Civil War Surgery and the Evolution of American Medicine*. New York: Random House, 2005, pp. 282–285.
8. Francis Ireland, letter, 7 February 1863.
9. *Annual Report of the Adjutant General*, 1863.
10. Francis Ireland, letter, 7 February 1863.
11. "91st Infantry Regiment, Civil War," New York State Military Museum, retrieved 12 August 2009, www.dmna.state.ny.us/historic/reghist/civil/infantry/91stInf/91stInfMain.htm. "131st Infantry Regiment, Civil War," New York State Military Museum, retrieved 12 August 2009, www.dmna.state.ny.us/historic/reghist/civil/infantry/131stInf/131stInfMain.htm.
12. Francis Ireland, letter, 7 February 1863.
13. "Civil War Slang," Civil War Preservation Trust, retrieved 12 August 2009, http://civilwar.org/education/pdfs/civil-war-curriculum-slang.pdf. "Slang," *Camp Chase Gazette*, retrieved 14 July 2006, www.campchase.com/Slang/Slang-A-F.html.
14. Dexter Historical Society.
15. Francis Ireland, letter, 10 February 1863, University of Maine.
16. Francis Ireland, letter, 13 February 1863, University of Maine.
17. Sifakis, *Who Was Who in the Union*. General Grover was an artillery officer from his graduation from West Point until 1855, when he transferred to the infantry. His Civil War career began as a captain in the 10th U.S. Infantry and continued with a promotion, in 1862, to brigadier general of volunteers. After serving most of his career in the Deep South, he ended the war as a brevetted brigadier general in the regular army.
18. Francis Ireland, letter, 13 February 1863.
19. John Ireland, letter, 29 February 1863, University of Maine.
20. Eben Day was the brother of John Ireland's wife, Martha Day: Dexter Historical Society.
21. John Ireland, letter, 29 February 1863.
22. William C. Davis, *Battlefields of the Civil War*, "The Battle of Stones River (Murfreesboro)," retrieved 28 December 2007, www.civilwarhome.com/stones.htm.
23. John Ireland, letter, 29 February 1863.
24. *Annual Report of the Adjutant General*, 1863 Dexter Historical Society.
25. John Ireland, letter, 29 February 1863.
26. Simon Jerrard, "Brief History." *Annual Report of the Adjutant General*, 1863.
27. Francis Ireland, letter, 9 March 1863, University of Maine.
28. *Annual Report of the Adjutant General*, 1863 and 1864. Dexter Historical Society.
29. Isaac Case to Governor Coburn, letter, Maine State Archives, Civil War Town Correspondence, Kenduskeag.
30. Isaac W. Case Memorial Library, Kenduskeag, Maine.

Chapter 11

1. *Annual Report of the Adjutant General*, 1863. Simon Jerrard to Hodsdon, 18 February

1864. Reports by General Banks, *Official Record*, Series 1, Vol. 15, pp. 1113 and on, pp. 251–254; Vol. 26, p. 9.

  2. *Annual Report of the Adjutant General*, 1863. Calvin D. Cowles, comp., *Atlas to Accompany the Official Records of the Union and Confederate Armies*. Washington, DC: Government Printing Office, 1891–1895, Plate 38. David C. Edmonds, *The Guns of Port Hudson*, Lafayette, LA: Acadiana Press, 1983.

  3. *Official Records*, Series 1, Vol. 15, p. 262. Lawrence L. Hewlitt, *Port Hudson: Confederate Bastion on the Mississippi*, Baton Rouge: Louisiana State University Press, 1987, pp. 72–95.

  4. Report by General Banks, *Official Records*, Series 1, Vol. 26, p. 9. Report by Captain William Rowly, U.S. Signal Corps, *Official Records*, Series 1, Vol. 15, p. 260. Report by Admiral Farragut, *Official Records*, Series 1, Vol. 15, p. 302.

  5. Simon Jerrard to Hodsdon, 18 February 1864. *Annual Report of the Adjutant General*, 1863. Hewlitt, *Port Hudson: Confederate Bastion on the Mississippi*, pp. 62–71. Edmonds, *The Guns of Port Hudson*. pp. 55–69.

  6. *Official Records*, Series 1, Vol. 15, p. 251.
  7. *Official Records*, Series 1, Vol. 15, pp. 271–275.
  8. *Official Records*, Series 1, Vol. 15, pp. 257, 255.
  9. Francis Ireland, letter, 19 March 1863, University of Maine.
  10. Hewlitt, *Port Hudson: Confederate Bastion on the Mississippi*. pp. 72–95. "Mississippi SwStr," Navy History, retrieved 23 July 2005, www.historycentral.com/Navy/Steamer/mississippi.html. "Mississippi," *Dictionary of American Naval Fighting Ships*, retrieved 23 July 2005, www.history.navy.mil/danfs/m12/mississippi-i.htm.
  11. Francis Ireland, letter, 19 March 1863.
  12. *Annual Report of the Adjutant General*, 1863.
  13. *Official Records*, Vol. 15, Chapter 27, p. 701. "The First Confiscation Act" (Confiscation Act of 1861), Freemen and Southern Society Project, retrieved 14 August 2006, www.history.umd.edu/Freedmen/conactl.htm. David Hamilton, "First and Second Confiscation Acts (1861, 1862)," *Major Acts of Congress*, retrieved 15 August 2006, www.enotes.com/major-acts-congress/first-second-confiscation-acts. The 2nd Confiscation Act was "An Act to Suppress Insurrection, to Punish Treason and Rebellion, to Seize and Confiscate the Property of Rebels, and for Other Purposes."
  14. *Official Records*, Series 1, Vol. 15, Chapter 27, p. 701.

  15. *Official Records*, Series 1, Vol. 15, Chapter 27, p. 706. From the *Official Records*, Vol. 15, Chapter 27, p. 702, Halleck to Banks: "Louisiana is essentially hostile territory, in the military occupation of the United States. The common laws and usages of war must govern. If it becomes necessary to seize transportation, provisions, etc., for the use of your army or the success of your operations, you will do so without regard to this court (the court established in New Orleans by the State Department) or its officers. Moreover, if they interfere with your operations, send them back to the city, or, if necessary, out of the department. The War Department has given you full power, and you have only to exercise it with discretion and justice."

  From the *Official Records*, Vol. 15, Chapter 27, p. 1119: "Special Order 106: The action of Brig. Gen. William Dwight, commanding First Brigade, Fourth Division, in causing Private Henry Hamill, Company D, One hundred and thirty-first New York Volunteers, to be shot to death in front of the brigade, at sunset on the 25th of April, for quitting his colors to plunder and pillage, while the brigade was on detached service in an exposed position and in presence of the enemy, is fully approved by the general commanding this army. The last warning against straggling and pillage has been exhausted. It has become necessary, to prevent demoralization, that the fate of this wretched man should be measured out to all who follow his example. The safety of this army is more important than the life of any man in it, from the humblest private to the commanding general. By Command of Major-General Banks."

  16. Simon Jerrard to Hodsdon, 18 February 1864.
  17. John Ireland, letter, 29 March 1863, University of Maine.
  18. John Ireland, letter, 29 March 1863.
  19. E.G. Libby, letter, 9 July 1863, Dexter Historical Society.
  20. John Ireland, letter, 29 March 1863.

Chapter 12

  1. *Annual Report of the Adjutant General*, 1863. Simon Jerrard to Hodsdon, 18 February 1864.
  2. Francis Ireland, letter, 4 April 1863, University of Maine.
  3. Irwin, *History of the Nineteenth Army Corps*, Chapter 9.
  4. Boatner, *The Civil War Dictionary*.
  5. Francis Ireland, letter, 4 April 1863.
  6. Winters, *The Civil War in Louisiana*, pp. 222–230.

7. Simon Jerrard to Hodsdon, 18 February 1864. Irwin, *History of the Nineteenth Army Corps*, Chapter 10. Winters, *The Civil War in Louisiana*, pp. 222–230.
8. Report by General Grover, *Official Records*, Series 1, Vol. 15, pp. 358–360. *Annual Report of the Adjutant General*, 1863. Winters, *The Civil War in Louisiana*, pp. 224–228.
9. Report by Colonel Holcomb, *Official Records*, Series 1, Vol. 15, p. 377. Winters, *The Civil War in Louisiana*, pp. 224–228. Cowles, *Atlas to Accompany the Official Records*, Plate 23. Irwin, *History of the Nineteenth Army Corps*, Chapters 10, 11.
10. Winters, *The Civil War in Louisiana*, pp. 226–228. Report by General Grover, *Official Records*, Series 1, Vol. 15, pp. 358–360. Simon Jerrard to Hodsdon, 18 February 1864. *Annual Report of the Adjutant General*, 1863, p. 93.
11. "Irish Bend," *CWSAC* [Civil War Sites Advisory Commission] *Battle Summaries*, retrieved 3 July 2005, www.cr.nps.gov/hps/abpp/battles/la007.htm. Simon Jerrard to Hodsdon, 18 February 1864. *Annual Report of the Adjutant General*, 1863, p. 93. Winters, *The Civil War in Louisiana*, pp. 226–228. Report by General Grover, *Official Records*, Series 1, Vol. 15, pp. 358–360.
12. Report by General Grover, *Official Records*, Series 1, Vol. 15, pp. 360–361. Winters, *The Civil War in Louisiana*, p. 229. Irwin, *History of the Nineteenth Army Corps*, pp. 117–120.
13. Francis Ireland, letter, 17 April 1863, University of Maine. As with the 2nd Louisiana mentioned earlier, the "1st La." he refers to is the 1st Louisiana Infantry, a Union regiment. They had been raised in New Orleans in July 1862. Irwin, *History of the Nineteenth Army Corps*, pp. 114–116. Nims' Battery was the 2nd Mass. Light Artillery, named for its first commander in the field, Captain Ormand Nims. The cavalry referred to was Captain Richard Barrett's company of Louisiana Cavalry. The *Diana* had been a civilian side-wheel steamship. It was captured by Union forces at New Orleans in April of 1862 and used as a transport. Transferred to the Union Navy in November, it was recaptured by Confederates in March 1863. It was destroyed by its crew at Irish Bend to prevent its again being captured by the Union troops. Report by General Grover, *Official Records*, Series 1, Vol. 15, pp. 360–361. "*Diana*," *Dictionary of American Naval Fighting Ships*, U.S. Naval Historical Center, retrieved 3 January 2006, www.history.navy.mil/danfs/cfa5/diana.htm.
14. *Official Records*, Series 1, Vol. 15, Chapter 26, p. 319. *Annual Report of the Adjutant General*, 1863. Winters, *The Civil War in Louisiana*, pp. 222–230. Report by General Grover, *Official Records*, Series 1, Vol. 15, pp. 360–362.
15. *Harpers Weekly*, 16 May 1863. Dexter Historical Society. U.S. Census for Maine, 1880.
16. Winters, *The Civil War in Louisiana*, p. 231.

Chapter 13

1. Francis Ireland, letter, 27 April 1863, University of Maine. As mentioned earlier, "Bobbin Boy" was a nickname for General Banks.
2. A statue of Evangeline, Henry Wadsworth Longfellow's heroine in his poem of that name, which tells of the removal of French occupants of Nova Scotia, stands in St. Martinville.
3. Francis Ireland, letter, 27 April 1863.
4. Captain Henry Wood to Colonel Jerrard, letter, 28 April 1863, Louisiana State University Libraries, Special Collections.
5. Boatner, *The Civil War Dictionary*. Richard Taylor, *Destruction and Reconstruction: Personal Experiences of the Late War*. New York: Appleton, 1897 (reprinted in 1973 by Arno Press, New York), p. 109. "Roster of the 7th Regiment, Louisiana Volunteer Cavalry," Retrieved 22 June 2006, www.acadiansingrey.com/7th%20Regt.%20Cav.htm.
6. Captain Henry Wood to Colonel Jerrard, letter, 28 April 1863.
7. Simon Jerrard to Hodsdon, 18 February 1864. Captain Henry Wood to Colonel Jerrard, letter, 28 April 1863.
8. Report by General George Andrews, *Official Records*, Series 1, Vol. 15, p. 715. Report by General William Dwight, *Official Records*, Series 1, Vol. 15, p. 305.
9. *Official Records*, Series 1, Vol. 15, Chapter 27, p. 163.
10. Francis Ireland, letter, 27 April 1863.
11. *Annual Report of the Adjutant General*, 1862 and 1863. For other regiments, the date of muster for the regiment as a whole and the individual soldiers who were mustered at the time the regiment was mustered is the same.
12. Francis Ireland, letter, 27 April 1863.
13. Charlie Farrar, letter, 28 April 1863, Dexter Historical Society.
14. John Ireland, letter, 3 May 1863, University of Maine.
15. *Annual Report of the Adjutant General*, 1863. The *Official Records*, Vol. 15, Chapter 27, p. 319, compiled from numbers gathered soon

after the battle, had listed casualties from the 26th Maine as 11 enlisted men and two officers killed and 48 men wounded. The report from the regiment itself would seem to be more accurate, since some of those listed initially as wounded presumably died of their wounds.
  16. John Ireland, letter, 3 May 1863.
  17. *Lewiston Journal*, 5 June 1893.
  18. John Ireland, letter, 3 May 1863.
  19. Carol Feurtado, Dexter Historical Society, personal communication, 6 July 2006.

Chapter 14

  1. Francis Ireland, letter, 5 May 1863, University of Maine.
  2. Francis Ireland, letter, 5 May 1863.
  3. Boatner, *The Civil War Dictionary*. A considerable force under General Smith did frustrate General Banks during the second Red River Campaign in the spring of 1864.
  4. Irwin, *History of the Nineteenth Army Corps*, Chapter 12.
  5. Irwin, *History of the Nineteenth Army Corps*, Chapter 12. Boatner, *The Civil War Dictionary*. Winters, *The Civil War in Louisiana*.
  6. Report by General Banks, *Official Records*, Series 1, Vol. 26, pp. 5–18.
  7. Ibid.
  8. Ibid. Irwin, *History of the Nineteenth Army Corps*, Chapter 12.
  9. Report by General Banks, *Official Records*, Series 1, Vol. 26, pp. 5–18. Taylor, *Destruction and Reconstruction*, p. 161.
  10. Report by General Banks, *Official Records*, Series 1, Vol. 26, pp. 5–18.
  11. *Annual Report of the Adjutant General*, 1863. Simon Jerrard to Hodsdon, 18 February 1864.
  12. Francis Ireland, letter, 12 May 1863, University of Maine.
  13. Edmonds, *The Guns of Port Hudson*, Vol. 1, pp. 226–233.
  14. Francis Ireland, letter, 12 May 1863.
  15. Ibid.
  16. Otis Roberts biographical material. Dexter Historical Society records. Carol Feurtado, Dexter Historical Society, personal communication, 6 July 2006.
  17. John Ireland, letter, 17 May 1863, University of Maine.
  18. *Annual Report of the Adjutant General*, 1863. Carol Feurtado, Dexter Historical Society, personal communication, 6 July 2006. Sylvia Sherman, Maine State Archives, personal communication, 3 Aug 2006.
  19. John Ireland, letter, 17 May 1863.

  20. John Ireland, letter, 24 May 1863, University of Maine.
  21. Ibid.
  22. Winters, *The Civil War in Louisiana*, p. 237. Simon Jerrard to Hodsdon, 18 February 1864. *Annual Report of the Adjutant General*, 1863.
  23. Simon Jerrard to Hodsdon, 18 February 1864. *Annual Report of the Adjutant General*, 1863.
  24. Francis Ireland, letter, 28 May 1863, University of Maine. While sporadic attacks against this supply column very likely did occur, a search of the movement of Confederate troops in that area did not turn up a force of 6,000 Confederates close at hand.

Chapter 15

  1. *Official Records*, Series 1, Vol. 26, pp. 526–528, p. 13. Edmonds, *The Guns of Port Hudson*, Vol. 2, p. 19.
  2. Boatner, *The Civil War Dictionary*. "Franklin Gardner," Civil War Preservation Trust, retrieved 22 August 2006, www.civilwar.org/education/history/biographies/franklin-gardner.html. "Mouton, Alexander," *Biographical Directory of the United States Congress*, retrieved 12 August 2007, http://bioguide.congress.gov/scripts/biodisplay.pl?index=M001050.
  3. Cunningham, *The Port Hudson Campaign*, pp. 20, 21. Edmonds, *The Guns of Port Hudson*, Vol. 1, pp. 45–52. Hewlitt, *Port Hudson: Confederate Bastion*, pp. 9, 10.
  4. Winters, *The Civil War in Louisiana*, p. 243. Cunningham, *The Port Hudson Campaign*, pp. 35, 36, 120, 121. Those 7,000 or so defenders inside the fortifications included armed civilians as well as regular soldiers.
  5. Winters, *The Civil War in Louisiana*, pp. 243, 260. Irwin, *History of the Nineteenth Army Corps*, Chapter 16.
  6. Irwin, *History of the Nineteenth Army Corps*, Chapter 16.
  7. Winters, *The Civil War in Louisiana*, p. 260. Irwin, *History of the Nineteenth Army Corps*, Chapter 16.
  8. *Official Records*, Series 1, Vol. 15, Chapter 27, pp. 164–166.
  9. Sifakis, *Who Was Who in the Union*, p. 446.
  10. *Official Records*, Vol. 15, Chapter 27, pp. 712–13. Joseph T. Wilson, *The Black Phalanx: A History of the Negro Soldiers of the United States in the War of 1775–1812, 1861–65*. Hartford, CT: American, 1888 (reprinted in 1968 by Arno Press, New York). Hollandsworth, *The*

Louisiana Native Guard. The 1st, 3rd, and 4th Native Guard Regiments were listed as "unattached" members of General Christopher Auger's First Division, and General Weitzel was one of the brigade commanders in that division. It was not these black regiments alone that were listed as unattached, but they were the only infantry regiments so listed. The other unattached units in the 1st Division were two companies of the 1st Louisiana Cavalry, a battalion of the 2nd Rhode Island Cavalry, the 1st Indiana Heavy Artillery, and the 12th Massachusetts Battery.

11. Winters, *The Civil War in Louisiana*, p. 259. Wilson, *The Black Phalanx*. Hollandsworth, *The Louisiana Native Guard*. Mike Walbridge, *African-American Heroes of the Civil War*. Portland, ME: Walch, 2002.

12. *Official Records*, Series 1, Vol. 15, Chapter 27, p. 68. John David Smith, "An Ironic Route to Glory: Louisiana's Native Guards at Port Hudson," in *Black Soldiers in Blue*. Chapel Hill: University of North Carolina Press, 2002. Howard Wright, *Port Hudson: Its History From an Interior Point of View*, reprinted, Baton Rouge: Committee for the Preservation of the Port Hudson Battlefield, 1961.

13. *Official Records*, Series 1, Vol. 26, pp. 526–528. "Port Hudson (Siege of) (1863)," eHistory Archive, Ohio State University, retrieved 18 July 2006, http://ehistory.osu.edu/world/Battleview.cfm?BID=39. Edmonds, *The Guns of Port Hudson*, pp. 1, 387. Cunningham, *The Port Hudson Campaign*, p. 82.

14. Simon Jerrard to Hodsdon, 18 February 1864. *Annual Report of the Adjutant General*, 1863. "1st Battery, 1st Maine Light Artillery," Summary Unit Histories and Related Materials, retrieved 18 October 2006, www.maine.gov/sos/arc/archives/military/civilwar/1bltart.htm. The 1st Indiana was commanded by Colonel John Keith, with the 22nd Maine probably attached to Cox's Battery. The 1st Battery, 1st Maine Light Artillery, commanded by Lt. John Morton, had been mustered in at Portland, Maine, in December 1861 and had been in Louisiana since March 1862; steamer *Fulton* mentioned in *Official Records*, Series 1, Vol. 26, p. 519.

15. Cunningham, *The Port Hudson Campaign*, pp. 76–77. Edmonds, *The Guns of Port Hudson*, Vol. 2, pp. 133–145.

16. *Official Records*, Series 1, Vol. 26, pp. 546–547. *Annual Report of the Adjutant General*, 1863. The Maine adjutant general's report gives the dates as June 9–10.

17. *Official Records*, Series 1, Vol. 26, pp. 131–132. Edmonds, *The Guns of Port Hudson*. pp. 160–161.

18. *Official Records*, Series 1, Vol. 26, pp. 132–133.

19. John William DeForest, *A Volunteer's Adventures: A Union Captain's Record of the Civil War, with an Introduction by Stanley T Williams*. Hamden, CT: Achorn Books, 1970, pp. 124–125.

20. Edmonds, *The Guns of Port Hudson*, pp. 163–169. Simon Jerrard to Hodsdon, 18 February 1864. *Annual Report of the Adjutant General*, 1863.

21. *Annual Report of the Adjutant General*, 1863. Edmonds, *The Guns of Port Hudson*, pp. 167–169.

22. Simon Jerrard to Hodsdon, 18 February 1864. Report by Col. Simon Jerrard, *Official Records*, Series 1, Vol. 53, Part 1, Page 472. Joseph Joy, letter, quoted in *Bangor Daily Whig and Courier*, 1 July 1863. Smith, *Leaves from a Soldier's Diary*. Report by General Weitzel (written by Assistant Adjutant General Graves), *Official Record*, Series 1, Vol. 26, pp. 131–132.

23. Joseph Joy and John Lincoln, quoted in *Bangor Daily Whig and Courier*, 1 July 1863.

24. *Official Records*, Series 1, Vol. 26, p. 132.

25. *Annual Report of the Adjutant General*, 1863.

26. Smith, *Leaves from a Soldier's Diary*, pp. 68–69.

27. Cunningham, *The Port Hudson Campaign*, pp. 78–79. William A. Spedale, *Where Bugles Called and Rifles Gleamed*, Baton Rouge, LA: Land and Land, 1986, p. 121.

28. Report by General Banks, *Official Records*, Series 1, Vol. 26, pp. 5–18. *Annual Report of the Adjutant General*, 1863.

Chapter 16

1. Cunningham, *The Port Hudson Campaign*, p. 79. Boatner, *The Civil War Dictionary*. Edmonds, *The Guns of Port Hudson*, p. 195.

2. "Glossary of Terms: Priest Cap," New York State Military Museum, retrieved 12 September 2007, www.dmna.state.ny.us/forts/glossary/priestCap.htm. Edmonds, *The Guns of Port Hudson*, Vol. 2, p. 196.

3. "Grenade! The Little Known Weapon of the Civil War," retrieved 15 October 2007, www.historynet.com/grenade-the-little-known-weapon-of-the-civil-war.htm. "Battle of 1st Bull Run Scientist Page (Hand Grenades)," http://kms.kapalama.ksbe.edu/projects/2002/civilwar/battle02/scientist.html. Cunningham, *The Port Hudson Campaign*, p. 87. Edmonds, *The Guns of Port Hudson*, Vol. 2, pp. 9, 196, 210, 213. *Official Records*, Vol. 53, Chapter 66,

p. 470. *Annual Report of the Adjutant General*, 1863, p. 95.

4. *Annual Report of the Adjutant General*, 1863. Simon Jerrard to Hodsdon, 18 February 1864.

5. Report by General Banks. *Official Records*, Series 1, Vol. 26, pp. 5–18.

6. Cunningham, *The Port Hudson Campaign*, pp. 82–93. For a detailed look at the various attacks of June 14, see *Guns of Port Hudson*, chapters 19–21.

7. Francis Ireland, letter, 25 June 1863, University of Maine.

8. Report by Colonel Morgan, *Official Records*, Series 1, Vol. 53, pp. 470–471.

9. Charles G. Wing, letter to *Dexter Gazette*, 7 August 1897. Henry Wood, letter, 20 February 1864, Dexter Historical Society. Cunningham, *The Port Hudson Campaign*, p. 89.

10. DeForest, *A Volunteer's Adventures*, p. 141.

11. Simon Jerrard to Hodsdon, 18 February 1864. *Annual Report of the Adjutant General*, 1863.

12. Simon Jerrard to Hodsdon, 18 February 1864.

13. Ibid.

14. *Annual Report of the Adjutant General*, 1863. Henry Wood, letter, 20 February 1864, Dexter Historical Society. John Lincoln, letter, 22 July 1863, *Bangor Daily Whig and Courier*.

15. *Official Records*, Series 1, Vol. 26, p. 204.

16. *Official Records*, Series 1, Vol. 26, pp. 205–206.

17. *Annual Report of the Adjutant General*, 1863. *Official Records*, Series 1, Vol. 53, p. 473.

18. Diane Monroe Smith, *Chamberlain at Petersburg: The Charge at Fort Hell*. Gettysburg, PA: Thomas, 2004.

19. Smith, *Fanny and Joshua*.

Chapter 17

1. *Official Records*, Series 1, Vol. 26, p. 557.
2. *Official Records*, Series 1, Vol. 26, p. 56.
3. *Official Records*, Series 1, Vol. 26, pp. 57–61. Edmonds, *The Guns of Port Hudson*, pp. 270–271, 338–339, 350.
4. Boatner, *The Civil War Dictionary*. Cunningham, *The Port Hudson Campaign*, p. 120. Edmonds, *The Guns of Port Hudson*, pp. 376–377.
5. E.G. Libby, letter, 9 July 1863, Dexter Historical Society.
6. Charlie Farrar, letter, 14 July 1863, Dexter Historical Society.
7. Francis Ireland, letter, 23 July 1863, University of Maine.
8. *Official Records*, Series 1, Vol. 26, pp. 5–18.
9. *Annual Report of the Adjutant General*, 1863.
10. Ibid.
11. Charlie Farrar, letter, 14 July 1863.
12. *Bangor Daily Whig & Courier*, 8 August 1864. *Annual Report of the Adjutant General*, 1863.
13. Chamberlain, "Dedication of the Maine Monuments at Gettysburg."
14. *Annual Report of the Adjutant General*, 1862 and 1863.
15. John Lincoln, biographical material, Bangor Theological Seminary. Obituary, *Bangor Daily Whig & Courier*, 23 May 1887.
16. Obituary, "Col. Jerrard Dead," *Brunswick* [Maine] *Record*, 5 February 1909. "Simon Jerrard," *History of Penobscot County, Maine*.
17. Dexter Historical Society.
18. Ibid.
19. Ibid.
20. Ibid.

Appendix A

1. *Annual Report of the Adjutant General*, 1861.
2. Ibid.
3. Regimental Correspondence, 2nd Maine, Maine State Archives. *Annual Report of the Adjutant General*, 1861, 1862. Diane Smith, *History of the 2nd Maine Regiment*, unpublished manuscript, author's collection. Sylvia Sherman, Maine State Archives, personal communication, 16 February 2009.
4. *Annual Report of the Adjutant General*, 1861. Sylvia Sherman, Maine State Archives, personal communication, 16 February 2009.
5. *Annual Report of the Adjutant General*, 1861.
6. *Annual Report of the Adjutant General*, 1861, 1862.
7. E.C. Blake, letter, 18 November 1861, Maine State Archives, Civil War Town Correspondence, Houlton.
8. *Annual Report of the Adjutant General*, 1862.
9. Ibid.
10. Josiah Crosby, letter, 4 August 1862, Maine State Archives, Civil War Town Correspondence, Dexter.
11. *Annual Report of the Adjutant General*, 1862, p. 159.
12. Ibid.
13. *Annual Report of the Adjutant General*, 1862. General Order 32, Appendix A, p. 13.

This list of persons exempt from the draft starts with the vice president of the United States (Maine's Hannibal Hamlin) and goes on to include members of Congress, pilots and mariners employed by U.S. citizens, postmasters, assistant postmasters and clerks, post officers, post riders and stage drivers, "in the care and conveyance of the mail of the United States," workers in U.S. arsenals, "persons of the denominations of Quakers and Shakers," justices of the supreme judicial court, and "ministers of the gospel regularly ordained." Men claiming a disability could also be exempt upon presenting a certificate from any surgeon within the county appointed by the governor for that purpose.

14. *Annual Report of the Adjutant General*, 1862 and 1863.
15. *Annual Report of the Adjutant General*, 1862, General Order 32, Appendix A, p. 15.
16. *Annual Report of the Adjutant General*, 1862, General Order 42, Appendix A, p. 19.
17. *Annual Report of the Adjutant General*, 1862, General Order 57, 23 October 1862, Appendix A, p. 23.
18. George Cutler, letter, 10 August 1862, Maine State Archives, Civil War Town Correspondence, Dexter.
19. Josiah Crosby, letter, 12 August 1862, Maine State Archives, Civil War Town Correspondence, Dexter.
20. John Elliot, et al., letter, 14 July 1862, Maine State Archives, Civil War Town Correspondence, Dover.
21. Josiah Jordan, letter, 18 August 1862, Maine State Archives, Civil War Town Correspondence, Dover.
22. C.W. Lowell, letter, 21 November 1862, Maine State Archives, Civil War Town Correspondence, Dover.
23. Edmund Dudley, letter, 15 September 1862, Maine State Archives, Civil War Town Correspondence, Hampden.
24. J.H. Gould, letter, 16 September 1862, Maine State Archives, Civil War Town Correspondence, Dexter.
25. C.W. Lowell, letter, 3 December 1862, Maine State Archives, Civil War Town Correspondence, Dover.
26. Sam'l Clements, letter, 20 November 1863, Maine State Archives, Civil War Town Correspondence, Palmyra.
27. Josiah Crosby, letter, 21 November 1863, Maine State Archives, Civil War Town Correspondence, Dexter.
28. Nathan Wyman, et al., letter, 23 November 1863, Maine State Archives, Civil War Town Correspondence, Dexter.
29. Samuel McClellan, letter, 28 November 1863, Maine State Archives, Civil War Town Correspondence, Dexter.
30. Samuel McClellan, letter, 8 December 1863, Maine State Archives, Civil War Town Correspondence, Dexter.
31. Nathaniel Dustin and Hiram Carr, letter, 22 December 1862, Maine State Archives, Civil War Town Correspondence, Dexter.
32. S.H. Hussy, et al., letter, 25 August 1862, Maine State Archives, Civil War Town Correspondence, Houlton.
33. E.B. Fifield, letter, 18 December 1863, Maine State Archives, Civil War Town Correspondence, Dexter.
34. Samuel McClellan, letter, 28 November 1863, Maine State Archives, Civil War Town Correspondence, Dexter.
35. Josiah Crosby, letter, 25 December 1863, Maine State Archives, Civil War Town Correspondence, Dexter.
36. E.B. Fifield, letter, 22 February 1864, Maine State Archives, Civil War Town Correspondence, Dexter.
37. Russell S. Merrill, letter, 21 July 1862, Maine State Archives, Civil War Town Correspondence, Dexter.
38. *Annual Report of the Adjutant General*, 1862 and 1863.
39. Boatner, *The Civil War Dictionary*. Sifakis, *Who Was Who in the Union*.
40. Smith, *Conflict in Command*. Diane Monroe Smith, personal communication, 12 August 2008.

Bibliography

Annual Report of the Adjutant General of the State of Maine. Augusta, Maine: Stevens and Sayward, 1861, 1862 and 1863.

Boatner, Mark M. *The Civil War Dictionary.* New York: Vintage Books, 1991.

Bundy, Carol. *The Nature of Sacrifice: A Biography of Charles Russell Lowell, Jr.* New York: Farrar, Straus and Giroux, 2005.

Butler, Benjamin F. *Butler's Book: Autobiography and Personal Reminiscences of Major General Benjamin F Butler.* Boston: A.M. Thayer, 1892.

Chamberlain, Joshua Lawrence. *Bayonets! Forward: My Civil War Reminiscences.* Gettysburg, PA: Stan Clark Military Books, 1944.

Cowles, Calvin D., comp. *Atlas to Accompany the Official Records of the Union and Confederate Armies.* Washington, DC: Government Printing Office, 1891–1895.

Cunningham, Edward. *The Port Hudson Campaign.* Baton Rouge: Louisiana State University Press, 1963.

Davis, William C. *Battlefields of the Civil War.* New York: Smithmark, 1991.

_____. *Fighting Men of the Civil War.* New York: Gallery Books, 1989.

DeForest, John William. *A Volunteer's Adventures: A Union Captain's Record of the Civil War.* Hamden, CT: Achorn Books, 1970.

Eastern Gazette (supplement), Dexter, Maine, August 4, 1904.

Edmonds, David C. *The Guns of Port Hudson.* Lafayette, LA: Acadiana Press, 1983.

Emerson, Paul. "Hampden, Maine, Soldiers and Sailors of the Civil War," non-circulating manuscript, Bangor (Maine) Public Library.

Harper's Weekly (A Journal of Civilization). New York: Harper and Brothers.

Hewlitt, Lawrence L. *Port Hudson, Confederate Bastion on the Mississippi.* Baton Rouge: Louisiana State University Press, 1987.

History of Penobscot County, Maine. Cleveland, OH: Williams, Chase, 1882.

Hollandsworth, James G. *The Louisiana Native Guard: The Black Military Experience During the Civil War.* Baton Rouge: Louisiana State University Press, 1995.

Irwin, Richard B. *History of the Nineteenth Army Corps.* New York: Putnam's Sons, 1892.

Kennedy, Randall. *Nigger: The Strange Career of a Troublesome Word.* New York: Pantheon Books, 2002.

McPherson, James M. *Battle Cry of Freedom: The Civil War Era.* New York: Ballantine Books, 1989.

_____. *Crossroads of Freedom: Antietam.* Oxford and New York: Oxford University Press, 2002.

Miller, Francis Trevelyan, ed. *The Photographic History of the Civil War.* New York: Review of Reviews, 1911.

Paine, Lincoln P. *Ships of the World: An*

Historical Encyclopedia. New York: Houghton Mifflin Harcourt, 2nd edition, 1997.

Rodriguez, Junius P., ed. "German Coast Uprising (1811)." in *The Encyclopedia of Slave Resistance and Rebellion*. Westport, CT, and London: Greenwood Press: 2007.

Rothman, Adam. *Slave Country: American Expansion and the Origins of the Deep South*. Cambridge, MA: Harvard University Press, 2005.

Rutlow, Ira M. *Bleeding Blue and Gray: Civil War Surgery and the Evolution of American Medicine*. New York: Random House, 2005.

Shaw, Horace, and Charles J. House. *The First Maine Heavy Artillery, 1861–1865*. Portland, ME: n.p., 1903.

Sifakis, Stewart. *Who Was Who in the Union*. New York: Facts on File, 1989.

Smith, Diane Monroe. *Chamberlain at Petersburg: The Charge at Fort Hell*. Gettysburg, PA: Thomas, 2004.

_____. *Fanny and Joshua: The Enigmatic Lives of Francis Caroline Adams and Joshua Lawrence Chamberlain*. Gettysburg, PA: Thomas, 1999.

Smith, George G. *Leaves from a Soldier's Diary: The Personal Record of Lieutenant George G Smith, Co. C, 1st Louisiana Regiment Infantry Volunteers During the War of the Rebellion*. Putnam, CT: G.G. Smith, 1906.

Smith, John David. "An Ironic Route to Glory; Louisiana's Native Guards at Port Hudson," in *Black Soldiers in Blue*. Chapel Hill: University of North Carolina Press, 2002.

Spedale, William A. *Where Bugles Called and Rifles Gleamed*. Baton Rouge, LA: Land and Land, 1986.

Taylor, Richard. *Destruction and Reconstruction: Personal Experiences of the Late War*. New York: Appleton, 1897 (reprinted in 1973 by Arno Press, New York).

United States War Department. *The War of the Rebellion: A Compilation of the Official Records of the Union and Confederate Armies*. Washington, DC: Government Printing Office, 1880–1901 (online at Cornell University Library, http://digital.library.cornell.edu/m/moa war/waro.html.

Walbridge, Mike. *African-American Heroes of the Civil War*. Portland, ME: Walch, 2002.

West, Richard S., Jr. *Lincoln's Scapegoat General: A Life of Benjamin F. Butler*. Boston: Houghton Mifflin, 1995.

Whitman, William, and Charles True. *Maine in the War for the Union: A History of the Part Borne by Maine Troops in the Suppression of the American Rebellion*. Lewiston, ME: N. Dingley, Jr., 1865.

Wilson, Joseph T. *The Black Phalanx: A History of the Negro Soldiers of the United States in the War of 1775–1812, 1861–65*. Hartford, CT: American, 1888 (reprinted in 1968 by Arno Press, New York).

Winters, John D. *The Civil War in Louisiana*. Baton Rouge: Louisiana State University Press, 1991.

Wright, Lt. Howard C. *Port Hudson; Its History From an Interior Point of View*; reprinted, Baton Rouge; Committee for the Preservation of the Port Hudson Battlefield, 1961.

Index

Acadian ("Cajun") 141
Addison, Maine 35
USS *Albatross* 109, 111, 112
Alexander, Maine 35
Alexandria, Louisiana 142, 144, 149
Alexandria, Virginia 41, 44, 47
Algiers, Louisiana 147, 148
Allen, John E., Sergeant, Co. E, 22nd Maine 170
Ames, Adlebert, Colonel, 20th Maine 23
Amherst, Maine 34
Andrew, John, Governor of Massachusetts 41
Anson, George, Lieutenant, Co. B, 22nd Maine 161
Antietam, Maryland 199
Applebee, Albert 195
Appomattox, Virginia 177
Arlington Heights, Virginia 37, 41, 50
Army of the Potomac 59, 67, 117, 180, 201
Arnold, Richard, General 159
Atchafalaya River, Louisiana 122
Atkinson, Maine 35
Augur, Christopher C., General 153, 154, 159, 166, 168, 169
Augusta, Maine 196
Aurora, Maine 34

Bailey, Lyman 18
Bailey, Nathaniel, Private, Co. B, 22nd Maine 164
Baker's Cavalry *see* 1st Maine Cavalry
Baltimore, Maryland 37
Bangor, Maine 25, 28, 29, 34, 116, 136, 137, 182, 187
Banks, Nathaniel, General 39, 40, 41, 44, 58, 67, 68, 69, 89, 96, 101, 107, 108, 109, 110, 116, 119, 122, 124, 127, 129, 133, 141, 143, 144, 149. 154, 155, 156, 157, 159, 160, 161, 166, 176, 178, 201; reports of 107, 110, 125, 142, 143, 168, 181

Baring, Maine 35
Barris Landing, Louisiana 147, 148
Batchelder, Hiram T., Sgt, 22nd Maine 31, 46
Bath, Maine 196
Baton Rouge, Louisiana 16, 74, 75, 76, 77, 78, 80, 81, 84, 85, 97, 98, 105, 107, 109, 110, 112, 116, 144, 148, 153
Bayou Boeuf, Louisiana 119, 121, 122, 137
Bayou Teche 119, 122, 123, 124, 128
Belfast, Maine 35
Berwick Bay, Louisiana 121
Berwick City, Louisiana 148
Bethel, Maine 101
Birge, H.W., Colonel 128
Blake, E.C.: letter of 188
Bolton, George, Capt, Co. C, 22nd Maine 34
Boston, Massachusetts 36
Bowdoin College, Maine 144, 176
Brackett, John O., Major, 22nd Maine 24, 31, 122, 131
Bragg, Braxton, General 102, 119, 121
Brashear City, Louisiana 119, 121, 122, 127, 144, 147, 148
Brawn, Sumner, Private, Co. E, 22nd Maine 96
Breckenridge, John, General 74
Brewer, Maine 34
Bridgewater, Maine 35
Brown, George, Sgt/Lieutenant, Co. A, 22nd Maine 45–46, 133, 179
Bull Run, First Battle of 48
Burnside, Ambrose, General 67, 201
Butler, Benjamin Franklin, General 40, 51, 68, 69, 71, 72, 74, 115, 136, 201, 202
Butte a la Rose, Louisiana 142

Cailloux, Andre, Captain 156
Cairo, Illinois 182
Calais, Maine 35

247

Calhoun, John C 10, 11
calomel 98
Camp Chase, Virginia 50
Camp New York, Baton Rouge, Louisiana 105
Camp Pope, Bangor, Maine 30, 31, 32, 182
Camp Seward, Virginia 38
Canaan, Maine 194
Carle, Van Buren, Private, Co. B, 22nd Maine 179
Carmel, Maine 34
Carpenter, Asa, Private, Co. E, 22nd Maine 90
Carr, Hyram 197
Case, Isaac, Captain, Co. C, 22nd Maine 35, 106, 179, 181, 182; letters of 37, 47, 48, 50–51, 53, 60, 71, 72, 76, 81, 84–85
Case, Isaac, Sr. 106, 182
Casey's Division, Reserved Army Corps 37
Centerville, Louisiana 122
Chamberlain, John Calhoun 10, 11
Chamberlain, Joshua, Colonel, later General 3, 11, 23, 176, 182
Chancellorsville, Virginia 145
Chaplin, Daniel, Colonel, 18th Maine 23
Charleston, Maine 34, 90
Chase, William 195
Cherryfield, Maine 36
City of New York (steamship) 37
Clack, F.H., Major 125
Clay, Henry, Colonel 28th Louisiana 125
Clements, Samuel 196
Clewley, Augustus, Private, Co. B, 22nd Maine 164
USS *Clifton* 122, 127
Clinton, Louisiana 152, 157, 158
Coburn, Abner, Governor of Maine 105
Columbia, Maine 35
Confiscation Acts of 1861 and 1862 115
USS *Congress* 52, 53
Connecticut Infantry: 12th 160, 161; 13th 124; 25th 124, 128
CSS *Connie* 142
Conscription Act of 1863 *see* Enrollment Act of 1863
Contraband Camp, Newport News, Virginia 50, 51, 58
Cook, John W., Assistant Surgeon, 22nd Maine 21
Cooper, Maine 35
Copperheads (Peace Democrats) 54, 87, 116–117, 180, 199
Corcoran, Michael, General 48
Corcoran's Legion 48
Corinna, Maine 34
Corinth, Maine 35

Crawford, James, Drummer, Co. E, 22nd Maine 90, 91
Crawford, Maine 35
Crocker, John 66
Crosby, Henry, Captain, Co. A, 22nd Maine 21, 34, 54, 163, 164
Crosby, Josiah 19, 20, 189, 193, 196, 199
croton oil 95, 98
USS *Cumberland* 52, 53
Cutler, George 191–193
Cypress Point, Grand Lake, Louisiana 122

Damons, Onslow W. 195
Danforth, Maine 35
Daniel Webster (steamship) 182
Davis, Jefferson 69, 122, 152, 153
Day, Eben 102
Deaf, Dumb, & Blind Asylum, Baton Rouge, Louisiana 79–80
Dedham, Maine 34
DeForest, John W., Captain, 12th Connecticut 160; report of 173
Dewey, George, Admiral 114
Dexter, Maine 25, 26, 34, 35, 66, 116, 117, 129, 139, 180, 183, 184, 194, 196, 197, 198, 199, 200
CSS *Diana* 125, 128
Dixmont, Maine 35
Donaldsonville, Louisiana 119
Dover, Maine 35, 176
Drake, Edward 200
Dudley, Edmund 194
Durand Plantation, Louisiana 135
Dustin, Nathaniel 197
Dwight, William, General 87–89, 121, 125, 127, 128, 141, 142, 166, 168, 169

Eddington, Maine 34
CSS *Ellen* 142
Enrollment Act (Conscription Act) of 1863 116, 190
Erwin, Timothy, Private, Co. G, 22nd Maine 179
USS *Essex* 75, 76, 111
Etna, Maine 35
Exeter, Maine 35, 200

Farragut, David, Captain/Admiral 69, 71, 107, 108, 109, 110, 112, 113, 116; reports of 110, 112
Farrar, Charles (Charlie), Private, 22nd Maine 32, 42, 78, 83, 89, 96,100, 114, 116, 137, 138, 139, 140, 145, 147, 148, 183; letters of 61–62, 137–138, 143, 180, 182
Fessenden, Francis, Colonel, 25th Maine 37
Fessenden, William P., Senator 37

Fifield, Edward B., Lieutenant, Co. D, 20th Maine 66, 199, 200
Fitzgerald, Charles H. 194
Flagg, Frank G., Adjutant, 22nd Maine 32, 61
Fogg, Jacob, Private, Co. E, 22nd Maine 148
Fort Bisland, Louisiana 119, 121, 122, 124, 125, 127, 129, 141, 143
Fort De Russy, Louisiana 142
Fort Fairfield, Maine 35
Fort Jackson, Louisiana 16, 69, 70, 71
Fort St. Philip, Louisiana 16, 69, 70, 71
Fort Sumter 185
Fort Washington, Maryland 44
Fortress Monroe, Virginia 44, 46, 47, 48, 51, 52, 64, 67
Foxcroft, Maine 35, 195
Franklin, Louisiana 122, 123, 124, 125, 127, 131, 134, 141, 142, 143, 144, 147, 148
Fredericksburg, Virginia 67, 81, 94, 145
French Plantations, Aroostook County, Maine 197, 198
USS *Fulton* 157
Fusilier, Gabriel Leclerc, Captain 135

USS *Galena* 53
Gardner, Franklin, General 149, 151, 152, 153, 154, 157, 165, 166, 178, 180; reports of 110, 111, 112
Garland, Maine 35, 200
German Coast Uprising 13
Gettysburg, Pennsylvania 180
Gilmore, Charles D., Major, 20th Maine 23
Glenburn, Maine 34
Godfrey, John 20, 21
Gordon, Nathaniel 7
Gould, J.H. 195
Grand Ecore, Louisiana 142
Grand Lake, Louisiana 122
Grant, Ulysses, General 143, 146, 149, 177, 202
Grierson, Benjamin, Colonel 158
Griffin, Charles, General 177
Grover, Cuvier, General 74, 75, 76, 78, 101, 121, 122, 123, 125, 127, 128, 133, 154, 157, 159, 166, 169, 170; reports of 129, 175
Guilford, Maine 35

Haines, Roscoe, Private, Co. E, 22nd Maine 86
Hall, Joseph, Maine Secretary of State 20
Hall, William, Private, Co. E, 22nd Maine 61, 129, 130, 145
Hamlin, Hannibal 11, 18, 190

Hampden, Maine 34, 163, 164, 194
hand grenades 167, 168
Hanson, Edward, Private, 22nd Maine 22
Harrington, Maine 35
Hart, Alfred, Private, Co. E, 22nd Maine 58
USS *Hartford* 109, 110, 111, 112
Hartford Convention 8
Hartland, Maine 35
Haseltine, William, Corporal, Co. C, 13th Maine 103, 104
Haskell, Isaac, Captain, Co. D, 20th Maine 66, 200
Helena, Arkansas 181
Hermon, Maine 34
Hersey, Justus 67
Hersey, W. Prince, 1st Lieutenant, Co. E, 22nd Maine 34, 103, 105
Hodgdon, Maine 35
Hodsdon, John, Maine Adjutant General 19, 20, 22, 173, 188, 193–196, 198, 199, 200
Holcomb, Richard E., Colonel, 1st Louisiana Infantry 124, 167, 172, 173
Holden, Maine 34
Hooker, Joseph, General 117, 201
Houton, Maine 35, 197, 198
Howe, Harrison, Private, Co. G, 22nd Maine 56
Hubbard, George 195
Huckins, Jason, Assistant Surgeon, 22nd Maine 85, 95
Hudson, Maine 34
Hutchings, Jasper 20
Hutchinson, Jonas, Private, Co. E, 22nd Maine 61, 90, 99

Indian Village, Charenton, Louisiana 124
Indiana: 1st Indiana Heavy Artillery 157, 159
Ireland, Eben 28, 63, 78, 184
Ireland, Flora 30, 63, 65, 83, 97, 118, 139, 147, 184
Ireland, Francis (Frank) 4, 6, 25, 28, 30, 34, 161, 184; letters of 30–33, 35–36, 41, 43, 44, 47–55, 56–59, 59–61, 64–65, 69–73, 74–78, 78–83, 84–91, 91–94, 95–97, 97–100, 101–102, 112–115, 119–121, 127–129, 131, 133, 136–137, 140–141, 143–145, 147–148, 169–172, 180–181
Ireland, Isaiah, Private, Co. E, 22nd Maine 90, 100
Ireland, James P., 2nd Lieutenant, Co. A, 22nd Maine 45
Ireland, John 28, 78, 184; letters of 39, 62–63, 65–67, 102–103, 116–118, 138, 139, 145–146, 146–147

Ireland, Martha 28, 63, 78, 137, 147, 184; letters of 139
Ireland, Olin 30, 102, 137, 139, 184
Ireland, Shephard 100
Irish Bend, Louisiana 122, 123, 124, 126, 127, 129, 130, 137, 138, 182
Irish Legion 48
USS *Ironsides* 53
Irwin, Richard, Assistant Adjutant General 115, 175

Jerrard, Anson, Lieutenant, Co. H, 22nd Maine 234*n*2
Jerrard, Simon, Colonel, 22nd Maine 22, 24, 25, 31, 53, 64, 67, 119, 122, 131, 144, 170, 171, 172, 173, 175, 176, 177, 183; reports of 44, 45, 64, 67, 74, 75, 78, 85, 107, 116, 119, 122, 125, 129, 136, 147, 161, 162, 168, 173–175
Jersey City, New Jersey 37
Johnston, Joseph E., General 152, 153, 165
Jonesport, Maine 36
Jordan, Josiah, Surgeon, 22nd Maine 21, 31, 85, 193–194
Joy, Joseph E. 18, 19, 21, 181; letters of 162–163
Juniper, E.S. 196

Keith, John, Colonel, 1st Indiana Heavy Artillery 242*n*14
Kenduskeag, Maine 35, 106
Kennedy, Randall 93
Knight, Charles H., Sergeant, Co. E, 22nd Maine 170
Knowles, Elkanah 42, 43
Knowles, Elkanah, Jr 43
Knowles, George, Corporal, Co. A, 22nd Maine 42, 43
Knowles, John 43
Knowles, Thomas, Lt, Co. A, 22nd Maine 42, 43, 45

Lagrange, Maine 34
Lambert, Archibald, Captain, Co. I, 22nd Maine 35
Lee, Maine 34
Lee, Robert E., General 60
Leighton, Daniel, Private, Co. E, 22nd Maine 137, 146
Leighton, Mary (wife of Charlie Farrar) 183
Leighton, Stephen 196, 199
Leighton, Wentworth, Private, Co. D, 22nd Maine 85
Levant, Maine 35, 183
Lincoln, John K., Chaplain, 22nd Maine 33, 60, 175, 183

Lincoln, Maine 34
Lincoln Gun 65, 66
Linneus, Maine 35
Logan, John, Colonel 157
Longfellow, Stephen 8
Lorenz Austrian Rifle 59, 61
Louisiana: election of 1860 14–15; French Acadians 13 population diversity 13, 14; secession 14, 15
Louisiana Cavalry: 2nd 125; 7th Volunteer Cavalry 135
Louisiana Infantry: 1st (Union) 124, 127, 157, 163, 167, 174, 175; 2nd (Union) 87; 28th 125
Louisiana Native Guard 68, 153, 155, 156, 157; 1st 155, 156; 2nd 156, 157; 3rd 155, 156
Lovejoy, William W., Reverend 199
Lowell, C.W. letter of 194

Macwahoc, Maine 34
Maine: election of 1856 11; election of 1860 12; map (1860) 27, 28; slavery 7, 8, 11, 12; soldiers as proportion of population 12; statehood 9, 10; states rights and secession 7, 8
Maine Cavalry: 1st 199, 200; 2nd 200
Maine Heavy Artillery *see* 18th Maine Infantry
Maine Infantry: 1st 186; 2nd 23, 186–187; 6th 94, 145; 12th 79, 87, 88, 183, 204; 13th 68, 71, 103, 204; 14th 75, 79, 204; 15th 20, 204; 16th 189; 17th 23, 105, 189, 204; 18th (1st Maine Heavy Artillery) 19, 189, 194; 19th 204; 20th 3, 23, 186, 189, 199, 200, 204; 21st 98, 203; 23rd 203; 24th 203; 25th 41, 42, 203; 26th 32, 41, 42, 56, 72, 124, 128, 138, 147, 148, 203; 27th 41, 42, 203; 28th 203
Maine Light Artillery: 1st 157
Maine regimental casualties 19, 20
CSS *Manassas* 71, 72
Mason, Samuel, Sergeant, Co. F, 22nd Maine 179
Massachusetts Infantry: 4th 181; 31st 71; 41st (referred as mounted) 147, 148; 52nd 131, 147, 148, 180
Mayne, Lieutenant, 1st Louisiana Infantry 172
McClellan, George, General 17, 40, 47, 59–60, 67, 201
McClellan, Samuel 196, 199
McPhetres, Daniel, Private, Co. B, 22nd Maine 179
Meade, George, General 201, 202
Meddybemps, Maine 35
Merrill, Alonzo 117, 145

Merrill, Ithamer, Private, Co. E, 22nd Maine 89
Merrill, Russell 200
Merrill, Sarah Maria 145
USS *Merrimack* see CSS *Virginia*
Miller, Cyrus 195
Millers Point, Grand Lake, Louisiana 123, 124
USS *Mississippi* 71, 111, 113, 114
Missouri Compromise 10
USS *Monitor* 51, 52, 53
Monte Sano Bayou 110, 116
Monticello, Maine 35
Morgan, Annie (wife of Francis Ireland) 184
Morgan, Joseph, Colonel, 90th New York 147, 160, 161, 166, 167, 172, 173, 174, 175, 176
Morril, Solomon (Sam), Private, Co. E, 22nd Maine 90, 99
Morton, John, Lieutenant 1st Battery, 1st Maine Light Artillery 242*n*14
Mouton, Alexandre 149
Mouton, Marie Celestine 149
Mumford, William 69

New Iberia, Louisiana 125, 129, 131, 133, 134, 136, 137, 140, 143, 181
New Orleans, Louisiana 68, 69, 70, 71, 72, 73, 74, 78, 98, 138
New York Infantry: 6th 87, 88, 100, 124, 127, 128; 69th 48, 96; 70th 89; 90th 147, 148, 157, 161, 167, 173, 175; 91st 100, 121, 124, 128, 157, 163, 167; 110th 147, 148; 114th 144, 147, 148; 131st 87, 88, 100, 116, 124, 157, 161, 167, 174, 175; 159th 124, 125, 128; 175th 144, 147, 148
Newburg, Maine 34
Newport, Maine 195
Newport News, Virginia 44, 47, 48, 50, 56, 59, 61, 64
Nimsi Battery (2nd Massachusetts Light Artillery) 128, 129, 148
19th Army Corps, Department of the Gulf 39, 58, 69, 119, 122, 138, 141
Norwich, Connecticut 36

Opelousas, Louisiana 140, 141, 142, 143, 144
Orrington, Maine 34

Paine, Halbert, General 158, 166
Palmer, Erastus, Sergeant, Co. H, 22nd Maine 171
Palmyra, Maine 35, 195, 196
Parkman, Maine 195, 197
Patten, Gipson, Sergeant/Lieutenant, Co. A, 22nd Maine 45–46

Pattersonville, Louisiana 122
Peck, Frank, Lieutenant Colonel, 12th Connecticut 160
Pekes, Thomas 21
Pemberton, John, General 110, 111, 112, 152, 153
Perry, Mathew, Admiral 113
Petersburg, Virginia 176
Plymouth, Maine 35
Pope, John, General 60
Port Barre, Louisiana 147, 148
Port Hudson, Louisiana 81, 92, 96, 107, 108–114, 116, 143, 144, 148, 149–165, 166–177
Porter, David D., Admiral 112
Portland, Maine 36, 182, 196
Powers, Frank, Colonel 157
Pruyn, Robert L., Captain, 4th Louisiana Infantry 165
Putnam, Aziel, Captain, Co. G, 22nd Maine 35
Putnam, Olonzo G., Lieutenant Colonel, 22nd Maine 22, 23, 24, 31, 119, 122, 125,128, 176; report of 176

CSS *Queen of the West* 121

Red River 112, 142, 149, 151
Reily, James, Colonel, 4th Texas 125
Remmick, Daniel, Private, Co. E, 22nd Maine 89
Richardson, Jefferson, Wagoner, Co. E, 22nd Maine 93
Ripley, Maine 194
Roberts, Otis, Sergeant 6th Maine 145
Roberts, Thomas A., Colonel, 17th Maine 23
Robinston, Maine 35
Rodman, Thomas J. 65
Rosecrans, William, General 102
Russell, Ellen (wife of Francis Ireland) 184
Rust, Albert, General 111

Saint Albans, Maine 35
Saint Martinville, Louisiana 131, 133, 134, 136, 140, 143
Sangerville, Maine 35, 196
Sawyer, J.S. 195
Scales, Augustus, Private, Co. E, 22nd Maine 85–86
Scott, Elen 105
Sebec, Maine 35
Shepherdstown, West Virginia 199
Sherman, Thomas W., General 154, 155
Sherman, William T., General 202
Ship Island, Louisiana 68, 70, 73
Shreveport, Louisiana 142, 143

Sickles, Daniel, General 201, 202
Silver, Samuel, Private, Co. E, 22nd Maine 96, 99, 115, 145
Smith, Edmund Kirby, General 141
Smith, Elisha, Colonel, 114th New York Infantry 167
Smith, John 117
Smith, Joseph, Private, Co. E, 22nd Maine 86
Smith, Melancton, Captain 113
Springfield, Maine 34
S.R. *Spaulding* (steamship) 44, 46, 47, 50, 64, 68
State House, Baton Rouge, Louisiana 75, 76, 79–80, 82, 87
Stetson, Maine 35
Stones River, Murfreesboro, Tennessee 93, 102
Stowe, Calvin 144
Stowe, Harriet Beecher 144
Strong, George, Chief of Staff to General Butler, Assistant Adjutant to General Banks 136, 155

Taylor, Richard, General 110, 111, 122, 124, 125, 127, 129, 130, 134, 135, 141, 142, 143, 180; reports of 143
Taylor, William, Captain, Co. F, 22nd Maine 35
Texas Infantry: 4th 125
Thibodeaux, Louisiana 119, 121

Union, Charles Captain, Co. D, 22nd Maine 35

Veazie, Maine 34
Vermillion Bayou, Louisiana 142
Vicksburg, Mississippi 112, 143, 146, 149, 152, 179, 180, 182
Vincent, W.G., Colonel, 2nd Louisiana Cavalry 125
CSS *Virginia* (USS *Merrimack*) 51, 53

Waite Plantation, Maine 34
Warren, Gouvenour K., General 177

Washburn, Israel, Governor of Maine 18, 20, 21, 22, 42, 189, 191, 197
Washington, D.C. 36, 38, 41
Washington, Louisiana 143, 144, 147, 148
Wass, David, Sergeant, Co. D, 22nd Maine 56
Waterhouse, Turner 19
CSS *Webb* 121
Webb, Amaziah, Private, Co. B, 22nd Maine 179
Weitzel, Godfrey, General 121, 133, 136, 142, 154, 155, 156, 160, 161, 165, 166, 167, 169; reports of 163
Whitehouse, Turner, Captain, Co. K, 22nd Maine 35
Whiting, Recruiting Officer, Newport, Maine 195
Whittemore, Charles, Private, Co. E, 22nd Maine 105, 118
Whittemore, Franklin, Sergeant, 17th Maine 105
Whittemore, Jacob, Private, Co. E, 22nd Maine 89, 96, 99, 105, 117, 118
Whittier, Jacob H. 194
Williams, James, Captain, Co. B, 22nd Maine 34, 61
Wilson, Henry, Private, Co. B, 22nd Maine 164
Wilson, William (Billy), Colonel, 6th New York 87–89, 96, 101
Wing, Charles G., Sergeant, Co. E, 22nd Maine 172
Wood, Benjamin 55
Wood, Fernando 54–55, 87
Wood, Henry L., Captain, Co. E, 22nd Maine 19, 20, 25, 28, 35, 96, 133, 134, 135, 136, 139, 179, 183; reports of 134, 135, 172, 173, 175
Wood, Mary (wife of Captain Henry Wood) 138, 139
Wyman, Nathan 196, 199

www.ingramcontent.com/pod-product-compliance
Ingram Content Group UK Ltd.
Pitfield, Milton Keynes, MK11 3LW, UK
UKHW041936140426
5217IPUK00014B/501